Daniel R.
Burkhart

March 2004

SOLO SAFARI

by

Terrance Cacek

with contributions by:

Jerry Weaver
Charles Craver
T.N. "Alex" Alexakos
Charles Puff
Reinald von Meurers

SAFARI PRESS, Inc.

WARNING!

This book contains data on handloading and firearms that reflect the particular experiences of the authors. The authors used specific firearms, ammunition, and reloading equipment under conditions not necessarily reported in the book. Under no circumstances should the reader try to duplicate the loads mentioned in this book. The handloading of ammunition and the discharge of a firearm should never be attempted without the supervision of an adult experienced in both handloading and firearms. The publishers can not accept responsibility for the firearms and handloading data in this book.

Cacek, Terrance

ISBN 1-57157-058-6

Library of Congress Catalog Card Number: 94-67699

1994, Long Beach, California, USA

10 9 8 7 6 5 4 3 2

Readers wishing to receive the Safari Press catalog, featuring many fine books on big-game hunting, wingshooting, and firearms, should write the publisher at the address given above.

This is the 50th title published by Safari Press.

Table of Contents

DEDICATION

To the brave men of Africa who somehow brought me back alive time after time: Mathias, who stood beside a proven bad marksman in the face of a wounded buffalo; Ceeasi who entertained me and James who fed me; Wiro, who knows what elephants will do before the elephants know; Pearson, who never learned that broken Land Rovers cannot be repaired in the bush; Jason Masonto, who shares my adrenaline habit; Friday, who has a working relationship with the God of the Leopards; Andy Kockott, who abided my wildest fantasies; Leslie Reed, who wrestles with cow buffalo and Mercedes trucks; Ibo Zimmermann and Segale Gobuamang, who didn't quite burn me up in the middle of the Kalahari; Victor Kgampi, who taught me how to hunt buffalo; Kgaodi and Muzila, who taught me how not to hunt buffalo; Freeman Malebogo, hunter, entrepreneur, and friend who taught me so much of Africa; Mosesane Pekeneng, who emptied my pockets with my permission; Eric Molelekwa, who still thinks I should have shot that lioness; and a dozen or more skinners and biltong cutters who shared my campfires but whose names I never knew. You gave me the best moments of my life. To every one of you, thanks.

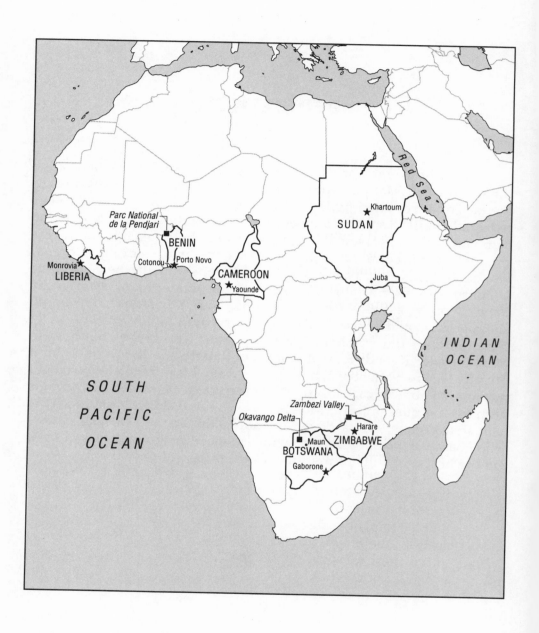

PART 1

PREFACE

Part one of this book is a collection of stories about the people of rural Africa, the wild animals of Africa, and my adventures with them. I'm not going to feed you the usual rubbish that this book recounts the adventures of the last man to know the "old Africa," Africa the way it was and always should be.

Sure, the naked savage has been replaced by a modern man who thinks and acts more like you and me, but that only makes it easier for us to relate to one another. Sure, black rhinos are being destroyed by poachers and elephants are just as surely being destroyed by well-meaning preservationists, but in many ways African hunting is better today than at any time in this century.

My stories are worth telling, I hope, because I did it my way, with little or no assistance from professional hunters. I've used terms like "solo safari" and "self-guided safari" only to distinguish my safaris from traditional safaris outfitted and guided by professional hunters. I almost never hunted alone; I was accompanied by black Africans. I never guided myself; my success and survival depended totally on the bush skills of my African friends. Had their skills failed, I would not be telling these stories.

So please join my friends and me as we leave our footprints beside those of the elephant and drink from the same waters as the lion. Perhaps these tales will move you to travel to Africa to see what I have seen and know what I have known. Perhaps you will then join me in the crusade to conserve African wildlife for all time.

SOLO SAFARI
FOR CAPE BUFFALO

I was pushing a bucket of bolts up the highway from Harare, capital of Zimbabwe, to the Zambezi River. It was a rented four-wheel-drive truck that the people at Land Rover were proud of ten years earlier, but it had seen too many of Africa's back roads. Tied on behind was a trailer full of rented camping equipment and a two-week supply of food. James, my Shona cook, sat beside me staring at the road ahead because conversation was impossible. I spoke no Shona and he spoke only a few words of English. I was going to the Zambezi to hunt buffalo, but I was going to do it my way— without assistance from a professional hunter.

The fact that dangerous game can be hunted in Zimbabwe without a guide is the best kept secret in the safari industry. While exploring possibilities for my buffalo hunt, I contacted several booking agents, including Chris Hallamore, a native of Zimbabwe and former professional hunter. When I explained that I was a wildlife biologist with considerable hunting experience, Chris suggested a self-guided hunt. Neither of us was sure it was possible to organize a safari from halfway around the world, but the idea had the allure of high adventure.

Africa is the home of the largest and most dangerous animals, so it becomes the ultimate goal of most experienced big-game hunters to hunt there. Ironically, African hunting traditionally requires little skill and involves little danger. Virtually all visiting sportsmen are guided by professional hunters who assure the outcome of the hunt. The professionals arm themselves with powerful rifles, which they do not hesitate to use.

I had hunted with professional guides and I intend to do so again, but I wanted to hunt on my own this time. I had never hunted dangerous game and I wanted to savor the fullness of the experience. I wanted the outcome to rest with the buffalo and me, not with a professional hunter, so I decided to try a self-guided hunt. I bid successfully on a ten-day hunt in the Sapi Safari Area in the Zambezi Valley. My license allowed one bull buffalo, one cow buffalo, and eight deer-sized impala.

I had been in Zimbabwe for two very hectic days. I had picked up the rented truck and dodged traffic in the outskirts of Harare to collect James. They drive on the wrong side of the road in Zimbabwe. We visited the bank, grocery store, Game Department, and the company that rents camping equipment.

The tarred roofs of Harare gave way to tin roofs and finally to thatched roofs. Then I knew we were in rural Africa. The left-handed traffic thinned out, giving me a chance to relax at the wheel and reflect on my situation. I was amazed and just a little scared.

I was amazed that I had successfully organized a safari from half-way around the world. I was scared because of the uncertainties that lay ahead. I was about to tackle one of the most dangerous animals on earth, knowing little about buffalo hunting. I had tried to calculate the odds. Buffalo have killed more hunters than any other animal. One safari company whose clients take about two dozen buffalo per year averages one charge per year. A friend who grew up in Africa has killed about sixty-five buffalo and has been injured twice.

I suspect that buffalo hunting is a little less dangerous than driving race cars at Indianapolis, but I would be hunting without a professional hunter as a backup. This would be like driving at Indianapolis without a seat belt. I was feeling brave about all this back in Virginia, but as the moment drew near, I was beginning to feel apprehensive.

Four hours later we reached Makuti, the last outpost of civilization. Makuti doesn't look like much—just a gas station, native bar, and a fairly good motel and restaurant. We topped off the fuel tank, filled three jerry cans, and bought loaves of fresh bread and a bag of ice. Two miles further on, we stopped at the Game Department Office to pick up the necessary permits. I met Mathias, a department em-

Solo Safari for Cape Buffalo

ployee who would be my tracker and would assure that everything was done properly and legally. I also met Ceeasi who would be on my payroll as a skinner.

The four of us, one white and three black, headed north. We soon reached the crest of the Zambezi Escarpment and the Zambezi Valley spread before us. The specific area known as the Valley extends from the Kariba Dam to the border with Mozambique. The entire twenty-five mile width of the valley lies in Zimbabwe. The Zambezi flows along the northern edge of the valley floor and forms the border with Zambia.

The blacktop road snaked its way down the escarpment. At the valley floor, we turned right onto a gravel road and headed toward Mozambique. We bounced and vibrated for fifty miles before reaching the Chewore River, where we turned off onto a jeep road. Six hundred yards further on we found camp. We pitched the tents in the dark and had boiled eggs and cornmeal for supper with the promise of meat for tomorrow.

The next morning Mathias, Ceeasi, and I drove a mile from camp to check the rifles. Ceeasi fastened a target to a dead mopane tree while I took the pair of Ruger Model 77s from their case. The big, new .458 had a heavy, reassuring feel and the .338 felt light and comfortable, like an old friend. Both were dead on.

"Today we will shoot only an impala for James," I declared.

"No buffalo?" Mathias asked.

"No. Just an impala for meat. We will hunt buffalo tomorrow."

Mathias and Ceeasi were puzzled. We had come to hunt buffalo, but now this strange white man said he would shoot only an impala. I had my reasons. I didn't want the buffalo to come too quickly. I wanted to enjoy the bush, get its feel, and shoot an impala to gain confidence in myself. The buffalo could wait.

The Africans climbed into the back of the truck for a better view and we turned onto a jeep track where I got my first taste of driving in the Zambezi bush. The valley floor looked flat from the escarpment, but it is crossed by dozens of gullies and several tributary rivers. All were dry from April to October. Black men swore and white knuckles turned whiter as the truck bounced up and down the stream banks and swam through the loose, dry sand in the riverbeds.

The good thing about impala is that they are very plentiful. You may see several small herds in an hour. The bad thing about impala is that they quickly drift into the brush when danger approaches. We

3

stalked to within a hundred yards of several herds, but intervening trees and brush always prevented a shot. Mathias and Ceeasi were becoming impatient. I was becoming impatient. I feared they would think I was gun-shy and I resolved to take a shot, any shot, at the next impala I saw.

The opportunity came quickly, but it was just a streak of gold in the sun-dappled forest. I hurried the shot and knew before the bullet left the barrel that it was half a foot high. We looked for blood, but I knew there would be none. I felt low, like a rookie quarterback whose first pass has just been intercepted. How can a guy kill one of the most dangerous animals on earth if he cannot hit a harmless impala? I was embarrassed and the Africans were embarrassed by my embarrassment.

"But I'm not a rookie," I thought. "I've been hunting for twenty-five years. Terry Bradshaw threw an occasional interception, but he won four Superbowls. He recovered from his mistakes and so can I." The argument seemed convincing and it worked. An hour later I made a perfect shot on a young impala doe. Meat!

The next morning Mathias demonstrated his methodical approach to buffalo hunting. We drove the roads and looked for tracks. We stopped to check dung piles, and he judged their age with the accuracy of carbon dating. We parked at places known only to him and walked a mile or more to water holes where we checked for fresh signs. All came up negative.

Then Mathias pointed in the direction from which we had come and said he knew a good spot some distance back. I had a hunch that we had been operating on a process of elimination and that he had zeroed in the only remaining possibility.

At a totally nondescript location, Mathias waved me off the road and we parked in the shade of a baobab tree. We ate impala sandwiches and took long draughts of water in anticipation of a long march. We had just left the truck when Ceeasi hissed and pointed into the bush. Huge black forms drifted toward us 150 yards away. Buffalo! We crouched down.

"The nearest one is a bull." Mathias whispered. "You look here," he instructed, touching my binoculars. Through the glasses the herd looked like an avalanche of black bodies. The bull's horns swept low to the line of his jaw then extended four inches past his ears. The tips curled upward for nearly a foot before turning inward.

"It's a good one. I'll take him."

4

Solo Safari for Cape Buffalo

Suddenly the world was reduced to a hundred yard strip of African bush with a buffalo at one end and a hunter at the other. The eye, the mind, and the body became one, with a single purpose. The eye spotted the trunk of a mopane tree fifteen yards ahead and the body drifted toward it. I squatted down and rested walnut against mopane. The bull saw me and made a quarter turn, presenting his right shoulder, a perfect shot. I took a deep breath and squeezed the trigger.

The big Ruger jumped high into the air and the entire herd executed a left turn in perfect unison. I reloaded from the shoulder, shoved the crosshairs onto the bull's fanny and pressed the trigger as it disappeared into a wall of bushes. The .458 roared again, then all was silent.

Damn! I wanted to see it go down hard but it had made it to cover without missing a stride. If hit properly, buffalo die as easily as any other animal. But if they live for five minutes after being hit, they become supercharged with adrenaline, which transforms them into the most indestructible animals on earth.

As I reloaded, I thought about the shot. Had I held in the right spot? It looked good. I hadn't jerked the trigger. Maybe I should have used a solid bullet on the first shot.

Somewhere behind that wall of brush the bull waited, perhaps dead, probably wounded and still alive. This was the moment I had waited for, the Indianapolis 500 of big-game hunting, the Superbowl of Africa. But more was at stake than a silver cup or a gold ring. In the next few minutes something, or someone, would die. When you strip away all the hucksters in the safari business and cut through all the hype and inflated egos, buffalo hunting is reduced to this marvelous simplicity: The hunter kills the buffalo or the buffalo kills the hunter.

I moved ahead with the .458 at high port arms, the safety off. The adrenaline running through my own veins brought me exhilaration and soothed my fear. I was exactly where I wanted to be, here in Africa, facing uncertainty, without full control over the situation, but with full control over myself.

Mathias moved to my side with my .338. I noticed that it had been cocked and I heard the safety click off. I wondered whether he knew how to use a rifle and hoped I wouldn't find out. We stopped five yards short of the heavy brush were the bull had disappeared. I listened. Mathias listened. There! We could hear the bull's lungs pop and gurgle not fifteen yards away. He was hit hard and his lungs were filling with blood.

Mathias and I stepped apart, each hoping for a better view into the brush, each knowing that the rifles should be separated if the bull charged. Then a long, low bellow rolled through the forest. It was the death song of the buffalo. Mathias's dead serious stare gave way to a broad grin. He knew that sound well.

"It is finished," he said in a relaxed voice.

The bull went down in such heavy cover that I could not walk around it. I had to literally climb over it. It died facing its attackers, ready for that last, vicious charge, but two bullets had done their nasty work and death had come too quickly.

It was huge, 1400 pounds I would say. It was so ugly and its horns were so beautiful. Mathias shook my hand African style, by grasping the thumb, and he thumped my shoulder. He told me what a fine hunter I was and I assured him that he was the greatest tracker in all Africa. Ceeasi appeared and there was more handshaking. I did feel good.

We cleared the brush to take pictures. The light was no good but we tried anyway. The crew set to work with knives and ax, and the half-inch hide slowly peeled away. I helped mostly by staying out of the way as they clearly knew how to butcher big animals. Within three hours they had disassembled the bull and loaded it into the truck. When we drove away, only the contents of the paunch and the sex organs were left behind. I razzed the men for not eating the testicles, but apparently this is taboo for the Shona people. We hauled out every other ounce of the animal and divided it three ways with one-third going to James and a third each to Mathias's and Ceeasi's wives in Makuti.

That evening, the camp looked like a butcher shop with strips of meat and intestine hanging from every tree to dry. With such huge quantities of meat in camp, everything had to be secured from predators. Hyenas had visited camp every night and lions had prowled within a mile. I drove the truck into the circle of firelight. We loaded all the meat into the back of the truck, covered it with several logs and topped it off with thorn branches. We placed the buffalo cape and skull inside the cab and closed the windows. Ceeasi gave me clear instructions to sleep with the .458 loaded, then made his bed beside the fire with plenty of wood within easy reach. The lions roared as usual, and a hyena whooped and howled within ten feet of my tent, but Ceeasi directed a few chunks of firewood its way and the night passed without further incident.

Our camp was a Spartan affair, more like an Alaskan spike camp than an African safari camp. It consisted of two tiny nylon tents, a fire, and the trailer which served as a hyena-proof storage bin. There was no shower tent, no mess tent, no sanitary tent, and no gas-operated refrigerator.

I had nearly panicked when we first arrived in camp and discovered that the Chewore River was bone dry. Mathias scooped out a two-foot hole in the sandy riverbed. This quickly filled with sweet-tasting water which we shared with the local wildlife.

The lack of facilities was no problem for my Shona cook. James's impala pot roast would receive compliments at the dining room at Meikles Hotel in Harare and his oxtail soup was flavored to perfection. I endured many hardships on this hunt, but monotonous food was not among them.

In the days that followed, I came to know my crew. Mathias was serious, conscientious, and deliberate. He was about my age, on the shy side of forty. He had been a small-scale poacher, then a skinner, before joining the Game Department seven years earlier.

Those American sportsmen who talk a brave hunt, while depending totally on their professional hunters for physical security, should contemplate this man of Africa, this Mathias. Based on the impala experience, he would have thought I was a mediocre rifleman. Yet, when I wounded the buffalo, he stood beside me with an unfamiliar rifle, ready to meet the charge of the bull. I know American hunters who might show such courage, but I can count them on one hand.

Ceeasi spoke the best English, so I came to know him better than the others. He was thirty-three years old and an ex-soldier. He was the court jester, a mime. Every evening around the fire he reenacted the day's events, mimicking the animals, himself, and me. Even without understanding Shona, it was clear that Ceeasi never understated the humor of a situation. He cut a handsome pose in the firelight and I suspect his wife keeps a close eye on him.

James spoke little English, so I learned less about him. In 1980, the blacks of Rhodesia gained majority rule and Rhodesia was renamed Zimbabwe. As thousands of white families fled from Zimbabwe, thousands of black cooks, including James, fell on hard times.

Solo Safari

The crew worked well together and became friends. When Ceeasi's shoes fell apart, Mathias loaned him a pair of old boots. Ceeasi alternately hunted barefoot or in the undersized boots, depending on which set of blisters hurt most.

I tried to treat them fairly, and I believe they realized that I was not another redneck. I truly respected their skill, knowledge, and labor, and I believe they came to respect me as a hunter and a person. We communicated much of this without words.

This relationship with my crew was the unexpected bonus of a self-guided hunt. On guided hunts, the visiting sportsman talks with the professional hunter and the professional yells at the blacks. When the gin bottle is opened, the blacks disappear and aren't seen again until morning. For two weeks, they are physically close, share skills accumulated over many lifetimes, risk their lives for the paying sportsman, but they remain socially isolated. Africa is a place of extraordinary wildlife, but it is also a place of extraordinary people. Anyone who fails to know them cheats himself of half the African experience.

We hunted day after day for a cow buffalo but found no fresh tracks. There were solitary bulls and small bachelor groups but no herds of cows. All the ladies between the Sapi and Chewore rivers were together having one hell of a tea party. We wanted to crash that party but we had to find it first. I shot another impala for camp meat and made a trip to Makuti for petrol.

There was one remaining possibility. The cows had to be drinking from the Zambezi. On two consecutive days we drove thirty miles to the river, using gallons of precious petrol. We then checked every inch of the dusty road that parallels the Zambezi, but it had not been crossed by a single cow. We sat around the fire on the ninth evening of the hunt sipping warm beer. Only one hunting day remained, so it was time to talk strategy.

"The cows are not coming near the roads," I explained. "They are not coming near the rivers. Tomorrow, we must walk a long way into the bush to find the herd."

Yes, Mathias agreed the herd was deep in the bush. Yes, he knew an area far away that had good water. We would hunt there tomorrow.

I lay awake that night, rolled up in a single blanket, shivering, listening to whoops and snickers of our now familiar camp hyena. Here I was in the middle of a bloody wilderness with three Africans who could barely speak English. I was looking after them and they were looking after me and somehow we were getting by. Days earlier I had injured my thumb in the door of the truck and it was beginning to smell like an overripe leopard bait. I had barely enough petrol to reach the nearest station fifty miles away. The nearest repair garage was a hundred miles away. I had no spare parts, no backup driver, and no telephone to call AAA.

The next morning I proposed to drive deeper into the bush on tracks that would make a goat think twice, all in the hope of doing bodily harm to one of the most dangerous animals on earth. Lord help me. The alarm went off about five minutes later it seemed.

Ceeasi breathed new life into the fire as I crawled from beneath my blanket. I choked down a bowl of cold cereal and we drove off into the night while James crawled back into his tent. Two bone-jarring hours later Mat waved me off the road. I nosed the truck into the bush and we set out on foot as the first rays of sunlight filtered through the mopane leaves.

We eased up to the first water hole and surprised a family of warthogs. A lion complained loudly from a clump of bush not more than 200 yards to our right. Had it been expecting pork for breakfast? Then another lion roared 200 yards to our left. Was it a love song or a challenge to battle? I glanced at the guys' faces to see if I was supposed to be scared, but they showed no concern. I unslung the .458 as we walked past the lions. I didn't like being last in line with two roaring lions behind me.

We saw zebra, impala, kudu, baboon, and more warthogs. We stepped over rhino dung so fresh that it steamed, but rhino can be very nasty and I was glad we saw none. A bull elephant the size of a cement truck pulled down branches that rose thirty feet into the air. An impala ram stood in clear view seventy-five yards away and watched us pass. Its horns would have placed it high in the record book, but it's best not to bother with impala when hunting big game.

Then there was the leopard. You don't expect to see leopards in daylight, ever, but we flushed one at twenty yards. It crossed in front of me and let out a deep, throaty growl that was intended to scare the daylights out of me. It worked. The cat missed running over Mathias by four feet. Ceeasi would have great material for his evening performance around the campfire—the cat's desperate move to avoid hitting Mathias and the horror reflected on Mathias' face as the cat crossed his path.

Solo Safari

For five hours we hunted from water hole to water hole with hardly a word. We all read from the same book, and the pages brought no word of female buffalo. We were hot, tired, and thirsty and we were many miles from the truck. Ceeasi took his boots off, slung them over his shoulder, and we headed back.

Time had run out. The ladies had eluded us. We were soundly defeated and our only solace was the satisfaction of having done our best. The guys still wanted fresh meat to take to their wives, so we spent the afternoon hunting impala.

The next day I was pushing the bucket of bolts back down the highway toward Harare. For reasons I cannot explain, the old machine was still running. We had said goodbye to Mathias and Ceeasi. They would spend the day making impala biltong, the African version of jerky.

James stared straight ahead. His expression was stoical, as usual, but the old cook was chuckling to himself. This crazy American had hauled him to the Zambezi Valley, given him a third of a buffalo and an impala, and paid him three times the legal wage while he made the meat into biltong. Back in Harare he would receive the last fresh impala and four boxes of leftover food. Miracles do happen, even to down-and-out cooks in Africa.

I had actually pulled it off. I had planned and outfitted a safari from halfway around the world, traveled to the Zambezi Valley, killed a fine bull without the help of a professional hunter, and lived to write about it. I had shared success and disappointment with my crew and earned their respect.

Some measure the success of a hunt with a tape measure. They praise grotesque animals that "make the book" and despise beautiful animals that fall an inch short. That's all wrong, I thought. Success should be measured in personal accomplishment and in companionship, in sweat, and in the appreciation of sunrises and sounds from the night. Success must be measured in gracious acceptance of defeat. I had not killed a world-class buffalo, but I'd had a world-class experience.

THE ENEMY WITHIN

The trackers and game scout gathered around the big oval foot-print. Ridges of dust, forced into the cracks in the elephant's foot-prints, still showed knife edges, not yet blunted by the morning breeze. The bull had passed only minutes before. I could not understand the rush of whispers in Shona and Tonka, but ebony eyes sparkled with excitement. Wiro, the head tracker, placed both of his bare feet, heel to toe, inside the elephant track to measure its length. The big oval easily contained both of Wiro's feet. It was a large bull.

The trackers spread out through the bush and I hurried to keep up. Any rookie tracker could have followed the trail, but none of the younger men ever stepped ahead of Wiro, the Tonka master. Every man, white or black, who knows Wiro, respects him and defers to his superior judgment. He understands his world of trees, grass, and animals, but he is too reserved to flaunt his knowledge. As with most rural Africans, Wiro's face reveals little about his age. He is middle-aged. I cannot say more. Wiro works as a tracker for several months each year. The remainder of the year he gets by, maybe growing a little corn to feed his wife and six children.

To me a vulture is just another bird, but to Wiro it is input for his computer. He notices which vulture is sitting in which tree, which direction it is facing and how many other vultures are in attendance. From the sum of this information, Wiro subtracts the angle of the sun and divides by the temperature (in Fahrenheit, I believe) and con-cludes that a lion came to the bait two hours earlier, fed, and is now lying on the north side of a bush twenty yards from the bait.

This track was too fresh, too easy to force Wiro to draw on his reserve of skills. Without breaking pace or looking back, he flashed two fingers over his shoulder and the signal was passed back. Two bulls.

Solo Safari

I originally had planned to hunt elephant on my own, without a professional hunter. I had joined forces with a friend from Washington, D.C., to share costs and ease the logistics problems associated with elephant hunting. (Have you ever tried to backpack an elephant back to camp?) My friend, a veteran of many African hunts, had developed a friendship with Andy Kockott, a professional hunter who knows every inch of the Nyakasanga River, a tributary of the great Zambezi. The plan was for me to hunt with a black crew and Andy to guide my friend.

Call it pride or ego or damn foolishness, but I did not want a traditional, guided elephant hunt. Generally, the nervous client fires one round at an elephant, hitting it anywhere between the brain and the left, hind foot, if he hits it at all. A half second later, the professional hunter fires and kills the elephant. Ten seconds later, the professional hunter and well-rehearsed trackers congratulate the dumbfounded client on a spectacular kill. I wasn't about to pay half a year's salary for the first shot at somebody else's elephant. I would do it myself and damn the consequences.

But my plans went sour. On the morning of our departure, my friend's wife became seriously ill and he had to remain at home. A few days later, I found myself in camp with an experienced but temporarily unemployed professional hunter. To Andy, hunting is more than a profession. It is a passion. I hunted one day without him, but the enforced confinement to camp was driving him bonkers.

I had doubts about my ability to judge ivory, to distinguish between mediocre bulls and trophy bulls, so I asked Andy to join my hunting party. He would help find a good bull, but he agreed to shoot only in self-defense. We stalked several bulls, but Andy always turned his thumb down. Now, with two large bulls somewhere in the bush ahead, Andy's experienced eyes would help decide which one to shoot. I decided I was glad to have Andy Kockott with me.

We wound our way through the bush for half a mile, then Wiro stopped. I did not know why. I listened, but there was only the innocent call of some distant dove. A flash of red and green feathers streaked into the heavy bush, then all was silent. Did the bee-eater know that drama was at hand? My eyes followed Wiro's gaze into the bush and searched for a patch of gray, a tree trunk that moved, the switch of a wire-haired tail. I probed the limit of visibility, about 20 yards, but found no clue.

The Enemy Within

Then I heard it too. A branch cracked somewhere behind the tangle of brush and trees. I looked over the crud and saw a thirty-foot mopane tree thrashing in the horizon seventy yards away. The bulls were tearing down branches and feeding on them. The dove called. We waited. Then only silence. I took a couple of deep breaths and tried to look calm. Wiro pointed to the left, signaling that the bulls had moved in that direction.

How did he know this? How does an astronomer know that a distant star has exploded? How does a surgeon know that an internal organ is filled with cancer? In the face of superior expertise, I accept Wiro's conclusions on faith. If Wiro says the bulls went left, they went left. Perhaps he heard the bulls. Perhaps he saw the bee-eater roused from its refuge.

We moved ahead at a crouching trot, watching, thumbs pressing against safeties, chests pounding. Puffs of dust from our ash bags drifted behind us, indicating a favorable wind direction. Then the bulls appeared fifty yards ahead, widely separated, moving away at a walk. Andy danced left and right for a better view of the gleaming white tusks. He pointed to the bull on the right and gave a firm thumbs up, but even to my untrained eye the choice was clear. The five-ton bulls faded into the bush like clouds of vapor in a breeze.

The ash bags now showed the wind moving from right to left. We needed to move alongside the bull for a shot into the side of the brain. In order to keep our wind from the larger bull, we would have to move up between the two bulls. Nice!

More crouched trotting, more pounding chests. Then a wrinkled gray form drifted into the open. We were alongside, about fifty yards away. I motioned to Wiro to lead us closer, but he seemed hesitant. Then the reality of the situation struck me square in the face. The tracker had done his job. It was now an affair between the elephant and me. In the next few minutes, I would succeed or fail on my own skill, nerve, and judgment.

I was overcome with a rush of consciousness as the mind kicked into overdrive. Every detail was in sharp focus, every thought relevant to the task at hand. I took two steps to my left to place a sapling tree between the bull and me. I contorted my form into a crouch, so I would not look like a human being, and scurried forward. At thirty yards I settled onto a knee and lined up the shot. No good. The

13

sapling that had covered my approach now concealed the side of the bull's head.

I scooted six feet to my right for a clear field of fire. The bull saw the movement, turned toward me, flared his ears, and took two elephant-sized steps toward me. Don't give me any textbook crap about mild threat displays. This is a real live elephant and he's coming toward me and he's the size of a cement truck and elephants stomp on people and I probably won't live through the next thirty seconds. Textbooks don't count at that stage.

He stopped. I exhaled. Hell, he's just another piece of cake. I focused on the point of aim for the frontal brain shot, just above the line between the eyes. No, too much bone blocking the bullet's path through that massive skull. Too much chance for error or a deflected bullet. Better wait. "But what if he comes?" I thought. "That's the shot I'll have to take." I looked for the heart. The big bone of the left foreleg showed through the hide, angling across the heart, protecting it from my bullet. Wait! I shifted my aim back to the head.

As I waited for a better shot, I reflected on my situation. "Here I sit, about to do bodily harm to the largest animal on earth. He may fall dead, he may run away, or he may charge. At least I haven't gone berserk and shot recklessly. I've analyzed the ballistics of this thing and I'm waiting for the shot I want." I took a deep breath, then another.

His trunk slithered through the air searching for a scent but it found none. Satisfied, the bull turned away and moved forward, offering me the side brain shot. I looked for the ear hole and eye, the reference points indicating the location of the brain, but they were lost in the dark gray silhouette. "Well, it isn't going to get any better than this," I thought. "The brain must be right THERE."

The .458 roared and the hulk leaned toward me. He fell against a clump of saplings, which crackled and gave way under his mass. I snatched the bolt back as the bull slid to the ground. I slammed the bolt forward, and for the first time in two years, the big rifle jammed. I muttered something very naughty about Mr. Ruger, cleared the jam, and ran forward. At ten yards, the bull tried to lift his head and I knew that I had missed the brain by a fraction of an inch. I drove another bullet through the spine into the chest. I stuffed a couple of cartridges into the magazine and moved around to the bull's front.

The Enemy Within

"Watch out for his trunk." Andy's warning pierced my consciousness and brought me back to the world of people. On Andy's advice, I put a couple of insurance rounds through the heart.

Trackers drifted in from the bush and there was handshaking and speculation about the weight of the ivory. All congratulations were freely accepted with no pretense of humility. It was my bull and it was my day. Wiro presented me with the severed tail, the traditional proof that an elephant has been killed. I climbed over the carcass, paced off the length, measured the feet, and did all the other things that novice elephant hunters do to impress themselves with the size of their trophies.

The hunt was over, but we devoted the rest of the day to the elephant. Ladies came from camp and posed for pictures. Wiro chopped out the tusks while a dozen men swarmed over the carcass. A half ton of hide was pried loose and salted and a dozen truck loads of meat were hauled to camp to be dried. I did not hunt any more that day.

I had spent thirty of my forty years dreaming of that day on the Zambezi. These had been dreams of anticipation, longing, and fear. Like an Olympic athlete, I had mentally rehearsed every possible contingency a thousand times. On the appointed day I had performed well enough, and I would have a pleasant memory to sustain me in my old age. This rite of passage separated thirty years of anticipation from thirty years of pleasant reminiscence.

I recalled the ponderings of another adventurer, George Leigh-Mallory, who might have been the first human to stand on the summit of Mount Everest. We will never know his thoughts, because he died somewhere on the high slopes of Everest. Earlier, having completed a very arduous and dangerous climb, Mallory had asked, "Have we vanquished an enemy?" Then he answered his question, "None but ourselves."

Mallory had tested himself on the mountain. I had tested myself against the elephant. The mountain and the elephant were not the enemy. The enemy was within. The enemy was fear.

DANGEROUS TO WHOM?

Hunters and writers have argued for decades about which of Africa's animals is most dangerous: elephant, lion, leopard, rhino, or buffalo. The argument has not been for naught. As more information is shared among hunters, a consensus is emerging, but the information is strongly biased toward the point of view of professional hunters. I want to reexamine the data from the sportsmen's point of view.

Most professional hunters rate the cats as most dangerous, with the lion receiving the most votes. A wounded lion is more likely to kill you than any other animal. It has the awesome strength and bite to do the job very quickly. Lions usually run in packs or "prides," so hunters often have to contend with several angry lions simultaneously. This is not a good situation. Alexander Lake, professional hunter and author of *Killers in Africa*, kept a tally of twenty-three hunters who had tragic encounters with lions. Eight were horribly mauled and fifteen were killed. That doesn't leave any good alternatives—thirty-five percent maimed and sixty-five percent killed.

A wounded leopard is a smaller target. It charges from closer range and gives no warning. Therefore, it is more difficult to stop than a lion. There is no escape. But the leopard lacks the tremendous strength of the lion. It tends to bounce onto its victim, savage him for a few seconds, then bounce off. A leopard may be far more likely than a lion to maul a hunter, but the chances of survival are greater with a leopard. So you can choose between a high probability of a mauling and a lower probability of a mauling but a much higher probability of getting the final chop. Nice choice.

In 1986, no fewer than three professional hunters in Zimbabwe were chewed on by wounded leopards. All survived. The folks who control international commerce in wildlife allowed Zimbabwe to export only eighty leopards in 1986. I would guess that the number of leopards taken by sport hunters was somewhat less than that. This gives an injury rate, for Zimbabwe for 1986, of something like one injury for every twenty-five leopards killed. I believe the long-term, Africa-wide average would be less striking than that, but think about it—one in twenty-five. Better yet, don't think about it, not when you have spots under the crosshairs, or you will get the shakes and ruin the shot.

While the leopards lack the awesome strength of lions, leopards are capable of astounding feats. A 100-pound leopard can carry an antelope carcass of equal weight up a vertical tree trunk. How can an animal that looks so delicate be so strong? This enigma, this golden spotted cat, is a bundle of contradictions. It is beauty. It is treachery. It is everywhere, but it is rarely seen. It drifts through the bush as silently as the fog, then its call rips through the night, sending a shock wave through those who might fall prey. The leopard lives on the filthiest carrion, but its body is immaculate. Unlike the lion, which fears nothing, the leopard fears man. Yet the leopard will slide through an open bedroom window and snatch a sleeping dog from the foot of your bed.

I'm not prone to emotional responses to dead animals, but I will never forget the day I first examined a mounted leopard. I touched my finger tip to the claw of the leopard. It was not sharp like a needle but was sharp like the point of a well-ground knife. The thought of the cat's multiple knife points ripping through my flesh left a hollow in the pit of my stomach and I said a small prayer to Diana, Goddess of the Hunt.

With the cats vying for first and second place, most hunters put the Cape buffalo in third place. For twenty years, Anthony Dyer, president of the East African Professional Hunters Association, kept a tally of professional hunters who were badly injured or killed by the so-called Big Five. Buffalo won first prize, having stomped and horned their way through ten professionals. Lion and leopard ran a poor second, tying at five victims each. Elephant and rhino also tied at three each.

Dangerous to Whom?

The preeminence of buffalo is not surprising. They are legendary for their ability to absorb lead and punishment. The killing of a buffalo is a race between death and adrenaline. If death comes within a few seconds, before the adrenaline hits the bloodstream, the buffalo succumbs as easily as any 1500-pound animal. But if the adrenaline gets into its blood, it holds death at bay, shrugging off multiple hits from the heaviest rifles. You must destroy its body, for you will not destroy its will.

I have been able to collect good data on the dangers of buffalo hunting. Joseph Gustav Gruex killed over 7,000 buffalo for meat in Mozambique and was tossed six times. John "Pondoro" Taylor killed 1,200 buffalo, apparently without injury, but he was charged repeatedly. Commander David E. Blunt, author of the famous book *Elephants*, killed fifty buffalo. He reported being charged once but was not injured. John F. Burger, author of the only book devoted primarily to buffalo hunting, was tossed once in over a thousand tries. However, two of his companions were seriously injured and a third killed. Overall, the injury rate for buffalo seems to exceed one injury per thousand animals.

Sport hunting is about ten times more dangerous, probably because of poor shooting by nervous clients. One safari company that hosts about twenty clients a year averages one buffalo charge per year. A friend who grew up in Africa has killed about sixty buffalo and has been injured twice! (I have been very careful to avoid buffalo hunting with this chap.) I personally have been involved with eighteen buffalo kills and have been charged once. I will guess that for every hundred buffalo killed by sportsmen, there are about five charges and perhaps one injured hunter. Despite claims to the contrary, buffalo hunting is a bit more dangerous than driving the Los Angeles freeways.

However, we must recognize that Anthony Dyer's data, ten hunters injured or killed by buffalo, reflects the greater hunting activity for buffalo. I suspect that more buffalo are killed annually than all the other Big Five combined. An avid American sportsman might take one lion, one leopard, and one elephant in his lifetime, but he could easily take half a dozen buffalo. Over a sportsman's or professional hunter's career, buffalo probably represent the greatest aggregate danger.

The notion that buffalo are dangerous only after wounding is nonsense. I tend to agree that bulls are dangerous only if they are provoked, but provocation can take many forms: a sportsman's bullet,

Solo Safari

a ball fired from a poacher's muzzleloader, a foot injury from a poacher's snare, a wound from the horn of another buffalo, injuries from lions, or a case of indigestion.

In 1985, I hunted out of the Chewore River Camp in the Zambezi Valley. The hunter who preceded me in that camp was from South Africa. On the first day of his hunt, he was walking through the bush, minding his own business, when a bull buffalo boiled out of the crud and ran over him. He got a shot into the bull, but failed to kill it. The chap regained his feet and was collecting his wits when the bull came again. He fired and killed the bull, but the beast fell on the hunter, pinning his legs to the ground. With the help of his crew, he extricated himself and returned immediately to South Africa, forfeiting the remaining nine days of his hunt. A week later, the Johannesburg newspaper advertised a .375 for sale, cheap! This chap did not personally provoke the bull. Presumably, the bull suffered from one of the ailments listed above.

Dr. Brian Bertram, who conducted research on lions in Tanzania, reported that the very presence of lions causes buffalo to become aggressive. Consider this scenario: Buffalo smells lion; buffalo loads bloodstream with adrenaline; buffalo sees American kudu hunter; buffalo tosses sportsman; sportsman goes to hospital for repairs, losing two days of kudu hunting. Excited buffalo can be a real nuisance.

On the northern Serengeti Plain in Kenya, my party came upon an hour-old buffalo calf. Our truck was the biggest thing that moved, so the calf thought that the truck was his mama and he wobbled up for a drink of milk. I scrambled to replace my telephoto lens with a shorter lens so I could take the calf's portrait. I looked up to see mama at fifteen yards and closing. By my recollection, that cow was eight feet tall and weighed about 6000 pounds. She turned off at fifteen feet. I was charged a second time by a cow buffalo in Zimbabwe, but that story is told in a later chapter.

The bull elephant may be less likely to stomp you than the others, but it is more likely to scare the hell out of you. Elephants are so big, and they are hunted at such close range, that elephant hunting is really in a class by itself. If we were to apply the normal criteria of bullet weights and foot pounds to elephant rifles, even the .460 Weatherby would be judged totally inadequate. Shooting an elephant with an express rifle is the ballistic equivalent of shooting a deer with a .22 rimfire. Move in to twenty-five yards, place the bullet perfectly, no

20

problem. But if you screw up that twenty-five-yard shot on an elephant, you lose more than seventy-five pounds of venison. You may lose your life! As with lions, I suspect that elephants kill most of their victims. I hope I never meet the man who can sneak up to an elephant with the intent of doing bodily harm and without feeling a twinge of anxiety.

The original Big Five included the black rhino, but poachers have nearly eliminated the black rhino from Africa. They are not hunted legally today and probably will not be hunted in the near future. When I first hunted the Zambezi Valley in 1985, rhino spoor was everywhere and I had to be constantly alert for the unpredictable beasts. The possibility of a nose-to-nose encounter with a rhino in thick brush added real zest to the hunt. By 1987, poachers crossing the river from Zambia had taken a heavy toll and I had to hunt hard to find rhino spoor. In 1988, I saw none at all. The Zambezi Valley has the last viable, free-roaming population of black rhino in Africa, but these rhinos are being hammered. The Zambezi Valley, and all of Africa, will be poorer for the loss of this extraordinary animal.

Today, hunters must settle for the much larger, but more docile, white rhino of southern Africa. In sharp contrast to their smaller cousins, white rhinos have to be the most laid-back mammals on earth. I once walked to within twenty-five yards of a wild, white rhino bull. It was lying on its stomach, resting. It opened its eyes to look at me but never even raised its head off the ground. A dozen people in my party sneaked up, two at a time, for a close look at the beast, then quietly backed away. For all I know, that big gray boulder is still lying nose down in the dust.

Yet, wildlife biologists in South Africa tell me that they have more dicey encounters with white rhinos than with black rhinos, indicating the potential dangers of the bigger animals. The reason for the increased number of nasty encounters is that people give less respect to the white rhino. If an experienced hunter encounters a white rhino, he makes a fifty-yard detour around the beast. If he encounters a black rhino, he makes a five-hundred-yard detour. It is this casual attitude toward the white rhino that gets people into trouble. The white rhino really belongs with the hippo in the second echelon of dangerous animals.

This ranking—lion, leopard, buffalo, elephant, white rhino—averages out over all hunting conditions. Local conditions affect the order. For example, a bull elephant in very heavy brush might be far more of a danger than a lion on an open plain. In the open, a stalk can be planned to the hunter's advantage, the shot can be carefully set up, and follow-up shots can be fired before the animal reaches cover or the shooter.

So hippo are less dangerous, on average, than lions. You may not consider this too relevant if a hippo has just bitten your native wooden canoe in half and is about to make a move on you. Wildebeest, on average, are quite harmless, but I know two professional hunters in Zimbabwe who have been charged by wounded wildebeest.

Almost everything that has been written about the dangers of the Big Five, including the above treatise, has represented the point of view of the professional hunter or that extremely rare individual, the self-guided sportsman. If we consider other points of view, the lineup changes dramatically. For example, crocodile are easily the greatest danger for the native people of Africa, followed, I believe, by hippo. This reflects the lifestyles of African women who spend much time on streambanks, washing clothing and fetching water. They are far more vulnerable than professional hunters to crocodile and hippo attacks.

What are the dangers for a visiting sportsman from America or Europe who hires a professional hunter? Again the list changes. The greatest difference is that leopard really should not be considered dangerous for most visiting sportsmen. Unwounded leopards are harmless except in very extraordinary cases, such as man-eaters, which are rare among the spotted cats. Elsewhere, I mentioned a leopard encounter in the Sapi Safari Area in the Zambezi Valley. I flushed a leopard at twenty yards. The cat took off at a gallop, growling like a lion. It hadn't gone twenty-five yards when my unsuspecting tracker, Mathias, stepped square in front of the leopard. In this situation a buffalo would have lowered its head and charged, but the leopard changed directions so fast that it probably gave itself a hernia. It missed Mathias by four feet. This is exactly the situation you would create if you wanted to provoke an unwounded leopard to attack— but in this case the leopard turned away. Still, I doubt that Mathias would like to repeat the experience.

I have never heard or read of a case where leopards charged at the first impact of a bullet. Wounded leopards politely retire to heavy cover and wait for someone to come after them. The follow-up, which is extremely dangerous, is done by the professional hunter while the client nearly always waits in the blind or vehicle. Leopard hunting is dangerous, but most of the danger is borne by the professional hunter, little by the client.

Contrast this with elephant hunting. Unwounded elephants are very dangerous, especially the cows. Even if the client shoots well and drops his bull, other members of the herd may press the attack, a situation that simply does not exist with leopard hunting. Therefore, elephants are a danger to the client both before and after the shot. The risks of elephant hunting are more equally shared between the client and the professional hunter.

A new dangerous animal was on license in Zimbabwe for several years—the cow elephant. Zimbabwe issued cow licenses in conjunction with their culling operations. These offered a true elephant hunting experience at a fraction of the cost of hunting bulls. Actually, to hunt cows is far more dangerous, on average, than to hunt bulls. To quote from the notorious ivory poacher, John "Pondoro" Taylor who killed over a thousand elephants:

> It has been my experience that (a bull) elephant shot through the heart or lungs will always clear off after his trunk— that is in the direction he is facing. He may slew around a mite and head directly away from you after running a short distance, but I have never known a bull to charge on receiving such a shot. A cow, yes; it's by no means unknown for a cow to whip around instantly on feeling the lead and make a most determined charge, but not a bull.

The reaction of the other animals compounds the problem. Bulls are often hunted as singles. No problem. Or, if a small herd of bulls is shot into, it's every bull for itself. Unwounded bulls typically head for the far horizon, but if you threaten a herd of cows, the entire herd may stage a mutual defense.

Unfortunately, lady elephants sometimes reckon that the best defense is a good offense, so things can become rather exciting. With cows, you face great danger from the animal you shoot but a far greater danger from the animals you don't shoot. Big bull elephants are great trophy animals, but cows offer far more interesting and exciting hunting experiences at much reduced costs. If you want the maximum surge of adrenaline for the least cost, go for the cows.

Of all the cow elephants in a herd, the cows without tusks have a firm reputation as the most treacherous. It is suggested that life is tough for elephants without tusks, and they have to get mean to survive. Those who crop elephants try to shoot the cows without tusks first to quickly eliminate the greatest source of danger. But the sportsman who wants to collect a pair of tusks must leave the most dangerous animals standing. Zimbabwe's Zambezi Valley is noted for its high percentage of cows without tusks. So it is likely that hunting there for cows may have been the most dangerous hunting ever known.

Regrettably, Zimbabwe no longer offers cow licenses. Zimbabwe experienced a series of accidents in which hunters were seriously injured or killed and the officials decided that sport hunting for cow elephants was simply too dangerous. Surprisingly, every accident involved professional hunters and none involved self-guided hunters.

The problem of multiple animals is also encountered in lion hunting. Female lions, like cow elephants, will rally to the defense of the group. Pursuing prides of lions is more dangerous than pursuing individual males.

Buffalo also run in herds, but buffalo herds never, to my knowledge, stage a common defense against human hunters. It is possible that a hunter could get in the way of a stampeding herd, but this would be very unusual. (Don't tell that to my friend who chased a herd of 400 buffalo smack into a pride of lions. The buffalo scented the lions and stampeded in every direction. In the confusion, my friend killed his buffalo at seven yards.)

From the point of view of professionally guided sportsmen, I would reorder the lineup of the Big Five. Lions and cow elephants are first and second. Buffalo come next, followed by bull elephants. Leopards and white rhinos are far behind the rest of the pack, along with hippos.

New patterns of human and wildlife encounters are emerging in southern Africa. For example, many Americans and Europeans are floating Zimbabwe's Zambezi River in canoes, where crocodiles occasionally chew up a tourist. It will be only a matter of time before a Zambezi hippo chomps his teeth through a canoeist.

The decreasing use of mobile camps and the increasing use of permanent camps has led to the development of a new phenomenon called "camp lions." With camps located permanently within their territories, lions become very familiar with man. They learn to feed on both garbage and trophy animals hanging in camp.

In 1987, while camped in the Zambezi Valley, a lion came into my camp and ate thirty pounds of meat from the hind quarters of my

Dangerous to Whom?

buffalo. The quarters were hanging about fifty yards from my tent. On a later hunt, a lion ate some zebra meat stored about ten yards from my tent.

Most of the lion maulings that I know about have not occurred in the hunting fields but in camps at night. These nighttime attacks are extremely dangerous. In the field, rifles are at the ready, the animal is wounded and close to death, and the advantage is with the human hunters. At night, the advantage is with Leo. He is hungry, but healthy. He has the element of total surprise and enjoys the cover of darkness. The survival rate for those mauled at night is less than those mauled in daylight. There is the added specter of being dragged off and eaten by your attacker, as happened to a black game ranger in the Zambezi Valley in 1987.

"Camp hyenas" are also a problem. They are even more bold than lions and more numerous. I don't know of a case where a European or American has been killed by a hyena, but several have been disfigured and injured. On several occasions, hyenas have cast moon shadows on my tent and one tried to open an ice chest setting six inches from my tent.

How do our grizzly and brown bears compare with Africa's adrenaline pushers? It is difficult to make a comparison, but I am inclined to suggest that they are typically less dangerous to man than lion, wounded leopard, buffalo, or elephant. Yellowstone and Glacier National Parks host about four million visitors annually, yet they experience only four or five maulings, on average, by grizzly bears per year. If that many people visited the Zambezi Valley, the accident rate from lions alone would be many times higher.

In Africa's national parks, tourists generally are prohibited from leaving their automobiles. Hiking is permitted only in organized groups led by armed rangers. In some parks, camping is permitted only in areas enclosed in game-proof fences or continually guarded by game rangers. The American data, one mauling per million visitors, just do not justify these restrictions.

I once showed a visiting professional hunter from Zimbabwe a full body mount of a brown bear. The beast stood at full height with its teeth bared, an impressive sight. In response to my question about weapons, he said that he would not touch such an animal with anything less than a .375 and he would prefer a .458.

Solo Safari

However, many American bear guides do not show that kind of respect for their prey. I know of one brown-bear guide who boasted that he backs up his clients with a .30-06. No African guide would use less than a .375 on lion, a much smaller animal, and they do not apologize for their choice of weapon.

The American literature on bears includes several accounts of guides who held fire on charging bears to give their clients every opportunity to kill the bears unaided, so that they could enjoy all the attendant self-satisfaction. This is a nice gesture that I wholeheartedly support. An African professional who holds fire on a wounded, charging lion would have his professional hunter's license revoked and would be given a one-way ticket to the funny farm, if not the cemetery.

Of eighteen people mauled by grizzlies in Yellowstone and Glacier Parks from 1984 through 1987, four were killed— about twenty-two percent. In his book, *Alaska Bear Tales*, Larry Kaniut documented dozens of bear attacks and calculated a fatality rate of twenty-seven percent. This is unimpressive compared with the sixty-five percent kill rate for lions. On the other hand, the kill rate for bears is very impressive if you happen to be part of the twenty-seven percent. Statistics really do not mean much when you have the animal's hot breath in your face. Indeed, bears seem more likely than cats to direct their attack at the victims' heads, causing horrible, disfiguring wounds.

Some anti-hunters have suggested that hunting should be an equal contest between man and beast and that anything less is not true sport. Fifty-fifty odds, live or die. Only a wimp would use a .458 on an elephant. Real men use spears and clubs. When I learn that one of these critics holds a Congressional Medal of Honor, or has killed a lion in bare-handed combat, I will listen seriously. Until then, I'd rather ignore them collectively.

No one doubts the courage of the drivers who race at Indianapolis, even though something more than fifty percent survive each race. The most dangerous sport I know of is mountaineering in the Himalayan Mountains. The casualty rate is roughly fifty percent (mostly frostbite) and the fatality rate is about ten percent, far short of fifty-fifty odds of survival. Would our critics call these men and women cowards? Would the critics have parachutists make every other jump with parachute packs stuffed only with confetti? It is not the certainty of death or injury, but the possibility of harm, that adds spice to African hunting. P.J. Pretorius, one of the greatest hunters and adven-

Dangerous to Whom?

turers in African history, captured the essence of living on the dangerous edge in the opening lines to his book, *Jungle Man*:

> Living dangerously is twice blessed—it blesses the moment with elation; it blesses the after-day with warm memories. If a man has trodden unknown trails and landed on lost beaches, when age comes the domestic hearth is a campfire where old dramas are relived.

But those who live dangerously are not twice blessed if they do not survive the dangerous moment.

We can control the danger involved in hunting, mountaineering, and other adventures somewhat. We can hunt more dangerous animals, hunt or climb more or less dangerous terrain, and increase our level of skill. An increase in risk is not my primary motive for hunting African game without a professional hunter, but the added risk contributes to my sense of self-accomplishment, which is my primary motive. Due largely to government regulations in most African countries, and due also to the nearly impossible problems of logistics, this option is not available to most Americans.

A few Americans are increasing the level of danger of African hunting by switching from rifles to handguns and archery equipment. I'm an advocate for personal freedom and free choice, but let's not fool ourselves. Most of the increase in risk is borne by the professional hunters and trackers, not by the clients. Inevitably, this trend will result in the deaths of professional hunters and trackers. They take most of the additional risks, but at $20,000 per safari hand gunners buy the rights to do additional bragging.

If a professional is long on debts and short on bookings, he should be free to take on a hand gunner or archer. Likewise, if a black tracker desperately needs cash to pay his children's school fees, and if refusal to lead a hand gunner to within spitting distance of an elephant would result in loss of his job, he should be free to choose continued employment. I personally would not force that decision on him.

Regardless of which animal is the meanest, the fact remains that big-game hunters must take adequate precautions at all times, including in bed at night. Adequate armaments should always be close at hand. That's why my favorite rifle for impala is a .338 Magnum!

HARVEST OF TRANQUILITY

Why do I return to the hunting fields? Why does a strictly middle-class wage earner spend most of his life's savings accumulating experiences important only to himself? Memories, unlike other investments, are not lost on a bear market, but can memories alone sustain me in my old age? These are things I understand poorly.

There are many things I understand poorly. I do not understand time. My watch tells me there are still twenty-four hours in every day. I would find my watch hard to believe if it weren't for a firm faith in mechanics, because the earth seems to spin more rapidly now than when I was a child.

Every year the deadlines grow shorter, the people crowd closer, and technology advances further beyond comprehension. Every month I travel across half a continent. Every week my telephone conversations span the entire continent and every day the knot in my stomach twists more tightly. Where will it end?

For most, there is no end. There is only temporary escape. Some people escape to louder music, drugs, and more crowded pubs. Others escape to nostalgia, solitude, and natural places. I am among those who need solitude and natural places.

Great grandfather grew his food and split firewood from trees grown on his farm. He lived very close to the natural system that supported him. Now beefsteak comes from a supermarket and heat from a gas furnace. The threat of these modern conveniences is that they divorce us from our natural life-support systems. Some of us have a deep inner need to regain contact with the land, to re-create the old ways. The venison steaks in my freezer have a value that cannot be measured in dollars or grams of protein. They are my tie to the land.

Solo Safari

How could I face another day of artificial work with artificial people? How could I tolerate the negotiations, the compromises, the back stabbing, if I could not foresee the occasional return to untamed places? Do those who hunt, fish, and wander through the hills have fewer ulcers or family arguments than those who do not? Do they commit fewer crimes? These are things I understand poorly, but I believe the answers are affirmative. The hunting fields yield a harvest of horns and meat, but more importantly they yield a harvest of tranquility.

Why is it that presenting one's physical body to danger, in the form of tooth and claw, rock walls, crevassed glaciers, or white water helps achieve a state of inner tranquility? A positive link between danger and tranquility seems unlikely, but if sought by choice under controlled circumstances, danger can sooth the mind.

I began my career as an environmental specialist with an agency that was responsible for development of water resources, but it had a reputation for using a heavy hand on Mother Nature. I was a good environmentalist. I was so good that my supervisors decided their lives would be simpler without me on their staff. I'm proud that I was fired by this agency. It documents the incompatibility between their approach to environmental management and mine. It was a frustrating three years.

I took up rock climbing during those years. I noticed that I attempted the most difficult (and most dangerous) climbs on weekends that followed the most frustrating weeks at the office. In the face of thirty feet of smooth, vertical rock, the frustrations at the office just melted away. The closer the brush with death, the more total the escape from the realities of everyday life. Danger forces the mind to block out everything but the immediate problem.

Having been fired by the nature rapers, I went to work for an organization with which I was philosophically compatible. I immediately gave up rock climbing and now consider the sport somewhat foolhardy. And so I returned to Africa to get the hell scared out of me by an elephant and to find inner peace and to try to understand it all. I would hunt cow elephants because they are scarier than bulls, and I would hunt in the Zambezi Valley because it has many cows without tusks that are even scarier than cows with tusks, and I would hunt without a professional hunter to back me up because I wanted this to be my very own scare. I was very brave about this at my local safari club meetings, but my perspective might change in the midst of a herd of angry elephants. Win, lose, or die, it would certainly be an effective diversion.

Hunting cows is different from hunting bulls. I would follow a big-toothed bull to the ends of the earth, but cows never produce really good ivory, so other considerations must be weighed. I resolved to road hunt for a cow, so we would have access to the carcass with a vehicle. This would enable Andy Kockott to recover the meat and hide, which are worth more than the ivory.

The first problem would be to find a herd close to a road or in easy terrain. The second problem would be to distinguish between cows and young bulls. Any rank amateur can tell a mature bull from a cow. The problem is the immature bulls that frequently accompany the cow herds. The cows have slightly pointed foreheads while the bulls' heads are more rounded. This is a moderately reliable indicator but it shows only if the animals are in perfect profile.

The other primary indicator is the thickness of the tusks. Cow teeth are never thicker than a bottle of Lion Lager. A young bull's tusks might be as thick as the heavy end of a baseball bat. Of course a bull may have its crank hanging out, or it may not. If it is hanging out, it may not be visible through the brush. Professional hunters, who live and work among elephants, sweat blood in fear of shooting a young bull by mistake. I'd had only a few opportunities to view elephants and I was really intimidated by the problem.

I had a good hunting crew. My partner was John Tautin, a wildlife manager from Maryland. John had hunted throughout the Rockies, Canada, and Alaska, but this was his first hunt in Africa. John was trim and fit, a superb woodsman and hunter.

The Zimbabwe Department of Parks and Wildlife provided two Shona trackers. Jason Masonto was thirty-something, competent, and cooperative. He brought both instinct and logic to the interpretation of nature's signs. The older man was called Friday. He had a spring in his step which belied his thirty years with the parks department. He was a heads-up tracker, reading the trail ten to twenty yards ahead. On good ground, he could track at a fast walk, forcing John and me to struggle to keep pace. The Tonka tracker, Wiro, was with us again. The three of them, Wiro, Jason, and Friday had more than sixty years of tracking experience. I rarely argued with their conclusions.

The final member of the team was Pearson, who was something of a mechanical wizard. Using wire, bits of broken nails, and unlimited ingenuity, he kept Andy's old Land Rover rolling. How, I'm not sure, but he got us back to camp every evening.

The first encounter with cow elephants was not entirely welcome. John Tautin was dragging his belt buckle through the dirt, trying to crawl up on a herd of buffalo. I was right behind him with a mouth full of dust and an insurance rifle. We were trying to sort out a good set of horns when a cow elephant without tusks stepped into view beside the buffalo, about 120 yards away. No problem, just something more to keep track of. John and I maneuvered for a better view of the buffalo and a second tuskless cow emerged, then a tusked cow and a heavy bull. We were too far from a road to recover an elephant carcass, so we concentrated on John's buffalo.

Then the lead elephant remembered some patch of good tasting saplings and stepped out with six-foot strides. It was coming straight at us with another tuskless cow and assorted other elephants in tow. Perhaps a professional hunter could have sorted this situation out, but I wanted nothing to do with two tuskless elephants at close range. I suffer badly from stage fright and the audience (about fifty buffalo) was making me nervous. When the elephants crossed the seventy yard mark, I grabbed John by the collar and we executed a hasty tactical withdrawal: We ran like hell. This spooked the buffalo, wasting a three-hour stalk.

The next herd was near a road, so we moved in to look them over. At thirty-five yards we saw a tuskless cow, a broken-toothed cow with a calf, and another cow with very good tusks and a calf. One just doesn't shoot cows with calves. Behind the herd was another elephant which looked promising, so we backed off, made a half-mile circle, and moved in for a closer look.

Jason called it a cow and urged me to shoot. It had a pointed forehead but the tusks were a bit too thick for a cow. I beckoned to John and he duck-walked up to my position. "Does that animal have a pointed forehead?" John consulted his binoculars.

"Yes, definitely."

"How thick are the tusks?"

"About like the thick end of a baseball bat."

The elephant had the head of a cow and the tusks of a young bull. If it was a cow, it would have huddled up with the herd. This one was feeding thirty yards out. It had to be a bull. We backed off twenty yards.

Harvest of Tranquility

Wiro came up. He was agitated. I couldn't understand every word but it translated something like this. "Look you sniveling amateurs, a cow has tusks like this." He grabbed his left arm. "A bull has ivory like this." He placed both hands around his thigh. "This one has tusks like this." The hand went back to the left arm. "Shoot quickly so we can make some biltong."

John and I thought it was a bull. The trackers thought it was a cow. We consulted Pearson, the mechanic, but he wisely refused to comment. I decided to trust my trackers' sixty years of combined experience.

"Okay, let's go shoot the bloody thing and then look between its legs."

We moved in to set up the shot, but then the herd spooked and ran off. Jason led the follow-up but lost the trail. Without a doubt he intentionally led us astray, and I was glad he did. To this day I am fifty-five percent certain that animal was a bull.

The next day we found another herd. We moved in and began to study their tusks, and when we could see them, their foreheads. At forty yards, with an ash bag constantly flicking out clouds of dust to test the wind, I slowly worked along the herd searching for a suitable cow. To the far left, hidden from view were several animals I couldn't see well. Forget them for now. There was a cow with calf, then an animal facing directly toward me so I couldn't see the profile of the forehead. The tusks were just a bit too good and I feared it might be a young bull. Then there was a broken tusked cow with a calf, a half-grown animal with nubbins for tusks, and a bull with about thirty-five pounds per side. I had spent about fifteen minutes working along the front of the herd but had seen nothing that made me comfortable.

I remembered the animals hidden to the far left, so I backed out, tested the wind for the hundredth time, and moved in for a closer look. There was a small cow with a calf and another unaccompanied cow. It was in perfect profile and showed a sharply pointed forehead. John confirmed my analysis. Its teeth were small, but at this point the certain identification of sex was more important to me than the weight of the ivory. We had inventoried three herds of cows and had not seen a classic pair of cow tusks, those long slender toothpicks. I wanted to be done with elephants and move on to other game. This cow would do.

I flicked the ash bag for the two hundredth time and the wind remained reliable. I crawled to the thirty yard mark and eased up the .460 Weatherby. It was in perfect position for a side brain shot, but I couldn't see the ear hole and eye in the scattered shade of the forest. It was the exact situation I had faced with my bull elephant a year earlier.

I lowered the .460 and raised my binoculars. A tiny, yellow leaf showed in the sunlight, three feet this side of the cow's head. If I held the front sight four inches to the left of the leaf, the bullet should find the brain. Fortunately, the elephants were falling asleep and the cow was completely motionless. The .460 came up again and this time it roared. The cow staggered and fell to the ground.

I snatched the bolt back and glanced around for immediate danger. Seeing none, I paused for a second to pull an extra cartridge from my belt, feed it up the snout, and quietly close the bolt. I was contemplating a second shot into the body but it was obscured by heavy brush. About five seconds passed, then all hell broke loose. Elephants were running and growling and trees were cracking under their weight. With only one elephant on license, I dared not shoot in self-defense. It was time to move!

Crouching, running, looking over my shoulder, I ran smack into John Tautin. "Let's get the hell out of here," I hissed, but John was mesmerized by the drama that was unfolding before his eyes. At the risk of being rude, I physically pushed him backward and he finally got the message and turned and ran. Ten yards farther on we picked up Jason who needed no encouragement at all. He had been through this drill before.

At thirty yards we straightened our backs and broke into a proper sprint. Now elephants were trumpeting and grinding small trees into the dust. Jason and I lengthened our strides, leaving John a few paces behind. I glanced over my shoulder, looking for any pursuing elephants, and made a mental note of the wisdom of selecting a hunting partner who cannot keep up with me in a foot race. At eighty yards we passed Wiro, who had climbed thirty feet up a tree so he could see over the bush. At 200 yards we stopped, chests heaving, and listened to the commotion.

Wiro frantically waved us to the right. Elephants were moving off and we were in their path. We ran. Then Wiro waved us to the left. More elephants were leaving. We ran again, then all was quiet. We waited fifteen minutes, giving the cow time to die and giving the other elephants time to leave.

We tiptoed forward, rifles ready. At least three elephants remained, protecting the fallen cow. We backed off and circled upwind, hoping that our scent would drive the animals away. We sneaked in the second time but the three animals remained. We backed off and waited another five minutes. Again we tiptoed in and could see only one elephant. "Shoot," Jason urged, "it's wounded."

"Are you sure it's the same one I shot?"

"Yes! The same. Shoot fast."

I remembered that the cow had not collapsed immediately from the shot, but had staggered slightly before it went down, so I suspected that I had missed the brain. It could have gotten up, but I didn't want to shoot a second cow by mistake. We moved closer.

"That's the cow," John said peering through his binoculars. "It has blood on its ear. Shoot."

"That could be another cow that rubbed against the wounded one," I argued. Elephants occasionally try to help a wounded companion. "We gotta be absolutely certain." We moved still closer and squinted through the binoculars.

"Its front leg is covered with blood," John said. "Shoot."

It was badly stunned and did not react to our presence. I lined up the .460 and dropped it just ten yards from the spot where it fell initially.

Our work was over. At dawn, Andy Kockott and the biltong crew would begin their work.

I was quickly becoming the world's foremost expert on how to miss the side brain shot and kill an elephant anyway, having done this twice. Nevertheless, we had handled the elephant well. For over an hour, we had waited when we needed to wait, and had run like scared impala when we needed to run. Good judgment had easily overcome mediocre shooting.

That evening I sat on the bank of the Zambezi listening to the ringed doves, watching the hippos, and sipping my second gin and tonic, complete with ice. Gin and tonic is always good, but it is even better after a successful elephant hunt. I felt perfectly at peace with this natural world.

The sun slid into the hills of Zambia, turning the Zambezi into a river of fire. The ringed doves were interrupted by the drone of a Cessna, up from Mozambique, hurrying to the airfield at Kariba to land in the red light of dusk.

There are many things I do not understand, I thought. I do not understand how airplanes fly. Only by the greatest faith can I place my life in the hands of the pilot and the aerodynamic engineer. I wished the Cessna well in its race with darkness.

But I understand elephants. While transportation evolved from horses to airplanes, elephants have not changed one iota. I hunt the same elephants that were hunted a hundred years ago by Neumann and Selous. Wild animals are a nerve-soothing constant, a never changing link to our past. They are my most reliable producers of tranquility. These things I understand perfectly.

FRIDAY'S PRAYER

Andy Kockott, our professional hunter, provided a well-stocked camp and gave John Tautin and me a taste of the traditional African safari. The two tiny nylon tents I had used on my first buffalo hunt were replaced by a half dozen wall tents. My cooking fire and wire grill were replaced with a properly stocked kitchen complete with a wood-burning stove. The camp staff provided hot water every evening for showers, so I never needed to unpack my fourteen-day deodorant. Andy's wife, Sharon, set a proper table with a white lace tablecloth and crystal wine glasses. We lived well.

During the off season, Andy makes a living growing tobacco. Many of his farmer friends visited us in camp, bringing their equipment and piling luxury upon luxury. One brought a boat and we fished for bream and tiger fish. The campfire conversation covered racial politics, life under socialism, tobacco markets, and of course, big elephants.

John Tautin and I worked out a unique and totally satisfactory relationship with Andy. We borrowed his Land Rover and highly trained staff. During the evenings, he often advised on hunting methods and locations, but during the days, Andy stayed in camp. John, the blacks, and I hunted on our own. Sometimes we were successful and sometimes we weren't, but our victories and defeats were our own.

Solo Safari

We were running a string of leopard baits along the Zambezi River, east to the confluence with the Nyakasanga River and west to the second donga past the gravel ridge. Five baits, seven days, no leopard.

The basic procedure is very simple. You hang baits, mostly halves of impala or whole baboons, high in trees. This simulates the leopards' practice of hiding natural kills in trees to protect them from lions, hyenas, and vultures. You check the baits every day. When one has been fed upon, you build a blind and wait, hoping the cat will return during the legal shooting hours from dawn to dusk.

Any professional hunter will tell you that enticing a leopard to feed is no problem. The problem is getting the nocturnal cats to feed during daylight. My luck was all bad. I was fattening two eagles, two tree-climbing lions, and a dozen vultures, but no leopards. The baits must be checked daily and replenished from time to time, so the whole business interferes with buffalo and elephant hunting. I was investing a lot of time and getting nowhere.

I mentally reviewed my procedures and criteria for selecting bait trees. I had selected trees with vertical trunks which would filter out lions but allow leopards to pass. A fully grown male lion scratched his way up one of these vertical trees, leaving deep chisel marks in the bark, and ate an impala. I placed the baits in the shade so they would be invisible to vultures and eagles. They found the baits anyway. I instructed Wiro, Jason, and Friday to suspend the baits below the limbs so the birds couldn't perch on the limbs and feed. They perched on the hanging baits and fed. I selected bait trees along well-traveled game trails and dongas. Fresh leopard tracks appeared within fifty yards of two baits, but the cats rejected my offerings.

Wiro, the Tonka elder, consulted with Jason and Friday, the two chaps from the parks department. "We should go to the old sugar estate," Jason said, "and hang a whole impala, not just half."

"No," I argued, when I should have listened, "the sugar estate is too far away. It's too far to drive every morning to check the bait."

"Eeeh, the old sugar estate is very good," Friday said. "We shoot many leopards there."

"You have trouble getting out of bed at five o'clock," I reminded the trackers. "If we go to the sugar estate, how will you wake up at four o'clock?" The men exchanged uneasy glances and I knew I had won the argument.

Friday's Prayer

On the eighth day, John Tautin, my hunting partner, clobbered a bull buffalo in *jess* so thick that it would turn a black mamba away. Predators would be attracted to the kill site, so I figured this would be a good place to hang a bait. Wiro hoisted a prime leg of buffalo into a tree thirty yards from the kill site. He then swept the area around the base of the tree free of vegetation and smoothed out the dust. If any predator came by, Wiro would easily read its tracks and determine its species and size.

I was optimistic. A leopard will come to a bait only under cover. The cover can be provided by darkness or by heavy vegetation. The thick *jess* would provide perfect cover, giving the cat enough confidence to come during daylight.

At dawn the trackers read the story in the dust. A female leopard had walked up to the tree, sniffed the rumen contents that Wiro had smeared on the trunk, stuck its nose into the air, and walked on. If these leopards want to simply ignore me, that's fine, but this was insulting.

The trackers decided that the leopard had fed on a natural kill. Its belly was full, so it passed up our bait. It might hit the bait the next night. But it did not take the bait that night, or any other night. "Where else can we hang a bait?" I asked the trackers.

"I think that if we go to the sugar estate and hang a whole impala . . . ."

"No way. That's too far to drive every day," I interrupted, overruling sixty years of collective experience. There were more baits and more disappointments, then the course of buffalo hunting took us to the old sugar estate. "This would be a good place to hang a bait," Friday reminded me.

"Okay, okay, I give up."

Jason led us on a short impala hunt that produced a strapping young ram. The trackers rummaged through an old campsite and found some wire to fasten the impala in a tree. Then they searched up and down a brush-filled donga for a suitable tree. Several were nominated and rejected. One was in the open, so the leopard would not come until after dark. One was so low that lions could reach the impala. I stayed out of the selection process. This sugar estate thing was the trackers' idea. If it failed, I would share none of the blame.

Finally the blacks agreed on a tree. It wasn't perfect, but it was okay. It had good cover and a horizontal limb twenty feet up for the bait. The approach route was completely concealed, allowing early morning stalks of the tree. However, the shot would be a long one, about 100 yards, twice as far as one would prefer for a cat that can turn dangerous if hit poorly. The bait would not be silhouetted against the sky. As the sun set, it would be quickly lost against a background of dark green leaves.

Wiro and Friday wrestled the ram up the tree trunk and out onto the limb. We did not have a rope and they could not place the bait far enough out on the limb. A feeding cat would be largely obscured by the trunk of the tree, but it was the best they could do. Jason and Friday cleared all the brush from the approach lane and swept away any leaves which might crunch underfoot. Never before had they shown such diligence in preparing a bait site. They really believed this bait would produce a leopard and I was buoyed by their confidence.

As we prepared to leave, Friday faced away from the group and spoke aloud to the trees or to a Shona god. He was praying for a leopard. I was touched. Was he praying on my behalf? Or had my quest for a leopard become Friday's quest also? Pursuit of the golden, spotted cat had created some sort of bond between two hunters from two very different cultures. I longed to understand that bond better, but I spoke no Shona and Friday spoke almost no English.

For two nights the leopards ignored the bait and I had nearly given up my quest. I began to question my decision to tackle leopard without assistance from a professional hunter. Leopard hunting is a highly specialized business, not something for beginners.

Then, on the third night, a leopard ate a portion of the back and flank and some internal organs. The track showed it to be a mature female. We had placed seven baits, and this was the first to be taken by a leopard.

Later that day I left camp with the Land Rover loaded with thatch for building a blind. Jason occupied the passenger seat while Wiro and Pearson bounced along in the back. Friday and John Tautin were off in another Land Rover, trying to sort out a hippo. It was a forty-minute commute in the slow lane, which was the only lane, from camp to the sugar estate, but the traffic was light. We dodged a couple of waterbuck, detoured around a tree which had fallen in the road, and ground to a dead stop behind a herd of elephants. It was stop and go traffic, African style.

We finished the blind by two o'clock. It was a proper affair with four sides, a hinged door, and a peep hole just large enough for the barrel of my .338. We retired to the truck and lounged under a shade tree for two hours. I contemplated the situation. The shredded impala meat was well-oxidized, indicating the cat had fed early the evening before. This suggested that it might be hungry and would return early this evening, perhaps before sunset. On the other hand, it had fed very heavily, indicating that it might not be hungry.

Wiro and Pearson would wait in the Land Rover for darkness. That means literally in the vehicle because any black in the valley who is not associated with a vehicle or a white person is assumed to be a rhino poacher and is shot on sight.

At four o'clock, Jason and I crept back to the blind and began our ordeal of boredom. Fortunately, I had brought the most necessary item of leopard hunting equipment, a Wilber Smith paperback. I mused at the title, *The Leopard Hunts in Darkness*, and hoped that my leopard would not wait for darkness.

By 4:32, Smith's hero, Craig Mellow, had shot another dozen bad guys and made love three times to Sally-Anne. (Oh, to be young again.) By 4:47 he had salvaged the diamonds and delivered his friends from the horrors of a bat-filled cave. By 5:17, Craig and Sally-Anne escaped across the border to Botswana and lived happily ever after. End of book, beginning of boredom.

I squinted through my peephole. The impala bait was growing dim. I cursed because it was not far enough out on the limb. If the leopard fed on the hind quarters, only its head and perhaps a bit of its shoulder would be visible. Its chest would be obscured by the tree trunk. At a hundred yards, in dim light, it would be a difficult shot, but possible. We waited.

I should not have worried about boredom. Africa is never boring for those who want to learn its ways. I listened to the cooing of the ringed doves. Would they stop cooing if a leopard walked by? A vulture soared overhead but did not land. Perhaps this was good. It suggested that the area was free of lion kills that might compete for the leopard's attention. A brown bird that I did not know, about the size of a starling, perched three feet from the blind and looked in. I froze, not wanting to elicit any alarm behavior that might be noticed by an approaching leopard. A minute passed before the brown bird became bored and left.

At 5:42, Jason suddenly sat upright and listened. I did not know why. He poked a finger-sized hole through the thatch and peaked out.

Solo Safari

I very slowly moved into shooting position and stared at the fading impala. Nothing. Sundown would come, legally, at 6:00. We waited.

The leopard did not climb the tree. It did not walk out on the limb. It just appeared. From where, I do not know. It was not on the limb with the impala but on another limb twenty feet away and higher. It was a light blotch against the fading green-black foliage. A three-second look through the binoculars, another three seconds to line up the rifle, then a shot ripped through the donga. The leopard toppled from the limb.

I did not reload. That would be too noisy. We just listened. The cat hit with a thud and there was no rustling in the brush. Was it dead?

I glanced at my watch, 5:53. It would be too dark to shoot in another ten minutes. I decided to wait four minutes to let the cat die, allowing five or six minutes to stalk the tree.

I reloaded the .338, dug out a flashlight and handed it to Jason, then we began that dreadful journey from the blind to the waiting cat. The .338 was up and ready as the light probed the bush, searching for a reflective eye. There was none.

I drew a line from the limb to the ground. The cat would have fallen into a two-foot-deep gully and would be hidden until we were within ten yards. In the fading light there was no time to detour around for a better view into the gully. Ten yards, less than a second for a charging leopard, maybe enough time for one shot. We baby-stepped up to the donga and strained on tiptoes to look in. The golden, spotted cat was dead.

Jason was ecstatic while yours truly was, of course, a picture of calm. We yelled for Wiro and Pearson. They came quickly and we babbled in English, Shona, and Tonka. The language didn't matter because each knew exactly what the others were saying.

This hunt was not, strictly speaking, a self-guided hunt. I was guided by Jason, Friday, and Wiro. They had argued persistently for a bait at the sugar estate, selected the tree, placed the bait, and prepared the site with meticulous care. They never doubted that it would produce a leopard.

It had been a textbook leopard hunt, well done by all, but I have one nagging regret. I wish that Friday had been with me on that fading day on the Zambezi to see his prayer answered.

NYAMA!

The old Land Rover coughed its way out of camp, still suffering badly from the cold morning air. John Tautin cinched up the drawstring on his hooded sweatshirt while Wiro and Pearson hunkered down in the back, trying to hide from the cold wind. A hundred yards from our camp, I turned into the wildlife department's camp and picked up Jason and Friday.

"Nyama!" yelled the trackers as we pulled out of camp. Meat!

It was the last day of the hunt and we had taken all the trophy animals. All that remained on our license were the meat animals: a cow buffalo and a couple of female impala.

"Nyama!" yelled the blacks in camp. They were the men who risked their lives daily, patrolling the Zambezi Valley for rhino poachers from Zambia. It was a small-scale guerrilla war. Dozens of poachers had been killed, but they kept coming. Sadly, the Zambezi Valley will run out of rhinos before Zambia runs out of poachers. At our invitation, the patrolmen fed heavily from our meat pole, so they wished us well on our meat hunt.

We headed straight for Mdzia Pan, where we had previously seen herds of buffalo. While easing the Land Rover down the bank of a donga, I stepped on the brake pedal and it went clear to the floor. The brake line to the rear right wheel had broken. No problem, we could limp back to camp without brakes, using low gear, low range for the downhill sections.

But Pearson had another idea. In the next few minutes, he gave us a lesson in bush mechanics. He scrounged through the collection of bolts and bits of scrap metal in the bottom of his toolbox and found a large nail which suited his purpose. He then removed the broken line to the right wheel, broke off a bit of the nail, and used the broken nail to plug the brake line. He rummaged around under the seat, found a can half full of brake fluid, and topped off the reservoir. Within thirty minutes, we were under way with perfectly functional brakes on three wheels. It would never have occurred to me that Pearson could fix the brakes in the field. It never occurred to Pearson that he might not be able to fix them.

Several miles farther on, finding a place where a herd of buffalo had crossed the road, we took up the track on foot. The bush was very open and we followed at a brisk walk for more than an hour, and then Jason spotted a tiny patch of black hide through a hole in the vegetation.

John Tautin crawled on his hands and knees, then his stomach, for fifty yards, with me and my insurance gun at his heels. The herd spooked before he could pick out a cow. We waited for ten minutes to allow the herd to settle down before we resumed the trail. The trackers spotted the buffalo only a few hundred yards from the point of the first contact. John picked out a cow and smacked her in the chest with his .375.

She disappeared with the others in a cloud of dust. She was hit hard but did not lose one drop of blood. Her tracks were hopelessly intertwined with the tracks of two dozen other buffalo.

We initiated the wounded buffalo drill. The blacks tore three-inch squares from a page of the Lusaka, Zambia newspaper. Onto these they placed a few scraps of tobacco and rolled them into long forms that somewhat resembled cigarettes. They smoked slowly, giving the cow plenty of time to die before we pressed on. No experienced hunter wants to stumble upon a live, wounded buffalo.

John and I entertained ourselves by watching a couple of hornbills scratching in the dead leaves for insects. Several species of hornbills are found in Zimbabwe that were unfamiliar to us. John memorized the color patterns so that he could check the bird book back at camp.

The last embers of the cigarettes finally died, robbing us of any further excuse for procrastination. The trackers could do little but follow the herd, keep a sharp eye, and hope for the best.

Friday and Wiro worked to the left, with John and his .375 for cover. Jason and I and the .460 drifted to the right. We had crept about 150 yards before Jason spotted the cow. It was lying down, facing three-quarters away, with its head up. From forty yards, I rested the .460 against a tree and slipped one into its chest. The cow rolled over and I reloaded.

Jason and I approached the inert cow as John and the others emerged from the bush. Carefully, I circled the cow about five yards out, rifle ready. As I stepped into its field of view, the cow found a new life and struggled to its feet. I stepped backward, tripped, but caught my balance, losing a precious second. The cow's eyes locked onto mine, leaving no doubt about its intent. It faltered on weakened legs, then it came. I'll never forget those eyes.

Instinct took control, fusing my body and mind for a single purpose. The .460 came up and the trigger finger did its work. Two shots rocked the bush. John's .375 ripped through its neck and my .460 slammed into its shoulder. The cow slumped back to the ground. If we had fired one second later, I would have had a buffalo horn sticking in my chest, with a very angry buffalo still attached! The cow had taken two .375s and two .460s and was still alive. John finished it with a fifth bullet to the brain.

I felt that familiar ache in the small of my back, where the adrenaline hits the bloodstream, and in a few minutes I felt alive. You can have all the cocaine in the world. My drug of choice is adrenaline. We laughed and joked a little too much, trying to relieve the tension.

I ran my hand over the cow's horns. They seemed about twice as long as bull horns and sharper. It was a hot day, but a cold chill went through my spine. There is no glory in being clobbered by a cow buffalo, since you're just as dead. In Africa, even a *nyama* hunt can be exciting.

SAND AND FIRE

I was in a rut. I was spending thousands of dollars a year for the privilege of spending a few weeks in Africa and I was headed for the poorhouse. I needed to find someone who would pay me to live in Africa.

I wouldn't be leaving much behind. My job in Washington, D.C., had gone sour. The most dangerous predators on earth are not found in Africa. They stalk the corridors and lobbies of Washington. I had suffered badly from their depredations and I wanted out.

You might think it would be easy for a wildlife biologist to find work in Africa. Not true. Wildlife biology is a very popular profession. In America, we have several thousand positions for wildlifers, but tens of thousands of trained biologists. This leaves dozens of biologists waiting in line for every vacant position. Given a choice, many of these would work in the glamour locations, Alaska and Africa. The competition for jobs is intense. I tried everything. I even applied for the United Nations Volunteer Program and the Peace Corps. Zip.

The good news came at the least expected moment. I was sitting in my room at the Jameson Hotel in Harare when the phone rang. The call was from the States, from a headhunter for the U.S. Agency for International Development. "Would you be interested in a two-year contract to serve as an instructor at the Wildlife Training Institute in Maun, Botswana?"

Solo Safari

Maun! Hot damn! Maun is today what Nairobi was thirty years ago, the jumping-off point for some of the best remaining safari country in Africa.

"Yes. Hell yes!" I shouted through the static. Not only would I live in Africa, I would have sufficient salary to live in comfort and do a bit of hunting. I completed writing the cow elephant and leopard hunts described in the previous chapters with the pleasant anticipation of returning to Africa.

In anticipation, I read everything I could find about Maun. It is a place of glamour, a frontier town that compared with Dodge City, Kansas, in 1870, except that horses have been replaced with four-wheel drive trucks. Never mind that Maun sits in the middle of a desert about fifty miles on the other side of infinity. It is known for its French wines, Russian caviar, and other imported luxuries to please wealthy tourists. It is the home of legendary hunters, such as Harry Selby and Wally Johnson. Toss in a collection of desert rats and other misfits, the odd American millionaire, and Maun promised to be a place of fascination.

I landed in Gaborone, the capital of Botswana and spent ten days meeting officials, cutting red tape lengthwise, and purchasing a four-wheel-drive Toyota Land Cruiser, the workhorse of Africa. I had the Cruiser fitted with an extra fifty-gallon fuel tank, a twenty-gallon water tank, a massive "bull bar" to protect the grill, and a second spare tire. At a glance, it looked like an American pickup truck, but it had sixteen-inch wheels, a one-ton rating, and a rugged design and construction that put the American trucks to shame.

It was two days from Gaborone to Maun. The final segment was five hours on the worst gravel road I'd ever seen. In America, a pothole will swallow a wheel. In Botswana, a pothole will swallow an entire truck. In those five hours, my new truck became a used truck and she earned her name, the Mean Machine. By the time I arrived in Maun, the Mean Machine had relocated my kidneys to the vicinity of my shoulder blades.

I found a large village with 18,000 Tswanas, several hundred Europeans, and more goats and donkeys than anyone could count. Maun, I discovered, is paradise only for those who enjoy sand, dust, heat, and more sand. I arrived in September, near the end of the dry season. Every sprig of green vegetation within four feet of the ground had been plucked by goats. The main street was paved with tar and the

Sand and Fire

side roads were paved with Coke cans flattened by passing Land Cruisers. Most side roads were little more than a pair of axle-deep grooves in the sand that quickly mired all vehicles lacking four-wheel drive.

French wine? Where? I couldn't buy good ground beef in Maun, nor clothes hangers, mosquito nets, nor hardly anything else on my shopping list. Clearly, those who found romance in Maun were short-term visitors hosted, at considerable cost, by a tourist industry with solid logistical connections in South Africa.

Maun is not paradise. It is tolerated because it is the gateway to paradise. It lies in the Kalahari Desert with its springbok, gemsbok, giraffe, ostrich, and other desert game. The mopane woodland lies to the northeast, providing a wet season range for elephants, buffalo, and attendant lions. The jewel of the Kalahari, the Okavango Delta, lies at Maun's doorstep, just to the northwest.

The Okavango River originates in the highlands of Angola and falls to the southeast in its frustrated search for the sea. In Ngamiland, in northwestern Botswana, the Kalahari sands are so flat that the Okavango cannot maintain a channel. The river divides and subdivides and spreads across 7500 square miles of sand. The porous sand and the hot sun drink up the water and the river is no more. This inland delta, the only one in the world, is home to hippo, crocodile, lechwe, sitatunga, and dozens of tourist lodges. Maun is where a desert, a delta, and a tourist industry come together.

I immediately busied myself writing course outlines and lesson plans and trying to acquire the equipment and ammunition needed to upgrade marksmanship training. My investigations revealed a government that was sincerely committed to wildlife conservation, provided, of course, that wildlife did not interfere with cattle. Tswana culture revolves around the cow. It is the Tswana's livelihood and bank account. Tswanas hunt wild meat so they can spare their cattle, but they place little value on wildlife. Subsistence hunting was out of control. The international poaching network, which had devastated elephant and rhino populations further north, was just beginning to cast its eyes into Botswana. The government had excellent conservation proposals on paper, but they were seldom approved or implemented. On the land, the cow was supreme.

Nevertheless, substantial wildlife populations remain in northern Botswana and that area offers some of the best safari hunting in Africa. Trophy quality is not exceptional for most species, but the safari companies are well organized, if expensive, and the wilderness experience is unequaled.

Then I discovered the harsh realities of resident hunting. Hunters are divided into three categories: citizens, noncitizen residents (including myself), and nonresidents. The citizens may hunt nearly anywhere except in national parks and game reserves. Nonresidents must hunt with safari companies, but the companies are allocated concessions in the very best game areas. The concessions are very large and the safari companies annually harvest only about half their quota of animals.

Noncitizen resident hunters, by contrast, are allowed a pitifully small quota of animals and most of the quota is subscribed every year. Even common species, such as lechwe, tsessebe, hartebeest, and leopard are not included in the residents' quota. Furthermore, we are restricted to poorly watered areas with little game.

Then there's the paper chase. To hunt, say, an impala, the noncitizen resident hunter must apply to Gaborone for a permit and survive the selection process. Heaven knows how permits are allocated, but I don't. Then he must buy a Controlled Hunting Area Access Permit available only in Gaborone. With this in hand, he can purchase the hunting permit, but this must be done only in Maun. Next, he borrows a rifle and purchases a temporary firearms permit from the police. Noncitizens are effectively prohibited from possessing rifles in Botswana. Then he goes to the Veterinary Department for a permit to transport the meat back to Maun. You'll have to consult with God for the reasons behind that one too. Then the hunter drives three hours to the hunting area to discover that the last pan dried up while he was chasing permits and all the impala moved out of the area. If he somehow manages to kill an impala, he will need a minimum of five documents from four different agencies to export the horns. Well, even poor African hunting is good and I resolved to make the best of whatever was available, however difficult.

It was September and hunting did not begin until April. I used my weekends to explore the area around Maun. One of the prime game viewing areas of Botswana is the Savuti area in Chobe National Park. My visit to Savuti came unexpectedly.

The message came on Thursday morning. Bushfires were burning out of control at Savuti and the staff and students at the Wildlife

Sand and Fire

Training Institute were ordered to pack up and report for fire duty. I had never fought a fire, so this had the allure of high adventure.

We piled camping equipment, shovels, and rakes onto a Mercedes-Benz five-ton, four-wheel drive truck, then piled twenty-three students, nineteen men and four women, on top of the gear. The other instructors breathed sighs of relief when they learned that Leslie Reid would be the driver. The Mercedes suffered from a bad clutch and only Leslie knew how to keep it rolling. I later learned that the truck also had a bad generator, bad brakes, and bad four-wheel drive parts, but these too fell within Leslie's mechanical capabilities.

Leslie nearly missed this party because he had been in the hospital recovering from a buffalo attack. He showed me the fresh scar on his chest, the size of a half dollar, where the horn had punched through the sternum. The buffalo's hooves had also sliced open his arm and leg.

At three in the afternoon we tossed the last tent onto the truck and headed across town to top up with fuel. This was snag Number 1. The electricity was off and the fuel pumps would not operate. At five the electricity switched on and we headed north with our tanks full and an extra fifty-gallon drum in reserve.

The road from Maun to Savuti isn't a road at all, but simply a pair of furrows through the sand. In some places, the original tracks are so bad that drivers have up to four parallel sets of tracks to choose from. The Mercedes alternately roared and groaned as Leslie shifted to lower and lower gears.

"Its 130 miles to Savuti," I reasoned. "With an average of four gear shifts per mile and two jabs of the clutch per gear shift, the faulty clutch will have to function more than a thousand times before we reach Savuti. No way!"

The clutch quit at half past dusk. Armed with a flashlight and a single adjustable wrench—variable spanner, as we called it—Leslie dove under the truck. Thirty minutes later we were under way, but only for another hour. The gizmo that engages the front wheel drive failed and we mired axle deep in sand. Out came the flashlight and variable spanner, and the mechanical wizard again disappeared under the truck. Thirty minutes later the Mercedes was functional and free of the sand, but one of the chase vehicles, a Land Cruiser, refused to start. In desperation, two Cruisers swapped batteries, matching the weaker battery with the stronger ignition system. We were under way,

51

three hours behind schedule. What Africa lacks in equipment, it compensates with manpower, ingenuity, and unlimited patience.

At the boundary of Chobe National Park, we began to encounter wildlife. The headlights revealed wild dogs, hyenas, a serval, dozens of impala, and a lion.

We arrived at Savuti well past midnight. Forty firefighters were already in camp, including all available Game Scouts and laborers from Chobe National park and the Anti-Poaching Unit. In support, was a fleet of vehicles including two Land Cruisers donated by American sportsmen. Too tired to pitch tents, we spread our cots under the stars and were serenaded by hyenas and lions.

At dawn, the Fire Boss, Kebalepile Nkwane, surveyed the situation from the air, a plane having been provided by a local safari camp operator. The report was not good. Mr. Nkwane reported thousands of acres of blackened bush, and several fires continued to burn at widely scattered locations. Fire causes both damages and benefits to the ecosystem, depending on timing, size, and intensity. These dry-season fires were too intense and had grown much too large.

For three days we swatted flames with broken tree branches. Those who were better equipped shoveled sand onto the flames. For three long days we choked on smoke, lived in sand and ash, jump-started reluctant engines, and set controlled backfires. We gulped hot water, missed meals, siphoned gasoline, and pumped up flat tires. In just three days, sixty-five hungry firefighters consumed two buffalo bulls that had been killed for rations. Our hands blistered, we poured sweat, we ached, and we failed. Sunday afternoon, the students piled onto the Mercedes and returned to Maun to resume classes Monday morning. Forty men stayed behind to continue the battle.

As Leslie pushed the big Mercedes through the loose sand, I considered the tragic cause of the fires. Several days after the fires began, Mr. Nkwane's men found four elephants that had been killed by poachers. Fortunately, they discovered the elephants before the poachers chopped out the tusks, so the ivory was recovered. Almost certainly, the poachers had started the fires to divert attention from their illegal activities. Their scheme had almost worked. The entire Chobe Park staff and the Anti-Poaching Unit were called to fire duty. Mr. Nkwane directed the Anti-Poaching Unit to spend a day tracking the poachers, but they had no success and quickly returned to the fire.

Sand and Fire

The costs of the episode were enormous: four dead elephants, possibly more; thousands of acres of blackened bush; five thousand man-days of hard work, hundreds of gallons of precious fuel consumed, and untold wear to a fleet of vehicles. The next year, we would do it all again.

LOST IN THE KALAHARI

The instructors from the Wildlife Training Institute were on an orientation tour of Botswana. Our two Land Cruisers were rolling down the northeastern boundary of the vast Central Kalahari Game Reserve. The sand road marking the boundary runs straight as a string for 175 miles. No one thought it was possible to get lost on such a marvelous road, but we managed to do it.

The marvelous road became more and more faint. All eyes searched the bush ahead for a tire track, but the old track wandered like a drunken sailor. Obviously, the previous vehicle had been lost, too.

We parked under a skinny shade tree and produced water bottles, lunch sacks, and maps. Amid much good-natured ribbing, Ibo Zimmermann, the group leader, assured us that the situation was in hand. Each Cruiser carried seventy gallons of gasoline and the leader carried an additional fifty-gallon drum of gasoline and fifty gallons of water. These ample reserves inspired great confidence.

Let me tell you about wilderness travel, African style. Now I'm talking about real, honest-to-goodness, down-home African travel, not these highly choreographed shows put on by safari companies. In spite of our reserves of gasoline, we faced potential problems. The slick safari companies put two or three spare tires on every vehicle. We had one spare tire for two vehicles and it was flat, having been victimized by the gravel road outside Maun.

If you think we were at risk, you haven't begun to comprehend the innovative abilities of the African bush mechanic. We had a pair of tire irons, a tire repair kit with three shiny new patches, and less than a thousand miles of bad road to go. Of course the hose on the tire pump leaked, but if one guy held the hose in the right reverse curve, the leak could be nearly sealed. If three strong men pumped like hell in quick relays, they could gain a little on the leaky hose and squeeze twenty-five pounds of air into a tire. No *mathatha*! You can fret about this sort of thing, or you can lie back, go with the flow, and somewhat enjoy the bush.

The map showed a fence thirty miles ahead that came in from the left and joined our lost track. If we struck a compass course ten degrees to the left of the junction, we would hit the fence, turn right, and find our lost track. But how do you follow a compass course through dense bush? The Cruisers could smash down bushes and saplings but had to twist and turn among the larger trees.

The tree huggers of the world would be appalled by the practice of "bush bashing" as practiced in Botswana. Where roads are lacking, you simply shift into low gear and grind your way through the bush. Unfortunately, this does no damage whatever to the shrubs. Okay, if you drove over a bush a dozen times, then backed over it a dozen more times, you just might kill it. This would be a blessing, because the relentless encroachment of bushes is seriously degrading Botswana's grassland. Bush bashing is damaging all right, but all the damage is suffered by the vehicle.

Several of us took turns as route finders. The guide perched atop the cab of the lead Cruiser and held a compass in one hand and a stick in the other hand. This was waved in front of the windshield showing the best route to Ibo or whoever was driving. With his other hand, the guide hung on for dear life. Slowly, the bush drifted by. Every thirty minutes we stopped to remove the mat of leaves, grass seeds, and sticks that blocked the radiators. Dusk would come in eight hours, but we would be far short of the fence.

An hour later we hit a cut line, a straight line graded through the bush by a mineral exploration company. This de facto road was used rarely by geologists and lost biologists, but frequently by poachers. One cut line crossed another and we zigzagged across the desert, finally hitting a sand road headed in the right direction. We now reassessed our situation. If we drove until midnight, we would arrive at our original destination for the day and our tour would be back on schedule.

As dusk approached, I climbed onto the back of the Land Cruiser where I could stretch my legs and watch for gemsbok and other game.

Lost in the Kalahari

I wedged myself between a fifty-gallon drum of water and a fifty-gallon drum of gasoline. My fourteen-day antiperspirant had failed after only four days and the cool breeze felt good against my salt-caked skin.

Suddenly, Ibo Zimmermann slammed on the brakes and he and Segale Gobuamang bailed out of the cab chattering about smoke. Ibo popped the hood open as flames shot out of the engine compartment. I jumped down, ready to sprint for the bush, but I saw Segale grabbing handfuls of the loose Kalahari sand and chucking them onto the engine. I screwed up my courage and joined in. Within a few seconds, we had killed the flames around the engine but could still see flames coming from deep underneath the Cruiser, from the area just in front of the fuel tank. This firecracker was about to explode.

Ibo snatched a siphon hose from behind the seat and jumped onto the back of the Cruiser. He was unscrewing the cap on one of the drums when Segale yelled at him. "That's the petrol drum. The water's in the other drum."

"Oh, sorry," Ibo replied as though he had reached for a coffeepot rather than a teapot at the club. He quickly shifted to the other drum and a minute later the siphon was working. It had five feet of head and generated enough pressure to direct a thin stream of water up and under the vehicle. In another fifteen seconds the fire was out.

The subsequent investigation revealed that dead grass had accumulated between the skid plate and the transfer case. Heat, probably from the muffler, had started the blaze. A few nonessential wires had burned, but the Cruiser was still operational.

Consider the possibilities. The fire was lapping around the half-full fuel tank and fuel line. The auxiliary fuel tank held nearly fifty gallons of gasoline and the drum held another fifty gallons. If Ibo hadn't immediately set up the siphon, the whole lot would have exploded and Ibo, Segale, and I would have landed in Angola, Zambia, and Zimbabwe, respectively. The resulting bushfire would have burned until the next rain fell about a month later. Yes, consider the possibilities. What if Ibo had stuck that siphon hose into the drum of gasoline?

A LESSON IN BUFFALO HUNTING

It was an odd sort of buffalo hunt with an odd cast of characters. It was organized on a one-day notice and shaped up more like a wild-goose chase than a buffalo hunt.

The Wildlife Training Institute planned a week-long trip to Chobe National Park in northern Botswana. This caused a conflict for me because I was entertaining an overseas visitor. Janet Bishop is a city girl. She is more comfortable at a New York opera than in the bush and she prefers Jaguars, the kind with wheels, over four-wheel drive trucks. When she came to Africa, I had to teach her how to urinate behind a tree because she had never done it before.

After considering the alternatives, we decided that Janet would accompany the Training Institute on the field trip. Due to rules concerning liability and nongovernment passengers, I had to drive the Mean Machine. With this extra vehicle, the principal asked me to shoot a buffalo for rations. Forty students, five instructors, and eight drivers and cooks can eat a buffalo in three days. The hunting area was seventy-five miles off our route on horrible sand tracks, but since I was providing the vehicle and gasoline, it was a good deal for the government. And, of course, I would be the one to risk life and limb in the face of horned death. It's tough duty, but. . . .

At Savuti, in the southern portion of the park, I began to gather information about the hunting area. The game scouts at Savuti had gone into the area, many miles west of the park, only two weeks before to hunt for rations. They had not seen a single buffalo and they advised me to abandon the hunt.

We would have to deliver the buffalo within two days or face sixty hungry faces. With driving time subtracted, we would have only six hours of effective hunting time. Was it worth the effort?

Victor Kgampi, one of my students, was familiar with the hunting area. "What do you think?" I asked him after hearing the pessimistic report.

"We can just go and have a look," he suggested. Well, that's hunting. All I ever asked for was a chance. Victor would be my tracker and we recruited a laborer to help with butchering and loading. The city girl, the instructor, the student, and the laborer piled into the Mean Machine and we raced off at twenty miles per hour to Linyanti Game Scout Camp, where we spent the night. The city girl didn't even complain about the cold shower or canned dinner.

At Linyanti, we met one of my former students who was leading antipoaching patrols. He briefed Victor on where to hunt. The distance was great and the buffalo were few, but he assigned one of the Linyanti staff to accompany us.

We left Linyanti camp an hour before sunrise. Hours later, Victor steered us to a couple of safari camps where he queried the black staffs. Their advice was consistent. "Go deeper into the bush." Somewhere near Zibadianja we came across two local chaps who were walking down the road carrying a ghetto blaster between them. Needless to say, the volume was on full. It was 500 miles to the closest ghetto, but the residents surely heard every drumbeat.

I stepped out of the Mean Machine to unknit my leg muscles while Victor yelled for the third time to turn off the radio. They bantered for five minutes, punctuating the palaver with wide sweeps of their arms. Victor reported that they worked at the safari camp we had just visited, they had seen a herd of buffalo earlier in the morning, and they had agreed to show us the location. Just what Victor promised them in return, I will never know, but I welcomed the help. "Hope they didn't have that damn radio playing when they saw the buffalo. It would have scared them all the way to the Caprivi."

So the city girl, the instructor, the student, the laborer, the Linyanti chap, and the two local chaps, seven of us in all, piled onto the Mean

A Lesson in Buffalo Hunting

Machine. We headed north for a couple of miles, then turned off the track into the bush.

Our first effort misfired. We saw something big and black moving through the bush a half mile away. What could be big and black except a buffalo? We performed a beautiful stalk, then watched the buffalo seemingly split in half as two jet black male ostriches stepped apart.

After that we found the tracks from a small herd of buffalo. The ever-helpful laborer scooped up a finger full of fresh buffalo dung, reached through the window of the Mean Machine, and held the dung three inches from Janet's nose. "See, it is very fresh," he explained. "The buffalo are very close."

"Yes, it certainly smells fresh," Janet said, casting a glance my way. I diverted my eyes to hide my embarrassment, but Janet laughed.

We tried to follow the tracks, but they were goofy. They dashed this way and that and led nowhere. Victor and the local chap in the blue shirt consulted, argued, decided, and reconsidered. I didn't agree with everything that was happening, but I believed an instructor's role was to let his students make mistakes, and critique his performance later.

Then we jumped four lions. That explained a lot. The lions had chased the buffalo this way and that. By now, the herd would have moved well out of the area and they would be spooky. To save time and cover distance, Victor suggested that we follow the track with the truck.

At first, the bush was open and the Mean Machine clung to the buffalo trail like a beagle hound on a rabbit track. Then the bush became heavier and the Mean Machine rolled over sapling mopane trees. Finally, we were forced to zigzag around larger trees and bushes. Still, we crossed the track every hundred yards or so.

The Mean Machine slowly ate up the bush as the route became more and more circuitous. We had gone a half mile without crossing the buffalo track and the heavy bush threatened to damage the Mean Machine.

"Enough," I cried. "Which way to the road?"

Victor pointed to the right and I followed. We hadn't gone a hundred yards when someone pounded on the roof and yelled, "Dust!"

A cloud of dust veiled the forest to our left, directly in our original path. Only a herd of stampeding buffalo could raise such a cloud. If I had abandoned the pursuit one minute sooner, the herd would have escaped notice. I cramped the steering wheel to the left and shifted up to second gear.

"Faster, faster," came a cry from the rear, but Janet was already bouncing off the roof. Someone spotted the fleeing buffalo and urged even more speed, but I hit the brake instead. This was a meat hunt, not a sporting hunt, and chasing buffalo with a vehicle is not my idea of an effective hunting method.

I slid out of the seat and loaded a .458. "Victor, you come with me."

"But, Doc, I have no rifle for protection."

"Come on," I insisted. "I'll protect you."

Experience has shown that two pair of eyes are more likely to spot buffalo than one. When facing buffalo, I want every possible advantage.

We hurried through the bush for seventy-five yards before Victor stopped and pointed. I saw nothing. Fifty yards further on he stopped again and this time I saw the black forms in the bush 150 yards away. Too far. A large tree stood fifty yards ahead. If I could reach it, I could look the herd over and try a shot. I told Victor to stay behind and I crawled on my elbows and knees to the tree.

The binoculars showed four animals standing in the shade a hundred yards away. Undoubtedly more animals were hidden in the bush. Three were broadside and I feared a bullet would shoot through them and wound another animal. One was facing me so the length of its body would easily stop the bullet. The fact that it was a good bull made the choice easy.

I raised the .458, but the front sight wandered all over the bull. I adjusted my position. That helped, but I was suffering from a case of jitters. I felt the wind on my face. No hurry. The bull would wait. I lowered the rifle and took a half dozen deep breaths. Then the front sight settled nicely in the center of the black and the trigger eased back. The bull moved exactly one yard, straight down.

I threw the bolt and watched. There was a pounding of hooves and a new cloud of dust, but one black form remained behind. I signaled Victor to stay back, reloaded the magazine, and crept forward. At twenty yards, I circled left and put a shot into the heart, just to be sure, but the bull was dead.

I was one happy hunter and Victor was one happy tracker. Janet took pictures and the butchering began. The laborer had plenty of help and the bull was dissected and loaded within an hour. We dropped the local chaps at their camp with a couple of generous tips.

A Lesson in Buffalo Hunting

We reached the Linyanti Game Scout Camp before dark. Janet shivered through another cold shower and I reviewed the events of the day to critique my student's performance. Victor Kgampi had led us into a vast area that contained few buffalo. He gleaned information from local residents on where to hunt and successfully recruited two knowledgeable local guides. Together, they found the tracks of a herd and managed to follow them through the confusion caused by an encounter with four lions. Victor matched our hunting method to the time we had available, a scant few hours, and positioned me within shooting range. There was nothing to criticize. The student had given his instructor a good lesson in buffalo hunting.

THE AFRICAN DREAM
IS ALIVE

Africa is changing and African hunting is changing. A major turning point occurred in the early 1960s when dozens of colonies gained independence. Some good things have happened since then. Education for blacks has improved in many nations and health care, although still dismal, probably has improved for many Africans. Most indicators, however, show that Africa is on a downhill skid. Many national economies are in shambles and are deteriorating. Corruption is common, many rural areas are unsafe for travel, and a half dozen wars are being fought around the continent. Africa is the only continent with a declining per capita food production, and starvation is rampant in some areas.

If you tell a hotel clerk in Zambia that the bulb in the bedroom has burned out, he will steal the only bulb from the bathroom and put it in the bedroom. Travelers in several countries must carry sufficient petrol, food, and water to last their entire trips. The national airlines in some countries will not accept their nation's currency. Maintaining a conservation program in this context is a tremendous challenge.

Much of West Africa was colonized by France and Belgium. As in Europe, they did little to preserve wildlife, and most of it disappeared long before the wave of independence swept across Africa in the early 1960s. Consequently, French West Africa is not the place for hunters looking for general bags and traditional African hunting. West Africa is of interest to serious collectors seeking species not found elsewhere, such as the forest duikers and dwarf buffalo. Cameroon has a small hunting industry. The Central African Republic is noted for its bongo and giant eland. Zaire has some large wildlife populations, but this troubled nation is closed to hunting.

Solo Safari

East Africa was colonized by the British and Germans who attempted to control overshooting and, later, to establish game reserves. From 1915 to 1970, elephant populations from Rhodesia (Zimbabwe) to Kenya grew enormously. This is the Africa of Teddy Roosevelt, Ernest Hemingway, Robert Ruark, and Stewart Granger. Kenya, Tanzania, and Uganda were classic safari countries and their hunting industries employed thousands of hunters, trackers, skinners, cooks, and personal servants. This is the Africa of our dreams.

The dreams turned into nightmares with the creation of the United African Corporation (UAC), which for many years dominated the poaching industry in Kenya. UAC's poachers combed Kenya and adjacent countries, devastating populations of rhino and elephant. While the price of ivory was increasing dramatically in the early 1970s, everyone in Kenya who owned or could rent a heavy rifle took out an elephant license, threatening UAC's attempt to monopolize the ivory trade. This was highly upsetting to the major stockholder in UAC, who also happened to be the mayor of Nairobi and the daughter of Jomo Kenyatta, the president of Kenya. In response to requests from his daughter, and also from the World Wildlife Fund, Kenyatta banned sport hunting for elephants in 1973. In the next four years, Kenya exported more than 650 tons of ivory to Hong Kong alone, requiring the slaughter of perhaps fifty thousand elephants. As a conservation measure, the ban on sport hunting was a total failure.

The international preservationists were overjoyed with the ban on elephant hunting. In 1974, the World Wildlife Fund bestowed upon Jomo Kenyatta their highest award, the Order of the Golden Ark. The real golden ark was Kenyatta's bank account.

Kenya's 106 professional hunters and their clients continued to patrol the game fields in search of lesser trophies. The problem was that every one of these hunters had been made deputy game wardens, and they interfered with UAC's field operations. The hunters and their clients led the public outcry against official poaching. They needed to be silenced. It is likely that Ms. Kenyatta appealed to her father to close all hunting, and what loving father wouldn't help his daughter. Exit 106 deputy game wardens. The flow of illegal ivory continued.

The 1977 ban on all sport hunting brought orgasmic joy to the international preservationists. We nasty hunters had been kicked out of a major hunting country. British animal rights advocates, zookeepers from around the world, researchers, and other preservationists poured in the "conservation dollars" and placed a stranglehold on Kenya, which has not been released to this day. Under their staunchly-defended preservationist policy, Kenya's elephant population fell from 169,000 prior to the ban on hunting to 17,000 in 1990, and they lost more than ninety-five percent of their black rhinos. Clearly, the prohibition of sport hunting again failed as a conservation strategy.

The generals and politicians in other nations quickly saw the benefits of official poaching, and a bloody wave of corruption spread across Africa. In some cases, even the staffs and vehicles of the game departments were used to poach elephants.

Uganda's wildlife heritage has also been decimated, the victim of war. The government is slowly attempting to reestablish the parks, but it will be many years before the biological and economic systems will support a hunting industry, if ever. Tanzania is limping along. Almost all its rhinos and big elephants are gone and about half of its smaller elephants, but other game remains abundant. Wildlife-based tourism is flourishing in Kenya, and this offers incentive for the conservation of wildlife and wildlands. Nevertheless, these resources are not being managed and are being led to destruction. Dozens of tourist-bearing vehicles crowd around a single pride of lions. This degrades the environment, the lions, and the tourists. This type of problem can be managed, but Kenya lacks the inclination to manage either animals or people.

But wait, all is not lost. Southern Africa is emerging as the stronghold for hunters and wildlife. Yes, southern Africa! Remember when the Kenyans were overrun with game and they sneered at the South Africans for having wiped out their wildlife. Today, South Africa is the only nation that offers hunting for all the Big Five. A few decades ago, the southern white rhino population had been reduced to a dozen animals. Today, several thousand are wandering around South Africa, enough to support a modest sport harvest. East Africa now has a few dozen northern white rhinos and several hundred black rhinos. Will they ever be restored to populations that can be hunted? Not likely.

A remarkable explosion of game populations has occurred on white-owned ranches in Zimbabwe, South Africa, and Namibia. In the 1970s, these countries revised their laws and gave landowners unrestricted interest in most game animals. For all practical purposes, they were granted ownership. Ranchers were then free to buy and sell most game animals, except for restrictions to control the spread of livestock diseases. Spurred by the profit motive, dozens of ranchers began to actively manage antelope and other "plains game." They opened their ranches to paying hunters and began exporting game meat to Europe.

Then in the early 1980s, southern Africa was hit by three years of drought, the worst in 300 years of recorded history. Ranchers were forced to sell their cattle, and cattle not sold soon died. Free of competition from cattle, the drought-resistant game animals flourished. Dollars from visiting hunters pulled many ranchers through the drought. When the rains came, many ranchers decided to restock with game rather than cattle. Although data are lacking, I would guess that parts of southern Africa have five to ten times more plains game today than in the mid-1970s. The capitalistic strategy for wildlife conservation was a smashing success.

The traditional African safari was a thirty-day, tented affair in East Africa, organized around the Big Five. The prized antelope was the kudu, and many hunters spent weeks to bag a forty-five-inch kudu. Today, the typical African hunt is a ten-day ranch hunt in southern Africa. The sportsman lives in the ranch house or an adjacent cottage and concentrates on the antelope. He probably never even sees any of the Big Five.

But the antelope in southern Africa are really fine. On a ten-day safari, you might hunt for kudu, wildebeest, impala, reedbuck, bushbuck, eland, duiker, zebra, warthog, and possibly sable, waterbuck, or tsessebe. In Namibia, throw in gemsbok, springbok, and Cape hartebeest. In Natal Province of South Africa, you can count on nyala.

Actually, trophy quality for the most highly-prized antelope, including kudu, sable, gemsbok, and eland, is much higher in southern Africa than in East Africa. I am amazed at the kudu that are coming out of Zimbabwe and the Transvaal Province of South Africa. The average size seems to increase every year. In the best kudu areas, hunters can expect to take bulls over fifty inches, if enough time is allowed. I have a hunch that antelope hunting is better in Africa today than any time in the last hundred years.

The situation is not as good with the Big Five. Rhino and elephants were cursed by the gods with horns and ivory, which are coveted in Asia. Rhino horn is used in the Orient as medicine and in

The African Dream is Alive

North Yemen for dagger handles. Poachers have nearly eliminated the black rhino from all areas but southern Africa.

Zimbabwe was the first black African nation to aggressively challenge poachers and protect its black rhinos. Despite limited funds and personnel, Zimbabwe is staging a small-scale guerrilla war against Zambian bandits who cross the Zambezi River to poach rhinos. More than a hundred poachers have been killed.

The Zimbabweans also captured dozens of black rhinos and translocated them to more secure areas. Where do you suppose those more secure areas were? The private game ranches! Black rhinos probably will not be hunted in the near future. Barring political chaos in South Africa, a modest number of white rhinos should be available indefinitely.

Poachers also hammered the elephant herds throughout East and Central Africa. Enormous populations of elephants remain in southern Africa and in the rain forests of West Africa and surrounding nations. Every scientifically based conservation organization in the world understands that controlled commerce in ivory and elephant hides, coupled with sport hunting, are essential incentives for the maintenance of elephant herds and their habitats.

One of these organizations, the African Wildlife Foundation (AWF), saw immense opportunities in the elephant. AWF was a small organization with offices in Washington, D.C. and Nairobi. Their public relations consultants saw that people could be swayed by the plight of the elephant. AWF assaulted the conscience of America with images of dead elephants, their faces hacked away by poachers to remove the tusks. In 1989, AWF's Year of the Elephant, the once small organization doubled its membership and budget and became a major player in international conservation.

The World Wildlife Fund (WWF), now the World Wide Fund for Nature, was the heavyweight in international conservation. WWF scientists knew that AWF's call for a ban on ivory trading was unfounded. An enormous internal struggle ensued between WWF's scientists and fund-raisers. The fund-raisers won. WWF echoed AWF's call for a prohibition of ivory trading and for donations. In 1989, WWF took in four million dollars more than it could spend.

Zimbabwe, South Africa, and Botswana, who had managed their elephants well and protected them from poachers, opposed the ivory ban; Zimbabwe was massacred by the world press for criticizing the ban during the CITES convention. The ban was imposed by international treaty, and a few weeks later, the U.S. Fish and Wildlife Service inexplicably banned importation of sport-hunted tusks from most nations.

Prior to 1990, elephants were mismanaged to line the pockets of corrupt politicians and ivory traders. Then, elephants were mismanaged to line the pockets of environmental organizations. The elephants and the people of rural Africa are the big losers. Enormous elephant populations remain and Africans are resilient people. Somehow, both will survive.

Lions are a true wilderness species and are incompatible with livestock and dense human populations. Their numbers probably will continue to decline in proportion to increases in the human population.

Leopards, in sharp contrast, are highly adaptable and may even help farmers by controlling baboons and other animals that are damaging to farmers. Leopards remind me of our coyotes. They can live under a person's nose without being seen. Like the coyote, leopards will be survivors, even in the face of severe persecution.

Listing the leopard as an endangered species was a mistake. The spotted cat was never near extinction, except possibly in local areas. The anti-hunters take great pride in placing the leopard on the endangered list, and they claim that the resulting restrictions on trade saved the leopard from extinction. This is simply not the case. The only thing that has changed is our knowledge of leopard populations. They will do just fine for the foreseeable future.

The buffalo has a lot going for itself. Its horn and hide have no real commercial value. It is too big to poach by snaring and too dangerous to poach with underpowered rifles. I know of no effort to monitor the buffalo's continent-wide population, but it probably is doing well.

If buffalo breeding stock were available, many game ranchers in Zimbabwe and South Africa would reintroduce buffalo. The problem is the European Economic Community (EEC) and their overly stringent requirements for controlling foot-and-mouth disease in imported beef. The nations in Africa are competing among themselves for shares of the EEC beef market. Any hint of foot-and-mouth disease in the producing areas would jeopardize the trade in beef. Since buffalo harbor the disease, it may not be transplanted and, in some cases, buffalo have been exterminated from beef-producing areas.

Fortunately, a two-part solution exists to this problem. First, the technology exists for producing disease-free buffalo, which may be used for breeding stock. Second, regional zoning could be implemented, creating disease-free areas for cattle, buffer zones, and wildlife areas. Since buffalo are not blessed with the "endangered" label, they receive little management attention. However, buffalo will respond better to management than any other member of the Big Five. A third part of the solution might be to bring some reasonableness to EEC's import policies.

No nation has responded more aggressively to the European beef market than Botswana. While the surrounding nations, South Africa, Namibia and Zimbabwe, are turning to wildlife, Botswana is devastating its wildlife resource to increase beef production. The EEC's paranoia about foot-and-mouth disease led to the construction of hundreds of miles of fence to separate cattle from wildlife. The fences probably have had little effect on the disease. The only real effect is the virtual elimination of migratory wildebeest from the central area of Botswana. Nevertheless, northern Botswana is a vast area blessed with abundant big game.

African wildlife faces many threats. The greatest long-term threat is the rapidly increasing human population. Nevertheless, contrary to popular belief, vast areas of Africa have very sparse human populations and a high potential to produce game. These areas will produce game in abundance if African people and their governments are convinced that game production is profitable. Conservationists in Africa and elsewhere must move beyond the bumper sticker mentality of the professional fundraisers, which is that "only elephants should wear ivory," and get on with the more complicated business of sustained yield management. A steady flow of sport-hunted tusks and horns, commercial ivory, hides, and meat will contribute enough money to the regional economies and to government coffers to convince Africans to maintain their herds of game. The sport hunter's dream of African safari merges with the conservationist's dream of abundant herds of game in natural ecosystems.

NORTH TO THE KWANDO

My buddy and I crawled through the steaming vegetation along the banks of the Thamalakane River. The African sun hammered down on us and sweat stung our eyes. Our quarry was still 150 yards away. We needed to move closer, but a shallow backwater blocked our path. There was nothing to do but to crawl through the six-inch deep water, pushing our faces through the tangle of grass, stinging nettles, and spider webs.

The water exploded five yards ahead. "Croc!" I yelled as I recoiled backward, smashing my elbow into my friend's face.

"Hey, hey, settle down, its just a monitor lizard," my friend replied.

"Oh." It wasn't the first time I had been scared by the six-foot monitor lizards on the Thamalakane. Considering the risk of heart attack, they probably are as dangerous as crocodiles. Fifteen minutes later we eased into position and focused our binoculars.

"What do you think?" I whispered.

"Fantastic," he exhaled. "The one on the left will easily go forty inches."

"Yeah, but the one on the right has better conformation." I have never believed that the tape measure is the ultimate judge of quality.

"I wouldn't pass up either one of them. Let's have a closer look."

My buddy eased ahead, but one of the African women saw the movement and let out a shriek. They splashed into the river, submerging their bare bodies up to their necks. The game was up. We stood up and waved and they waved back with giggles and catcalls. Their laundry could wait while they took time for a swim. Okay, Maun does offer a few pleasant diversions.

Life in Africa consisted of occasional moments of intense excitement separated by endless periods of sheer boredom. Most monotonous was the food. A fair variety was available, but I'm a poor cook even when I have an American supermarket close by. I would have paid fifty dollars for a Pizza Hut Deep Dish Supreme. The Island Safari Lodge showed two scratchy movies every week. Most were pretty poor, but of course Charles Bronson never disappoints.

The Wildlife Training Institute has the largest swimming pool in Botswana, so I invited friends over for Sunday afternoon dips. No one in Maun had proper swim suits, so they showed up in shorts, T-shirts, underwear, and intimate apparel. Those wearing the latter always received return invitations.

A steady stream of students and villagers came to my door, and I never tired of them. They needed aspirin, ice, loans, lifts to the hospital, more loans, and my tire pump, used mostly to inflate soccer balls. Radio reception varied from poor to nonexistent, but I tried to catch the news on BBC every evening. I had a portable tape player and a fair selection of Peter, Paul and Mary, Simon and Garfunkle, the Carpenters, and others of my generation. But mostly I read. In two years, I devoured well over a hundred books and I reread the better ones.

There is some advantage, I suppose, to living away from television and newspapers. It does allow time for introspection, time to reassess one's life and recall what is really important. While living in the United States, I spent my time dreaming about leopards and elephant. Now, in Africa, I daydreamed about ring-necked pheasants and beagle hounds.

Yes, beagle hounds. Rarely have I been without one, in part because they are the best company a man can have, and in part because a beagle hound keeps me in touch with the essence of life.

Think about it. What does a beagle hound do? He eats, sleeps, hunts, and conceives little beagle hounds. What else is there? A beagle hound reflects what man always has been and what he should continue to be. For millions of years of human existence, man has been an eater, a sleeper, a hunter, and a lover. I need beagles to remind me of these simple joys of life that we constantly stray away from.

I was sitting on my front stoop enjoying two of the other joys of life, a gin and tonic and a month-old *Time* magazine, when an old

North to the Kwando

Land Cruiser rattled into my driveway. It was my African friend, Freeman Sewadimo Malebogo.

Freeman had drawn a lion permit in the far north, on the Kwando River. It is a fair lion area but is very far from Maun. Freeman doubted that his old Land Cruiser was fit for the long journey and his aging 9.3x62 isn't anyone's idea of a lion rifle. Under Botswana law, one hunter can assist another, so Freeman asked if I could come along and shoot the lion for him. He knew where to buy a couple of buffalo permits and a zebra permit, so he suggested that we take both his old Cruiser and the Mean Machine to haul biltong.

A two-day holiday was coming up. If I took three days of leave and tacked on the two weekends, we would have nine days. Allowing a full day to drive to Area 5 and a full day to return, we would have seven days to hunt, not enough time for lion. Lion hunting in Botswana is especially difficult because it is illegal to use bait, which is the common practice in other countries. The Botswana lions must be hunted by tracking, but following the spoor of a single, soft-footed animal is extremely difficult.

Still, Freeman had asked for assistance and I had come to Africa to help these people. Overcome by a fit of altruism, I agreed to a lion hunt.

The Malebogos are a family in transition. Freeman's son is a top student at the University of Botswana. His cousins, Allen and Boemo, live at his remote cattle post and tend his cornfields and herds. Freeman had just retired as manager of the Maun Cooperative Store. He was building a new butchery and take-away restaurant and he needed cash. He would sell the buffalo biltong and the zebra and lion hides and raise enough money to buy cement and metal door frames for his new building. Dried buffalo meat was sold to pay for cement and corrugated sheets for the roof. He has a bottle store that is complete and open for business, but completion of the butcher shop awaits more cash. Hunting and education are lifting the Malebogo family into the African middle class.

Freeman has years of experience as a hunter. As a young man, before the days of licenses and quotas, he organized a great hunt. He and friends assembled a string of twenty-five horses and donkeys and traveled deep into the Okavango Delta to hunt buffalo and other game. Their route was blocked by a belt occupied by tsetse flies, carriers of the sleeping sickness, which is sometimes fatal to man and is nearly always fatal to domestic stock. They camped on the edge of the fly belt, then crossed the belt in a single push during the night when the flies are inactive.

Weeks later, with the pack animals heavily burdened with dried meat, the nimrods retraced their route. While making the nighttime crossing of the fly belt, they ran smack into a pride of lions that stampeded the twenty-five pack animals and forced the men to build fires to ward off the predators. At first light, they rounded up the stock and hurried on, but the animals had been bitten by the deadly flies. All the pack animals survived the lions and delivered their loads back to the village, but in the following weeks most of the animals died of the sleeping sickness.

We left Maun on African time, three hours late, then stopped at Freeman's cattle post to pick up Allen and Boemo. The biltong crew was still insufficient, so we stopped in Mababe Village to recruit some local labor. Freeman engaged an old man in conversation who assured Freeman that he not only would cut biltong until the wee hours of the morning, he would also show us the secret roads leading to buffalo and lion. What's more, he could track lions until they dropped of exhaustion. These services would be provided for eight days for the paltry sum of twenty-five dollars. The deal was made.

The residents of Mababé are from the tribe of northern or River Bushmen. For several hundred years, they have mixed their blood with Tswana and other Bantu tribes and, to my untrained eye, are indistinguishable from the Bantu. They speak a language of clicks, like the true Kalahari Bushmen, and they are favored as trackers.

By now it was dusk, so we pitched our tents beside the donkey corral at Mababé Village. I could very well have lived my entire life without sleeping next to a donkey corral. Donkeys make a braying sound that is about as pleasing as fingernails on a chalkboard. Every twenty minutes, another one would let loose. They worked in relays, one waking the next before going to sleep. Just about the time I'd start counting sheep or impala or whatever, another donkey would cut loose. This is just another of the joys of Africa you miss entirely if you book with a safari company.

At five in the morning the donkeys finally packed it in. Why not? The roosters had begun to crow.

We jump-started Freeman's truck and five of us resumed the journey. Freeman's old Cruiser traveled just fast enough to raise a cloud of dust. It coughed and sputtered for six hours before we crossed the Selinda Spillway and entered Area 5. I broke out my borrowed rifle, a Brno .375 with a gritty trigger and a backward safety—you pull it backward to fire.

Now the old Bushman took over. His name was Mosesane Pekeneng but we called him the Old Man, a term that connotes respect in Africa. I doubt he weighed as much as a doe impala and his head was the color of the fish eagle's. His clothes were little more than rags, except for a sweatshirt from Tulane University. Words in seTswana spilled from his mouth like water spilling over Victoria Falls. He spoke of the bridge over the Selinda Spillway, which had burned in a bush fire. Minutes later, we came to the pile of ashes. He predicted that a track would join ours from the left, and there it was. This guy knew Area 5 in and out. He was taking us to the west. I'd been told that the good hunting was in the east, along the Kwando River, but I wasn't about to argue with the local expert.

There was just one hitch. The further west we went, the less game we saw. We camped by a small lagoon on the Selinda Spillway. There were no sounds from donkeys or roosters, but there were no lion sounds either, only a chorus of frogs.

The next morning, Freeman and I agreed that the Old Man was not a good tracker and we abandoned his leadership. We jump-started Freeman's truck and retraced our route, arriving at the Kwando past noon. The one day I had allocated to the trip in had stretched to three days, and it clearly would take two days to return to Maun. The seven hunting days had shrunk to four days.

That evening the blacks gazed into the fire, contemplating a three-legged pot full of fresh impala meat. Mostly they listened while the Old Man pontificated. I had now spent enough time in the bush with blacks that I was no longer self-conscious about being the odd man out. Being somewhat of a loner by nature, I appreciated the semi-isolation provided by the language barrier. I finished my can of chicken curry and crawled into my tiny nylon tent.

The roar of a lion rolled through our camp. "Is that my lion?" I wondered. "Will he know he is being hunted? Will we meet tomorrow?"

The moon shone through the red nylon tent, creating a surrealistic effect that set my mind into motion. It was one of those rare occasions when I contemplated my mortality. The presence of danger, the nearness of death, evokes these thoughts. Lying there in the moonlight, I recalled a night in Vietnam twenty years ago when death came near. I was a young supply lieutenant in charge of a reactionary force and the Viet Cong were probing our perimeter wire. If they found a weak spot, they would attack and I would lead my twenty-five supply clerks in a counterattack to restore the perimeter. Most of my force had never fired their rifles, and they had no reason to trust my leadership. Neither did I.

Like millions of soldiers before me, I thought seriously about life and death. My thoughts were not what I would have expected them to be. I decided that I had no fear of the physical pain of death. A disabling injury was more frightening, but even that was not foremost in my mind. Mostly I thought about all the beautiful women I had not known and all the bull elk I had not hunted. Like millions of other soldiers who have waited for battle, I decided that I would regret the end of living. I also thought about those twenty-five supply clerks who might or might not follow me into a firefight. If they followed, they would be badly shot up and their blood would be on my conscience. I regretted having these lieutenant's bars. Give me a private's stripes and a dozen magazines of ammo and bring on the enemy. I'll shoot it out with them. But please, God, don't make me lead these men to the ends of their lives. I feared that I would lead them poorly, but I never doubted that I would try.

My prayer was answered. The Viet Cong backed off. The order to counterattack never came.

Now it was twenty years later. The lion roared again, reminding me that this land was his. I felt the hard lump of the .375 lying against my sleeping bag. I thought about the several beautiful women I had known and all the bull elk I had hunted. "Okay, my friend, I am ready for you. Perhaps tomorrow we will do battle."

My thoughts drifted to a day ten years earlier when two buddies and I tied our fates together with a nylon rope and climbed high onto Mount Rainier. It was a dangerous route on a dangerous mountain. Windblown snow slashed horizontally across our field of vision, limiting visibility to a few yards. The snow and the sky were white and my friends appeared to float on the rope like astronauts attached to an umbilical cord. We pushed the route onto a sixty-degree slope. The new snow was knee-deep and ripe for avalanche. I wanted to turn back but was outvoted.

Then the sky cleared beneath us and I could see 500 feet of air under the heels of my boots. The broken glacier below looked cold and stark, but I did not fear the 500-foot plunge. I thought about all the mountains I had not climbed and could find no reason to die on this one. The end of living was too near. I staged a temper tantrum to convince my friends to back off.

Now, ten years had passed and the lion roared again. I thought of the many mountains I had climbed. "Tomorrow, my friend. Are you ready?"

I remembered the death of a co-worker five years earlier. He had worked for the government for thirty years and was planning an adventurous retirement. His retirement party was held on a Friday. Saturday morning he competed in a ten-kilometer race, and Saturday night he died in his sleep. The message of death is that we have only a limited amount of time and we must live life fully. So, the following Monday morning, I began seriously planning my first trip to Africa. Now five years had passed and a lion was close. I was exactly where I wanted to be.

I had faced five buffalo, two elephants, and a leopard without serious mishap. The problem was that I knew the numbers on lions. On a per capita basis, lions kill more hunters than any other animal. Were the numbers about to catch up with me? The difference between adventure and suicide is the probability of survival. Lion hunting is adventure. I had to assume that I would survive, but my dignity was at risk.

I had seen the film *Out of Africa*, which shows two lion charges. If you are going to hunt lions, don't view this film. The speed and determination in these lion charges will scare you beyond belief. Of course Meryl Streep and Robert Redford faced their lions with total dignity. Would I do as well? Would I calmly squeeze the trigger with death a half-second away? The primary task of a professional hunter is to salvage his client's dignity, to never disclose that the insurance broker from Chicago muffed the shot and wet his pants. The taxidermist will repair the bullet hole from the professional's .470 and the lion will look just fine in the trophy room back in Chicago. I had no one to guarantee my dignity on this trip.

The teapot was steaming as the first rays of light slithered over the eastern horizon. I rattled the pot a bit, hoping that the racket would wake up the rest of the crew. No luck. We finally left camp an hour late, but it did not matter. We had agreed to concentrate first on buffalo. The biltong must dry three days before it can be moved, so we needed to kill the buffalo early.

Solo Safari

The Mean Machine eased into the open bush. With five sets of eyes watching, it did not take long to find buffalo tracks. We had a fifteen-mile-per-hour trailing wind, very unusual for Africa, but we decided to follow the track a short way on foot. The Old Man led.

We hadn't gone 200 yards when another set of buffalo tracks crossed the ones we were following, then another. We could not go a hundred yards in any direction without stepping in fresh buffalo dung. "So this is what heaven is like," I thought to myself.

And there were lion tracks. No females or cubs. Just the big, buffalo-hunting males. The buffalo track continued downwind. Why follow a track with the wind when so many buffalo are about?

We turned into the wind to return to the truck. I noticed a faint tendril of smoke from a bushfire several miles away. No problem, but we were down wind from the fire. Good knowledge to keep handy.

Freeman guided the Mean Machine through the scattered bush while I perched in the back to watch for buffalo. A half hour later I spotted black heads and horns straight ahead, but downwind. We bailed out of the Machine and quickly circled wide to the right to keep our scent from the buffalo, then we stalked back into the wind. Boemo saw them first.

It was a classic buffalo stalk. I did fifty yards on my hands and knees before stopping to check through the binoculars. The Old Man crawled up to me with Freeman's 9.3x62. Bad luck. At this point the Old Man could contribute nothing and he might even bugger the whole operation.

I could see black forms in the bush but could not pick out a bull. A twenty-five yard, low crawl put me on the shoulder of an anthill. With this slight elevation, several cows came into view 120 yards away. The binoculars showed the heads of several bulls who were lying down, their chests hidden by the low bush.

"Shoot. Shoot," the Old Man urged from five yards away. These were the first English words I had heard him utter. Without the benefit of binoculars, he could not know that the only available targets were cows. I waited, hoping the animals would move.

Now the Old Man crawled up to me and caught the attention of a cow. "If we don't move," I thought, "it will lose interest and ignore us." The cow didn't. What if it spooks? The bulls will jump up. If they freeze for ten seconds, I will pick one out and shoot. If they run immediately, I will have lost a chance.

North to the Kwando

"Shoot," the Old Man begged. The cow's stare was boring holes through me. Biltong is biltong. I already was in a prone position, so I only needed to raise the .375 and squeeze the trigger. The cow fell in its tracks and the herd bolted into the bush.

Freeman and the others ran up and we listened to the grunts from the herd that had stopped 300 yards away. I dispensed with the customary insurance shot to avoid frightening the herd. We would try for another buffalo. Freeman was a bit miffed because I had shot the cow. Biltong is biltong, but cows yield less than bulls. I promised that the next one would be a bull.

We started after the herd, but I noticed that the tendril of smoke from the bushfire had grown into a billowing cloud, and it was directly upwind from us. "Let's get that cow butchered and get out of here." There were no arguments.

We began doing a proper job. The Old Man knew his way around a carcass and his knife slipped through the seams between the joints. With skill such as this, the ax was unnecessary. The Old Man dipped his hand in blood and smeared it across a big front hoof. He kicked some fine Kalahari sand over the sticky hoof and sharpened his knife on this improvised whetstone.

Now the smoke was no longer on the horizon. We could see it drifting through the trees. Knives flashed and huge chunks of meat were wrestled into the box of the Mean Machine. The smell of smoke entered our nostrils and the ax began to swing. Now we could hear the fire crackling 200 yards away and I dodged a piece of sopping wet tripe as it arced toward the Machine. "Gather up the knives. Where's the ax? Lets get out of here."

The fire came within fifty yards before the last man jumped on board and the Mean Machine charged ahead. We alternately tried to work across the wind to flank the fire, then charged downwind just to escape the flames. Somebody once said that life is more valuable if it has been put at risk. Just then I was worth about a million bucks. "Lord, keep this Machine rolling. Don't let us get stuck now." After fifteen minutes of tense bush bashing, we drove into fresh air.

We were taking the shortest route to camp when we ran smack into a herd of a hundred buffalo. I looked around for smoke. No *mathatha*. It was two in the afternoon. We had plenty of time. The wind was right. Besides, I needed to reverse my reputation as a cow shooter. "Let's do it."

Solo Safari

I checked the stack of solids in the magazine of the .375, then fed a blue nose into the chamber. I sneaked up on the herd several times, but they faded into the bush. Finally, I was almost running behind them, with the Old Man at my heels. "They go to water," he panted.

"Go to hell, you old pest," I thought. "How could you possibly know where the herd was going?" The chase continued another five minutes, then it stopped. I crawled to a double mopane tree, laid the .375 between the two trunks, and peered through my binoculars. The herd was milling around a water hole. A huge bull was facing directly toward me at 200 yards. Its horns extended six inches past its ears, making it the largest buffalo I had ever seen. I picked up the rifle and squeezed the trigger. Then I pressed the trigger. Then I pulled it like crazy. It was the backward safety. The prize turned away and drifted into the herd.

Another bull stepped into view broadside. I couldn't see its spread, but the width suggested a mature bull. This time the .375 fired, the bull staggered a few steps, then ran with the others toward the crud. I threw the bolt, swung the foresight ahead of the departing bull's shoulder, and fired again.

Freeman and the others drove up and everyone fidgeted for the customary twenty minutes, giving the bull plenty of time to die. I sat apart, wanting to avoid the strained conversation, wanting to gather my thoughts because I knew I had messed up. I knew my first shot was good and the bull probably would be stone dead. The second shot was unnecessary and I should not have fired again. No one can guarantee a hit on a running buffalo at two hundred yards. The bull was closely surrounded by other animals and I might have wounded a second buffalo.

"Well, time to go have a look," I said.

"I'll go along," Freeman offered but his heart wasn't in it.

"No, I'll just go look." There was no further argument. I wanted to go alone anyway. If I had really ruined things, I would sort it out myself.

I found the blood trail and followed it for forty yards into the thicket. The bull was dead, as I expected. Like so many buffalo, it had turned around and died facing its enemy. Was there another buffalo, wounded, watching from the bush? I tracked the herd further into the bush, my thumb on the safety, trying to concentrate on pulling the thing backward. There was no blood. After 300 yards, I had not jumped a buffalo or drawn a charge. If I had hit another animal, it apparently left with the herd. I probably would never know.

North to the Kwando

But the skinning knife solved the mystery. We found my solid bullet, the second one, in the far side of the animal. It was a perfect hit and good shooting had made up for bad judgment. I remembered the cow elephant hunt where good judgment had made up for bad shooting.

"When will the day come," I wondered, "when bad shooting and bad judgment will join against me?"

It was nearly dark when we loaded the second buffalo. I noticed that I was faint with hunger. I had packed a lunch but had forgotten to eat it. It had been an exciting day. With two buffalo on board, plus a quarter ton of fuel and five men, the Mean Machine inched toward camp. A quarter mile from camp, the left rear wheel and the right front wheel fell simultaneously into two springhare holes. The Machine was hopelessly stuck. Well, better now than when we were outrunning the bushfire.

The biltong crew was overloaded with work for the next several days and they rarely left camp. Freeman and I shot a zebra and hunted for lion. The shooting and fire had driven the buffalo from the area and we never saw another buffalo. Strangely, we continued to see fresh lion tracks, and we heard them at night, but my encounter with fanged death would have to wait for another hunt.

MARAUDERS ON THE THAMALAKANE

I rolled the focusing wheel on my binoculars and a pair of black tits birds sprang into focus. They were beautiful, absolutely gorgeous. Small, but beautiful just the same. Magnified ten times, they looked as though I could reach out and touch them. They were a breeding pair and they were building a nest.

Southern black tits, *Parus niger*, are small, insectivorous, arboreal birds. They are uncommon in Maun, so it was a rare treat to have them nesting nearby. Southern white tits, *Homo sapiens*, are more common, but are seen only rarely. For two consecutive years, they reportedly showed themselves in the wee hours of the morning of 1 January beside the swimming pool at a tourist lodge. During these occasional displays of aberrant behavior, thought by some to be mating displays, *Homo sapiens* mimic the calls of the white-rumped babbler, *Turdoides leucopygius*, and the laughing hyena, *Crocuta Crocuta*. However, I must caution my readers that this is hearsay. I have not observed this behavior myself.

Wildlife, that is birds and animals, was a constant part of my life in Maun. My house was located on the grounds of the Botswana Wildlife Training Institute, across the Thamalakane River from the main part of Maun. Just across the road was a 400-acre educational park, which was well-stocked with game. After work, I often strolled through the park and viewed lechwe, zebra, wildebeest, giraffe, kudu, and warthogs. Come May, if I put an extra blanket on my bed, I could sleep with the windows open and awaken to the grunts of impala rams as they fought for rights to lady impalas. A young bull elephant took up residence in my neighborhood for two weeks and gave chase to one of my neighbors. The local kids thought it great fun to practice their tracking skills on this elephant. Fortunately, no one was killed.

Ibo Zimmermann often canoed on the river, and he was mock-charged twice in one day by a hippo. A crocodile, recognizable by his bobbed tail, injured two adults and killed a child, all within two miles of my house.

The education park was a paradise for birds and they spilled over into my yard. In addition to black tits, there were Myer's parrots, red-billed buffalo weavers, woodland kingfishers, grey-headed helmetshrikes and dozens of other species. Doves are the voice of Africa. They spoke to me every morning and every afternoon, every day of the year.

A pair of gray hornbills claimed my yard and all mopane trees for 200 yards to the south as their private aviary. They allowed me to come and go freely but declared all other gray hornbills *persona non grata*. The male, with its heavy black bill, became very tame and would allow me to approach within ten feet. His lady, with its red, streaked bill, remained aloof.

In November, as the rainy season began, I noticed that the female had disappeared and I suspected that she was incubating some eggs. I watched the male for several days and noticed that it returned repeatedly to a certain mopane tree. Closer investigation revealed a circular hole, about two inches in diameter, leading to a hollow in the trunk of the tree. Inside, the female hornbill was incubating eggs.

The hole had been half closed with mud, so the female was sealed in and predators were sealed out. The remaining slot had the same vertical and horizontal dimensions as the male's bill. Using his long, horn-shaped bill, it fed its mate through the slot. This, I suppose, is why hornbills have horn-shaped bills. The female's favorite morsel was fresh scorpion, which I assume to be the hornbill's equivalent to our favorite foods.

Then one day in December, the female appeared outside the nest. The male resealed the entrance and the nest contained a single young hornbill. For several weeks both parents fed their chick through the slot. Then it too appeared outside. For another two days, the parents instinctively continued to thrust insects and scorpions into the now empty nest. Hornbills aren't too bright.

Marauders on the Thamalakane

Life with hornbills isn't without frustrations. They decided that the window sills of the Mean Machine were perfect potty chairs. This would have been okay if they had sat with their bills in and their tails out, but they sat in the opposite direction and deposited their business inside the Machine. This stance allowed them to admire themselves in the side mirrors while they did their chores. Not that there is anything wrong with their little deposits, which wash off easily, but it caused occasional embarrassment for my passengers.

When not messing up the Machine, the rascals entertained themselves by perching on the windshield wipers and pecking at the rubber blades. Within two weeks, they destroyed both rubber blades. No one in Maun stocked them, so I had to buy new wipers. Ngami Toyota stocked these for twenty-six dollars each, fifty-two for a pair.

I wrapped the new wipers in paper and plastic to protect them from the birds. The marauders quickly tore the covers off and began working on the new rubbers. Debit another fifty-two dollars and now we're talking big money. Ornithologists will be pleased to know that I learned the reason for this devious behavior. It was because these two hornbills were the most malicious, malevolent, mendacious birds ever to fly across the face of the earth.

Then I learned that Riley's Garage carried wiper blades that were quickly detachable. I made a quick trip to the bank and then to Riley's Garage. The new blades were perfect. I carried them safely in the cab until it rained. Of course, I got completely soaked by every shower as I dashed around the Mean Machine installing the blades. No one said wildlife management was an easy profession.

One day, quite by chance, I left the Machine with one window closed and the other open. The male hornbill flew through the open window and was trapped. In time it would have rediscovered the open window and escaped but I came along first. "Gotcha!"

I rolled the window up and fetched my camera and a student to take pictures. I figured I would get some snaps of me and the bird to convince the folks back home that I am a genuine nature lover. Then I would dismiss the student, take the villainous bird behind my house, and wring its neck.

I gave the student a two-minute short course in photography and retrieved the hornbill from the Mean Machine. I was lovingly stroking the bird and grinning like a Cheshire cat for the camera when it bit me. It felt like a Mississippi snapping turtle had clamped down on my finger. I wrenched free, the bird wrenched free, and away it went, off into the blue skies, leaving me with a red finger and hurt pride.

For the next fifteen months, I always parked the Mean Machine with one window up and one window down, hoping to recapture the marauder. It continued to sit on the window sill and leave deposits inside, but it never again flew into the cab to trap itself. Maybe, just maybe, hornbills are smarter than I thought.

WHOSE ELEPHANTS?

The lion's roar ripped through the village but the children didn't interrupt their play. The sound of a lion was as familiar to them as an ambulance siren is to the children in New York City. The village was called Mababé, the country was Botswana, and the children were Bushmen.

Two dozen cook fires were sufficient to light up the entire village. I shared a fire with two hunters I yearned to know better, one a Bushman, the other a Tswana. The best way to learn about hunters is to go hunting with them. We had shared many campfires and knew one another well. That morning my companions had followed spoor without error, my aim had been true, and now the three-legged pot overflowed with buffalo meat.

Freeman Sewadimo Malebogo, the Tswana, asked in English if I might have one more packet of potato chips. I dug them out and tossed them to him. He pulverized the barbecue-flavored chips and stirred the improvised seasoning into the pot of meat. The old Bushman, Mosesane Pekeneng, waved a thank you. He spoke no English, but it didn't matter. After days together in the bush, we read each others minds, with occasional translations by Freeman.

The lion roared again, closer now, and caught the Old Man's attention. He spoke in seTswana to Freeman: "It would be good if the *Lekgoa* (that's me, the white man) could shoot that lion for us. Botswana Game Industries is paying 500 pula ($250) for good lion hides." Under

Solo Safari

Botswana law, I could help citizen hunters fill their hunting licenses, but I could keep only the photographs and the memories. The meat, hides, and trophies belonged to the citizens.

Wildlife was important to these two Africans, but for very different reasons. I popped the top of my last warm Coke, leaned back against the wheel of my Land Cruiser, and contemplated the relationship between Africans and wild animals. The relationship had changed a lot over the millennia.

Twenty million years ago, there were no Africans, just wild animals. One of these animals was a large, vegetarian ape. The climate dried and the forest gave way to grassland, no place for a vegetarian. The ape was forced to hunt. To hunt he had to cooperate, so he invented language. He had no claws or fangs, so his paws evolved into hands, which could hold weapons. The vegetarian ape became a hunter, a human being.

A few of the humans left Africa over many generations and underwent minor changes. A very few of these later migrated back to Africa. That's how I came to Mababé Village. But most Africans stayed in Africa and lived by eating wild animals, except when the wild animals got lucky and ate the Africans. That relationship continued for millions of years, then we invented commerce.

No one knows what commodity was first exported from Africa, but it was probably ivory, the teeth of elephants. Certainly this trade extended far back into Old Testament times. In the thirteenth century, Marco Polo, the Italian explorer, was astonished by the volume of ivory passing through the ports in Zanzibar and Madagascar. By the sixteenth century, the ivory traders had extended their networks into the deepest interior of Africa. Most African villages in the interior experienced their first contact with the outside world when they bartered ivory for trade goods.

This early commerce in ivory brought enlightenment and comforts to Africans, but things quickly turned sour. Throughout much of the known history of Africa, ivory was linked with the gruesome traffic in slaves. In much of Africa, the big money was not in slaves. It was in ivory.

Arab raiders drove deep into the continent in search of ivory or "white gold" and amassed huge stockpiles. The tusks had to be transported to the coastal ports, so the raiders captured natives and pressed them into service as pack animals. At the ports, the natives were sold as slaves, as "black gold." In much of Africa, slaves were largely a byproduct of the ivory industry.

Sound incredible? Samuel Baker, the English explorer and hunter, recorded in 1873 that a healthy young girl was equal in value to a single tusk. Each elephant has two tusks, so one elephant was worth two human beings. Other records put the ratio at ten humans for a very large bull elephant.

In 1867, David Livingstone blundered into Tippu Tip, the most powerful of the slavers, near Lake Nyasa, now Lake Malawi. Tippu Tip had amassed thirty tons of ivory and was "recruiting" hundreds of people needed to carry the hoard to the coast and then be sold as slaves. This and other experiences led Livingstone to conclude that the only way to stop traffic in slaves was to first eliminate the traffic in ivory.

I looked across the fire and watched my African friends divide the barbecued buffalo. I hoped none of their ancestors fell prey to the slavers, but they probably weren't so lucky.

Some say these modern Africans hunt only for meat. That is not true. They are sportsmen, and like all sportsmen, they hunt for many reasons. All three of us hunt because our ancestors hunted, because the urge runs in our blood. I've seen the predator's stare in their eyes, the quickening pace of their throbbing veins, the joy over a successful hunt.

Freeman and the Old Man hunt for other, more pragmatic reasons. The Old Man, the Bushman, is a true subsistence hunter. He hunts for meat to feed his family. When he hunts well, he shares meat with others in Mababé Village. In one way or another, these favors will be repaid later. Several times each year, the Old Man hitchhikes to the larger village of Maun where he sells hides and trophy horns and uses the money to buy clothes, matches, staple foods, and other necessities.

Both of my friends have a great interest in elephants. Freeman hunted elephants legally as a young man and made good money selling the ivory. Botswana stopped elephant hunting in 1983 and the country now is overrun with elephants, in sharp contrast to other parts of Africa. In 1989, Freeman heard rumors that Botswana was going to reopen elephant hunting and he planned to be first in line to apply for a license. A good pair of tusks would finance the completion of his butcher shop.

Conservationists in the United States and Europe had other plans for the elephant. Responding to devastating poaching, which occurred in other parts of Africa, they banned worldwide commerce in ivory. The price of ivory crashed, Botswana canceled its plans to reopen elephant hunting, and Freeman's butcher shop remains uncompleted.

Freeman's interest in zebra hides, buffalo meat, and ivory has political consequences. Botswana is a small country with a truly democratic form of government. Freeman is personally acquainted with the man from Maun who represents him in Botswana's parliament. Freeman lobbies his representative to do all he can to take care of Botswana's wildlife and to reopen elephant hunting. But with no market for ivory, the parliament cannot justify spending money to manage elephants and they do not want to anger the preservationists in the wealthy countries.

The Old Man has a somewhat different perspective on elephants. The people of Mababé plant fields of corn and sorghum every year, but their success rate is low. Elephants love to raid the fields, trampling far more than they eat. A herd of elephants can destroy a field of corn in a single night. If the rains come and the elephants don't come, the citizens of Mababé harvest a crop. Any other combination of events leads to failure. In the old days, the people of Mababé hoped that a hunter would kill an elephant nearby and give them the meat. Since the ban on hunting, there is no elephant meat and sometimes no corn.

With Freeman translating, I tried to explain to the Old Man that the people of America think that every elephant should be saved. Old elephants, I explained, should be eaten by hyenas and vultures and ivory should be allowed to decay in the bush. The Old Man does not understand American logic. For a thousand years, elephants were both a blessing and a curse for Africans. Today, for the Old Man and the others in Mababé Village, elephants are only a curse.

HOW TO SKINNY-DIP AT THIRD BRIDGE

The Third Bridge is located deep in the Moremi Game Reserve. Some claim it can be reached in four hours from Maun, but I found too many diversions along the way. Three impala rams with enormous headgear hung out just outside the South Gate, and they always need photographing. There were several kudu bulls along the way. Who can pass up kudu bulls? The saddle-billed storks never let me stalk within camera range, but I kept trying. There were lion tracks to examine and hawks to identify. The four-hour journey stretched to seven or eight hours.

The Third Bridge is a loose pile of poles held together by wire. With luck, it just might hold up while one more truck crosses the crystal clear waters of an unnamed stream. Never mind a little water over the running boards. The bridge sags a bit in the middle. And you will need to engage the four-wheel drive if you are crossing from west to east because you must climb a fifteen-inch-high step hidden below the surface.

I liked Third Bridge because I was hot and tired and I could stretch my legs and splash the cool Okavango water on my face. With luck, I might catch a South African lady skinny-dipping or at least one or two in a bikini. I liked Third Bridge because it was part of the history of Africa, although it was a grisly history. Several years ago, a French doctor, a woman, went to the water's edge to bathe and never returned. They found her soap, washcloth, and clothing, but no trace of her. Crocodile.

The crocodiles at Third Bridge seem to prefer women. Their sexist attitudes were confirmed in January, 1989, when another lady was submerged in the water, wiggling her toes in the sandy bottom, and resting her elbows on the bridge. She was chatting with her boyfriend who was sitting on the bridge, when a crocodile clamped onto her buttocks. A hell of a tug of war followed, with the crocodile pulling down and the boyfriend pulling up. A stout fellow, he pulled the woman and the six-foot crocodile half out of the water before the crocodile gave up. The woman was very seriously injured and spent many months in the hospital.

I always wondered if I should warn the skinny-dippers and bikini-wearers about the crocodiles, but there were never any crocodiles in sight. I thought they would think I was trying to frighten them, and I figured the odds were slim, so I never said anything. However, I did all my skinny-dipping when no ladies were about, not because of modesty, but because the ladies seemed to attract crocodiles.

I liked Third Bridge because it is surrounded by tsessebe, impala, warthogs, lechwe, and elephants. I camped at the bridge and listened to the sounds of Africa. Hyenas whooped, lions roared, hippos grunted, and zebras made sounds that you must go to Africa to hear because it cannot be described. At dusk, the big trees loaded up with birds coming in from the swamp for the night. At dawn, the birds discussed which lagoon was most likely to offer a good catch of insects. The discussion turned into heated arguments, which quickly awoke all campers.

If you poke around the tall grass and bush across the road, you will find the white-spotted, dainty bushbuck. Most campers are too preoccupied with baboons to notice the shy bushbucks. If I ever write a fairy tale about Africa, the lady bushbuck at Third Bridge will be the heroine and a big-dog baboon will be the villain. Some people like baboons because they remind us of people. Unfortunately, they always remind me of some person I would like to forget. Nevertheless, if you want a baboon experience, Third Bridge is the place to have it. They come into your camp, climb over your truck, and invite themselves into your tent.

During a moment of poor judgment, I decided that I needed some photographs of baboons. I was standing at the open door of the Mean Machine fiddling with f-stops or whatever when I heard a thump. I looked up to see a big male baboon sitting on the tailgate picking at my only package of chocolate cookies. These weren't just lemon creams. These were real chocolate cookies. This was serious.

"Get away, you pesky rascal," I yelled as I bolted toward the thief. The baboon hit the ground running, chocolate cookies in hand. I gave chase for twenty-five yards then heard the thump of a soft body hitting metal. Another dog baboon had climbed onto the Machine where I had been standing three seconds before.

I skidded to a halt and did a quick 180-degree turn. The baboon scooped up a quart bottle of iced tea and a carton of eggs and hit the ground. At thirty yards in a full gallop, the two objects began to slip from the grasp of the second pesky baboon so it dropped the slick plastic bottle. Gone were the chocolate cookies and my carton of eggs, two days' breakfast, were never recovered.

They had made a fool of me. They must have planned the whole thing. One hit the back of the truck and when I chased after it, the other one hit from the front. They probably rehearsed this maneuver a hundred times. Cheeky baboons!

The native people of Africa believe that baboons occasionally rape women. I believe it. They are thieves, why not rapists? Who knows what those perverts at Third Bridge are capable of doing?

BUSHED

The airstrip at Xakanaxa Lagoon in Moremi Game Reserve had flooded and a couple of dozen men were scratching out a new one with hoes and axes. The game scouts, who supervised the job, had obtained ration permits for two buffalo to feed the crew, and they asked me to help hunt the buffalo.

If men are going to work hard, they need a good protein diet. Extended labor under the blazing African sun could lead to nutritional depletion in their bodies. Who knows what diseases and pestilence could set in and spread to surrounding communities? These men needed buffalo meat. What could I say? As a humanitarian gesture, I volunteered to help hunt the buffalo.

I drove to the Khwaai River Game Scout Camp after work on Friday, arriving well past dark. The next morning, three game scouts, four laborers, and I climbed into a parks department Land Cruiser and drove into the hunting area north of the reserve. I noticed that the spare tire was flat, but that is not unusual for a government vehicle. I assumed they had tire levers, patches, and a pump.

It was one of those exhilarating African mornings when a man just belongs in the back of a hunting car, with the wind on his face, cruising for game. We saw plenty, and I marveled that Harry Selby and his clients must have easy hunting. Harry is the hero of Robert

Solo Safari

Ruark's classic book *Horn of the Hunter* and is manager of Safari South, which has the hunting concession along the Khwaai River. However, I also noticed that the area had received rain, the pans were full, and the buffalo would be scattered.

At nine o'clock we spotted a herd of buffalo. I assumed we would proceed on foot, but I was outvoted seven to one. We charged the herd with the Land Cruiser and of course the herd fled before we could shoot. Despite all their extraordinary bush skills, most Africans couldn't stalk a broken-down Chevy sitting in a crowded parking lot.

Four of us took up the track on foot, Game Scout Kgaodi with a .375 and I with a .458. In less than a mile, we bumped into the herd and Kgaodi and I duck-walked to within seventy-five yards. I lined up a bull and put three pounds of pressure on a four-pound trigger when Kgaodi leaned over and suggested that I move to another tree about three yards closer. The bull detected Kgaodi's movement or voice and twenty buffalo disappeared. Now I was irritated, but complaining wouldn't bring the herd back.

The herd moved into more open terrain and twice more we spooked them, both times at long range. The crew wanted to swing wide, run ahead of the herd and intercept them unaware. I've seen professional trackers attempt this, but never successfully. I took the opposite tack and called a halt to give the herd time to settle down. Fifteen minutes later we resumed tracking, but I insisted that my three companions stay fifty meters behind me. I carried the big rifle at the ready but never felt the weight. It's like closing up on a bird dog on point. The shotgun is part of you, but you don't feel it.

The trail continued for another two miles, then began to thin out on harder soil around several dry pans. I slowed to sort out the spoor and the support crew closed up. Perhaps it was just as well because Game Scout Muzila was the first to spot the herd.

This is the frustration of hunting with semiskilled Africans. I can spot game as well as any tracker, but to be successful, you must spot the prey at the very limit of visibility, with two or three pairs of eyes being better than one. But if you keep your people close by, they get excited, move around too much, and spook the game.

I waved the men down and began to move forward, but couldn't sight the buffalo. Again the crew moved up and again they spotted the buffalo. I waved them down and edged toward the black shadows. I could just keep up with the tail end of the herd as they slowly

Bushed

drifted through the bush. At a low crawl, I probably could manage about a half mile an hour but I wasn't closing the gap. Then something big and black moved to my left. This was my best chance, so I moved in that direction. Out of the corner of my eye, I saw Kgaodi scurrying up with the .375. I had no more than fifteen or twenty seconds before he would mess up the works.

A bull stepped into view about seventy-five yards away and locked his gaze onto me. From a kneeling position, I raised the .458, but a bush obscured the line of sight. If I moved, he would be gone in a half second. Slowly, I leaned just three inches to the left to clear the bush. Now off balance, the foresight wobbled badly, but within the vital target area. Not perfect, but good enough. I fired and immediately reloaded from the shoulder.

The bull collapsed as I scooted left and swung my feet around to a steadier sitting position. The bull lunged, trying to regain his feet, but another 500 grains of lead slammed him to the ground a second time. Again he lunged and I hammered a third bullet into his chest. This time he stayed down. I stuffed a couple of cartridges into the magazine and approached the bull. He was still breathing, so I waved Kgaodi and Muzila back and carefully aimed the insurance shot, the fourth one, into his chest. He was an enormous bull, the largest I have ever taken.

It was now ten o'clock, still early. Muzila and a laborer began skinning the bull while Kgaodi and I resumed the track, hoping for a second bull. We followed for nearly an hour in the growing heat of midday, but the herd had been badly spooked by the four shots. We returned to the fallen bull and Muzila and I assumed the skinning chores while Kgaodi and the laborer set out to fetch the Land Cruiser, which was many miles away.

We skinned and waited and watched the vultures gather and waited some more. I hadn't had a drop of water since sunrise, and it was now past noon and uncomfortably hot. Where were those guys? The flat, spare tire, that must be it. They had punctured another tire while bashing through the bush and had stopped to repair it. I hoped they had the necessary equipment. The marabou storks carved giant circles in the sky, their eyes on the pile of meat they hoped to share. They were as impatient as I.

At one o'clock, Kgaodi and the others walked in. The battery was dead and the vehicle refused to start. It was sitting in soft sand and could not be push-started. Nice! We were completely bushed. They had brought my pack with a bit of lunch and an old plastic jug about half full of water, about a pint each for Muzila and me. I glanced at the label on the recycled plastic jug. "Rat Finee, A Product of Canada." Well, life is so simple when you have no choices. I gulped my half then redried my throat trying to choke down half a sandwich.

The debate ebbed and flowed, all in seTswana, but one of the local laborers clearly was regarded as the expert. "This one is a walking road map," Kgaodi translated. "He says we are about twenty-one miles from the Khwaai Game Scout Camp. If we leave now, we will arrive by six o'clock."

There was no way we could cover twenty-one miles in four and a half hours, but what did it matter. There was no choice but to start out. The African mind never questions fate. There was no complaining or casting of blame, only frank discussion of how to proceed. The "Walking Map" would make the trek. He claimed to know where to find water along the way. I would go to fetch the Mean Machine, and Muzila would go as interpreter. The other four men would stay back to keep the vultures, hyenas, and lions from the carcass. They would keep the .375 and I would carry the .458. And so at 1:30 on a hot African afternoon, already badly dehydrated and tired, equipped with a .458 and an empty rat-poison jug, three men began a twenty-one mile hike.

The Walking Map set a brisk pace through the loose sand. I tried to divert my thoughts from my dry throat, to separate the mind from the body. It was a mental trick I had learned when carrying heavy loads up big mountains, but today the dry throat would not relinquish its hold on the mind. The .458 weighed about twenty pounds and pressed down mercilessly on my shoulders. Still, there were flycatchers to be admired and enough elephant spoor to keep me alert. We skirted several pans. Six hours earlier I had cursed the water-filled pans because they had dispersed the herds. Now, every pan we encountered was dry.

After an hour we hit the sand road. A road! Roads carry vehicles and vehicles give lifts. Unfortunately this was a hunting track that led nowhere and the hunting season was over for the safari companies. That's the trouble with Harry Selby. The guy is never around when you need him. Once the hunting season closes, this road might carry one vehicle per week. Best forget about a lift and keep walking.

Bushed

I tried again to separate the mind from the body. The mind trudged across the Sahara desert, but that was the wrong kind of fantasy. That was too close to reality. So I sent the mind on a trek up Mount Everest. I could at least daydream about being cool. The .458 grew progressively heavier and crushed my bony shoulder. Muzila, a man of great compassion, offered to carry it and thereafter we took turns. I tried to take a leak but could force only a few drops of yellow-brown urine. This was my kidneys' way of telling me that I needed a drink. The news didn't surprise me. The December sun was a blast furnace. December! The hottest month of the year. Why couldn't we get bushed in July when it's cool.

After another hour and a half, we entered a large clearing. At its center a pair of saddlebilled storks strutted through the mirage. Saddlebills! Wonderful! Saddlebills don't live in mirages. They live in water, real water. My hopes soared, but Walking Map led up past the pan. There was water all right with a world-class bull hippo right in the middle of it, and you know what hippos do in the water.

"Is there better water ahead?" I asked.

"Yes, just a short way." I had doubts about passing up any kind of water. I was thirsty but not desperate. I swallowed hard, or tried to, and fell in line.

I checked my watch. It was 3:30 and I tried again to separate the mind from the body. I sent the mind chasing after a beagle hound who was chasing after a rooster pheasant on a crisp October morning. Now that's living. I've got to get out of this Africa business and get back to Nebraska for some serious pheasant hunting. My mouth tasted of copper, dry sticky copper. "Go away mouth. Go away body. You're bothering me."

When I looked at my watch again, it was 3:35. Another six hours and we would arrive at Khwaai. I doubted I had enough fantasies to keep the body away from the mind for another six hours.

We trudged on. Was that track from a leopard or a hyena? Who cares? You can't drink a track. Just keep moving.

Then Walking Map turned off the sand road and headed through the bush. I looked up and there it was, a beautiful blue-water lagoon surrounded by green reeds. Not a dust-edged, brown-water pan, but a real lagoon with blue water.

Muzila kicked off his shoes and waded down a dung-filled hippo path into the clear water where he filled the Rat Finee jug. The water was cloudy but surprisingly cool. The flavor was slightly off. Who cares? Ignorance is bliss and water is water. I swilled a quart, ate the last half of my sandwich, and poured down another quart of water.

We lounged in the shade and contemplated our situation. The hottest part of the afternoon was past and we had our bellies and the Rat Finee jug full of water. Only five or six hours of slogging remained. Never mind that we were hungry and dead tired. We would make it. I resolved to quit the game department and move to the city. I would swear off hunting and curse the days of my birth, but we would make it to Khwaai.

Muzila sat upright, then Walking Map. I heard it too, a metallic rumble in the far distance. Could it be? Muzila grabbed the Rat Finee jug and I grabbed the .458 and we ran back to the road. "Listen, man, that's a truck. If it doesn't stop, it's getting a .458 solid through the engine."

The Mercedes seven-ton bounced into view and stopped beside us. The sign on the door read, "Northwest District Council." I always knew the Northwest District Council was the finest organization in Botswana. The Africans exchanged greetings in seTswana and we climbed on board. The Mercedes shook and rattled and tossed us every which way, and the driver spat tobacco juice with not enough force to clear the back of the truck, but we didn't offer to get out and walk. We arrived at the Khwaai Game Scout Camp an hour later.

We poked some food down our throats, then loaded the Mean Machine and headed back into the bush to rescue our companions. I checked the distance on the odometer from the camp to the point where we had been picked up. It was more than seventeen miles, much farther than we had expected. Thank you, Northwest District Council.

We found the stalled Land Cruiser and tried to jump-start it without luck. We towed it back to the sand road, then towed it some more trying to start the engine. No luck. We towed it back into the bush to hide it from vandals and abandoned it. Four men sitting atop a thousand pounds of lion bait still needed rescue.

Walking Map figured the carcass was five miles into the bush. The night bird's first song floated through the forest as we nosed the Mean Machine into the mopane. We wound our way between the bigger trees and smashed over the smaller ones. The headlights were pitifully inadequate for finding a route through the maze and we often had to back up and swing the lights left and right in search of a passage. The short, fire-hardened mopane spikes threatened to punc-

Bushed

ture the tires and the longer spikes screeched along the sides of the Machine like fingernails on a chalkboard.

I have no explanation of how these Africans found their way in the darkness. I was totally lost. "That's where we stopped to rest when you wanted to let the herd settle down," Muzila reassured me. "Don't you recognize it?"

No, I didn't recognize it and every tree looks like every other tree and we probably will drive off the end of the earth and wreck the Mean Machine. Walking Map uttered something in seTswana and I picked up the words *lekgoa* (white man) and *tseana* (stupid). Then straight ahead came the faintest ray of light from a fire. Five minutes later we arrived at the carcass. It had taken over an hour to cover the five miles of bush.

The Rat Finee jug was passed around and quickly drained. Roasted liver was retrieved from the coals and the carcass was loaded. There was another hour of bush bashing to regain the road, then the long drive back to Khwaai. We arrived at 11:00 P.M.

I suggested that we might try for the other buffalo the next day, but my suggestion found little support. The game scouts pointed out that their only vehicle was broken down in the bush and would I please haul the meat to the starving crew at Xakanaxa. It would add three hours to my drive home, but I said yes. We agreed to sleep late and leave at 8 A.M.

The next morning I remembered the huge set of horns and gave instructions for the skull to be skinned. Bad luck. Someone had already split the skull open to remove the brains for breakfast. I would have paid a thousand dollars for that skull, but someone destroyed it for fifty cents worth of brains. I did not have even a photograph of my best buffalo.

That was not the only problem. We discovered that the pile of poles that serves as a bridge across of Khwaai River had collapsed, stranding us on the wrong side of the river. Well, it had been one of those weekends. But we were alive, the Mean Machine was intact, and we had fresh meat which we would somehow deliver to Xakanaxa. Let's call the weekend a success.

THE FAINT-HEARTED PHOTOGRAPHER

I'd had bad luck photographing elephants and I needed to try again. Many of these beasts lived in Moremi Game Reserve just three hours from my home, so I planned a weekend safari. The headlights of the Mean Machine pointed north in search of the sand track. At Matlapaneng, a red rubber ball bounced over the eastern horizon and a pair of hitchhikers waved me over.

"*Dumela morena.*" (Hello, lord) Hitchhikers are always respectful. "I am asking for a lift to Shorobe." Fifty years ago, a poor linguist must have written an English grammar book which began every request with, "I am asking for. . . ." The phrase has stuck.

"Okay," I said, pointing with my thumb to the back of the Machine. One chap started loading battered suitcases and baskets while the spokesman continued. I knew what was coming.

"Could my brother just come along, too?" What he meant was his brother, his brother's wife and five kids, and a couple of cousins.

"*Go siame.*" (Okay)

The spokesman beckoned toward the hut and the brother bolted out with a packed canvas bag and hurled himself into the Machine. Next came a woman with a baby tied to her back and two bags in each hand, followed by a girl with more paraphernalia. It had happened a hundred times before. One or two hitchhikers turned into a half-ton payload. The Kalahari Transportation Service was back in business, but it was operating on zero gross income.

The lady with the baby took the seat beside me and we headed north. The sand track tossed the Mean Machine like a bucking bronco tosses a greenhorn rider. The baby's head rolled so violently with each bump that I feared its neck would break and I eased off the accelerator.

My mind wandered ahead to Moremi Game Reserve. I was cataloging the best location for the photos I needed when the baby began to cry. How I hate that sound. I gave the mother a scornful look, she produced an ample milk supply and the baby was silenced. Two potholes later, I shifted my eyes back to the road.

The passengers unloaded at Shorobe and another chap approached. *"Dumela ra."* (Hello, sir)

"Dumela ra."

"Are you going to Kasane?" A handful of people loitered nearby anxiously awaiting the reply. No doubt a half ton of luggage was packed and carefully hidden nearby, out of view of unsuspecting motorists.

"Sorry, I am going to Moremi."

My shirt was already damp from perspiration when I entered Moremi Game Reserve at 8 A.M. I spent the first day photographing antelope and marabou storks but found no elephants.

The next day I spotted a mixed herd of cows, calves, and a bull about a half mile south of Xakanaxa Lagoon. They were drifting away from the road in scrub mopane and the wind was wrong. I remembered a junction in the sand road several hundred yards back. The alternate track might carry me into the herd. I turned the Mean Machine around and measured the distance back to the junction, then proceeded an equal distance down the other track. Standing at my full height atop the cab, I could see mopane trees swaying as feeding elephants pulled down branches. After about five minutes, I determined the direction of their movement and moved the Machine 200 yards ahead to intercept the herd. I found a clearing with several larger trees that would make a more photogenic backdrop than the scrub mopane. The wind was on my face and the sun on my back. Perfect. I waited while a half dozen vultures rode the morning thermals, eyeing the bush to see who had died overnight.

The first patches of gray appeared fifteen minutes later. I started the engine and engaged the four-wheel drive in case a quick departure might be required. In another five minutes, the elephants surrounded me on three sides. The closest were within sixty yards, close enough for my 300mm lens.

I focused, glanced left and right, and shot. Then I glanced left and right again. I had watched about a dozen animals at once. It was

The Faint-Hearted Photographer

a bit tense, but I was perched on the running board with the door open. If an elephant charged, I would drop into the seat and escape down the road. I watched for any sign of aggression, flaring of the ears, a raised trunk, rocking back and forth, or shaking of the head. All the animals were calm.

Then a bull charged. It came from sixty yards without the slightest warning. I paused for a precious half second to center it in the frame and jab the shutter. Fifty yards and closing. I dropped into the seat pulling the door shut behind me. Forty yards.

"Okay, Dummy. You've got lots of time. Left and ahead for low gear. Now don't get in a hurry and kill the engine." I glanced out the window and saw that the bull had turned. The sound of the slamming door had broken its nerve. Africa just isn't what it used to be. The bull elephants are turning into cowards.

I looked left and right. All the other animals remained calm. No mathatha. I resumed photographing but took additional precautions. I remained in the seat with the Machine in gear and with my foot on the clutch. Again I looked left and right. There were no flared ears, no raised trunks, no shaking heads. Then he came again, this time from seventy-five yards.

The engine screamed, dust flew from all four tires, and the Mean Machine charged ahead. The noise and flying sand again broke the bull's nerve and he turned away. I looked over my left and right shoulders. All the other elephants were calm, so I hit the brake. I could play this game as well as this cowardly bull. I shifted into reverse and eased the Machine back toward the herd.

A cow and calf emerged from the bush. I looked left and right and leveled the long lens on the calf. I tried to focus, but now the camera was shaking too much. To hell with it. It was getting late, and I needed to get back to Maun.

CAMPFIRE STORIES

There were many other adventures in Zimbabwe and Botswana that I will not describe in detail. Pleasant days in the warm African sun, shooting impala for the pot, fishing for bream, identifying birds, and sharing the bush with Andy's many friends who were rotating through our camps.

There was the day when Andy, Wiro, and my hunting companion left camp at dawn to check lion baits. They would return at 8:00 A.M. for breakfast. Andy's Number 2 tracker and I packed our lunch, expecting to be occupied all day on a buffalo hunt. But we found the fresh track of a single, large bull a half mile from camp. I waved down Andy's vehicle and told him to hold breakfast for a half hour so I could join him. I need not have bothered. I bagged the bull within twenty minutes and beat the lion hunters back to camp.

One of the rare animals in the Zambezi is a beautiful antelope called the grysbok. We were searching for elephant when we flushed a bull grysbok and I hurried a 500-grain bullet smack into its chest. The bull jumped three times its height straight into the air and hit the ground at a full gallop. Andy swung his .375 around, just in case, but the bull fell dead. Andy knelt beside the grysbok and measured its horns against the last two joints of his trigger finger. "Fantastic. I think this bull will make Rowland Ward." The tape measure later confirmed that the horns exceeded one-and-a-half inches. "He's heavy in the body too. He'll go seventeen, maybe eighteen pounds," Andy guessed.

"He weighs twenty pounds if he weighs an ounce." No one was going to cheat me out of two pounds of grysbok flesh.

Solo Safari

Later in that hunt I killed my bull elephant, so I collected the smallest and largest game animals in Zimbabwe on a single hunt.

One of the most sporting hunts I've been on was John Tautin's bull buffalo hunt. We found a pair of bull tracks crossing the road that runs along the Zambezi River. The tracks led into a tangle of bush that would have repelled a bull rhino. Jason and Friday wanted to push off. They had families to look after and they rightly calculated that they weren't paid enough to track buffalo into such crud. John and I were both bachelors, so we had nothing to lose. With two superb trackers and plenty of firepower, what could possibly go wrong? We prevailed.

Visibility ranged from ten to twenty-five yards and we had to step over, dodge around, and duck under the wait-a-bit thorns. We managed a slow 200 yards, then something crashed ahead. Two safeties clicked off, then all was silent. Buffalo. Another hundred yards, and more buffalo broke the silence. Then another.

"This is just like flushing rabbits back home," John whispered.

"Yea, Jason and Friday make a pretty good pair of beagle hounds."

Jason leaned sideways allowing John to peer past him through a seventy-yard tunnel into the bush. There was no light at the end of this tunnel, only a black hulk, the front half of a buffalo. John sent a .375 down the tunnel and the bull wheeled and disappeared into the tangle of thorn.

We initiated the wounded buffalo drill. Jason rolled a newsprint cigarette and smoked the butt down to the last line of type. "Ready?" John asked, but now Friday was rolling a smoke. Friday is no dummy. He prefers his buffalo very dead. A bataleur eagle rode the winds 500 feet into the air and looked down on the scene. Oh, to have known what that eagle knew. Five minutes later, John asked again, "Time to go?"

"Well, I was thinking of taking up smoking," I quipped. Come to think of it, I wasn't paid at all for this. Jason and Friday drew the bolts on the semiautomatic assault rifles and snapped fresh cartridges into the barrels. John checked his .375 and I checked my .460 for the fourth time. I was the organizer of this safari, so I took charge and gave the order.

"It's your buffalo. You go first." Like all good infantry generals, I would control this operation from the rear.

Fire Team Alpha tiptoed the seventy yards and found the tortured tracks where the bull had spun from the shot. Jason and John eased forward inch by inch. Ten yards later they found the first splash of blood.

Campfire Stories

Visibility generally was less than thirty yards, so the point men shifted left and right as they attempted to gain a visual edge over the quarry.

"Who ever got the silly idea that fair chase is a good thing?" I wondered. Shooting from the back of a vehicle was looking better and better.

Now the point men eased forward centimeter by centimeter. Five minutes and twenty-five yards later, Jason spotted the black hulk another fifteen yards ahead. It was down and very dead.

It was an old bull, a veteran of many battles. It had sacrificed its tail to a lion and broken a horn tip on the boss of another bull. The scars in its hide recorded the violent story of its life. John challenged the warrior on the best defensive terrain in Africa and won the challenge.

The really joyous African hunting is on the game ranches. During my three trips to Zimbabwe, I managed to hunt on four ranches. The wilderness hunts for dangerous game are too intense, too obsessive, and too expensive. On the ranches I hunted eland, sable, zebra, wildebeest, warthog, and duiker for less than half the cost per day of hunting in the Zambezi Valley. I stayed in the ranchers' homes and was pampered with good food and wine. Game was so plentiful that dawn to dusk hunting was unnecessary. We hunted three or four hours each morning, returned to the house for lunch and a nap, then hunted a couple of hours in the afternoons.

Every hunt in Botswana involved some degree of frustration. The biggest single problem was borrowing rifles. I had a dozen top-quality rifles stored in a warehouse in Virginia, but the Botswana police would not let me bring even one rifle into their country, so I had to beg friends to lend me rifles. One chap told me, "There are two things I don't loan, my rifle and my wife."

All rifles I borrowed had open sight, and all were to some extent unsatisfactory. Imagine shooting springbok, about the size of a whitetail button buck, at 200 yards with an open sighted .375. I break into a cold sweat when I recall some of the rifles I used on buffalo. I spent dozens of weekends sitting at home reading dime novels, all for want of a rifle.

Several hunts fizzled on Saturday mornings as I sat around Maun with a fully-packed truck, waiting for some friend who had decided at the last minute that he would rather go to his cattle post to count his cattle or visit his rural wife. Other hunts failed for lack of game.

There were some rich experiences, like the evening just after dusk when I drove the Mean Machine into a muddy elephant wallow. We dropped in at 7:00 P.M. My tracker and I worked until 9:30 before we gave up, pitched camp, and cooked supper. The next morning, we wrestled in the mud for another four hours before liberating the Machine. Essentially, we jacked up one wheel at a time and built a corrugated wooden road under the Machine. We then spent an hour taking baths and doing laundry.

A couple of interesting hunts came my way. The Wildlife Training Institute planned a big open house and invited the minister and other dignitaries from Gaborone. You just cannot feed the minister goat meat, so we obtained ration permits for two gemsbok and six springbok. It was a three-hour drive to Puduhudu, a Bushman village at the edge of the hunting area. The next morning I put down eight animals in just two hours. It was hot-barrel hunting, a rare and interesting experience that I'm glad to have had but would not care to repeat. For years to come, that hunt will be relived around the fires at Puduhudu.

Then a couple of South African researchers contacted HQ and asked to collect a lechwe and tsessebe. They needed tissue samples for genetic research. HQ agreed, but stipulated that the shooting must be done by a department employee. Mustn't let foreign sportsmen hunt in the guise of research. I had established my reputation as a marksman, so I was nominated for the job. Since I had not hunted either species, I gladly accepted the assignment.

"Don't mess it up," came the order from the deputy director. "We don't want you chasing wounded animals all over the Okavango with visiting scientists looking on."

I usually do rather well with a rifle, but now the pressure was on. I shot the first tsessebe and the first lechwe we saw. Both were instantaneous one-shot kills at over 200 yards and both animals easily qualified for the record book. I didn't admit to my new South African friends that all this was pure, dumb luck.

Through all this, I lived in fear of the law. I did most of my hunting under Paragraph 11 of the 1979 Amendment to the Faunal Conservation Act. This allowed me to "assist" a citizen hunter provided that he accompanied me in the field and I did not retain either meat or trophies. All I kept were the memories and photographs. The citizens kept the meat and most of the trophies were thrown away. The problem was that most policemen were unfamiliar with Paragraph 11.

It happened thirty miles south of Sehitwa while I was hunting springbok for a local Bushman. The police caught me red-handed obeying the law, but because I couldn't produce a license in my name, they hauled me to the Sehitwa Police Station. There I showed them Paragraph 11. They must have been convinced that I was legal, because they brought no charges, but they confiscated my borrowed rifle, my friend's license, and a springbok carcass. No entries were made in the Exhibit Register, and no receipts were given, but they were going to teach us that you should never prove the Sehitwa Police wrong. Two days later, the police officer in charge of all Ngamiland returned the rifle, with apologies.

Freeman Malebogo, Mosesane Pekeneng (the Old Man from Mababé Village), and I planned a four-day buffalo hunt in the area north of the Khwaai River, the same area that Muzila and I favored for hiking (see chapter 12). Here I scored my first double on buffalo, two buffalo from one herd. The proper way to do this is to knock down one animal with a single shot, dispense with the insurance shot that would further spook the herd, then immediately follow the herd and kill a second animal.

We killed the two buffalo before we had even made camp. The problem was that the Mean Machine could not haul two buffalo, six men, and our luggage and camping equipment. So we off-loaded the luggage, loaded the buffalo, and hauled them to a likely camping area. Then I returned to fetch the luggage and equipment. The next morning we decided to move camp, so I shuttled loads to the new location. The next day we could not find buffalo but shot five impala. Freeman and I returned to Maun for the workweek while the Old Man and three others stayed in camp to cut biltong.

The next Friday evening, Freeman and I returned to camp, arriving at 1 A.M. Saturday morning we overloaded the Mean Machine with two dried buffalo, five dried impala, six men, all our gear, and the usual quarter ton of petrol and water. "The vehicle looks like the hyena," Freeman said, observing that the front end was higher than the rear.

We were crawling toward Mababé Village when we crossed the fresh spoor of a herd of buffalo. It's not rational to pass up a fresh buffalo track when you have an open license. It just isn't done. An hour later, a big-bodied, small-horned bull fell to my shot. Now we really had a problem.

Freeman and the Old Man stayed behind to butcher the bull while the rest of us pushed on to Mababé. We unloaded the dried meat and turned back to rescue our friends from the marauding predators, arriving at dusk. The odor of the butchered bull had indeed drawn lions, so Freeman had gathered enough wood to keep four fires burning throughout the night. He was glad to see us.

Now in total darkness, we loaded the bull and bashed through the bush for an hour before reaching the road. We arrived in Mababé at 11 P.M., totally exhausted. I pitched my tent, remembering to keep well away from the donkey corral. That night the donkeys were silent, but Mababé's twenty dogs barked constantly from 1 A.M. to 4 A.M. The next morning there were only nineteen dogs and a spot of blood in the sand. Leopard.

At first light, we popped a couple of local impala for fresh meat, bringing the total contribution of meat to three buffalo and seven impala. That was more meat than the entire village of 150 people had killed in the entire previous year. In the months that followed, I delivered five more buffalo, three lechwe, two zebra, and a kudu, making Mababé the best-fed Bushman village in Africa.

I thought back to my first meeting with the Old Man when he demanded twenty-five dollars for a week's work. I had felt pangs of conscience, fearing that I was taking unfair advantage of a naive Bushman. In the months that followed, I burned hundreds of dollars worth of fuel delivering tons of dried meat to his village. I spent several half days hunting impala so he could have fresh meat and I fired many three-dollar .375 rounds at baboons so he could collect the skulls and sell them for two dollars each. Next time someone lectures you about how the white man has exploited the black man in Africa, please tell them about the Old Man and the biologist.

The Old Man, Mosesane Pekeneng, was prone to telling stories, but Freeman and I grew fond of him and the three of us joined in many hunts. I provided transport and marksmanship. Freeman was the overall organizer and interpreter. The Old Man organized trackers and biltong cutters and provided many of the licenses that are freely available to rural dwellers. The other residents of Mababé Village considered him somewhat of a wizard for his ability to extract services from the visiting American. From their point of view, the Old Man was ripping me off, but I was a willing victim.

HOW AN ADRENALINE JUNKIE HUNTS BUFFALO

I have not spent a single day hunting buffalo with a professional hunter. I am strictly self-taught. The fact that I have handled seventeen buffalo and the fact that I am still ambulatory suggests that I'm doing something right. Here's how it's done.

You can either hunt the herds or the old bachelor bulls. In Botswana, the buffalo tend to be migratory and all the buffalo stay in herds. In the Zambezi Valley, with its permanent water sources, the buffalo are more sedentary. The old bulls leave the herds and live alone or with one or two buddies. These old gentlemen are survivors. The scars in their hides tell of battles with lions and other bulls. Their horns may be broken and they may be carrying a bullet or two. These gentlemen have character. With all their aches and pains, some of these gentlemen aren't gentleman at all. Their tempers are nasty and their patience is limited. Most hunters consider the bachelors more dangerous than the bulls in the herds.

Whether hunting the herds or the bachelors, the first step is to locate fresh spoor. This is done by driving the roads and walking around the water holes, watching carefully for tracks in the dust. Buffalo that have been hunted rarely drink during the day. They come down only between dusk and dawn, so water points must be checked in the mornings. During the day, the animals move from one to ten miles into the bush.

If you are driving a river road and find spoor headed toward the water, you must drive on for a mile or two to see if that same spoor recrosses the road, returning to the bush. If not, you will have a quick hunt along the river. If the spoor crosses the road twice, you must follow the outgoing spoor only.

Step 2 is to figure out whether the spoor is fresh. An experienced tracker can judge the age of a footprint. Most of us need to follow the spoor until we find some dung, which is easier to age. You are searching for dung that hit the ground since dusk yesterday. Scrape the bottom of your boot over the dung. If the surface has the same color as the interior, the dung was laid down after midnight. If the surface is darker, but still moist, it fell between dusk and midnight. No problem. If the surface is dry and crusted, pass it up and look for something fresher.

Now let's assume the spoor is that of a bachelor. Step 3 is to listen to the tracker's various arguments for not following this particular spoor. Every tracker knows of less dangerous ways to hunt buffalo. No tracker has life insurance, and all have at least one wife or girlfriend who wants to see them alive once more. Trackers have a catalog of about twenty reasons for abandoning spoor. The more common ones are: The wind is wrong; the spoor is too old; there are sure to be many more buffalo a few miles ahead; and lions are following the buffalo and will spook them before you find them.

Step 4 is to determine if the track is from a really big bull. If it is, become stubborn and tell the tracker to get on with the job.

Hunting the bachelors does indeed require a brave and skillful tracker. Any amateur can follow a herd of fifty buffalo. More skill is required to follow a single set of tracks. Then the tracker must spot the prey before it spots him. This too is more difficult with a single animal. If all goes well, the bull will lie up within two miles of water, the tracker will spy it while it is unaware, and you will low crawl the last thirty yards and set up a successful shot.

Hunting the herds may be less dangerous, but it usually is more exciting than stalking the loners. Okay, you've found a fresh spoor and have followed it for four or five miles. The large herds must range more widely to find sufficient forage. Now you must detect them before they sense you. With fifty pairs of eyes at their advantage, you hope to detect them beyond the limit of visibility.

Herds are very vocal. With luck, you will hear their grunts from 200 yards away. You must be constantly alert for the switching of a tail, the angle of a back leg, or simply a spot of black that is too big to be a burned stump. The crackling of branches and a cloud of dust tell you that you blew it.

This time your tracker got it right and spotted a patch of black hair at a hundred yards. The tracker's job is largely over. Hopefully there won't be a wounded buffalo to track. Now you or your professional hunter must take over. You check the wind and concealment, then proceed at a crouch, on hands and knees, or on your elbows. At fifty yards, you peek around a tree with your binoculars and see a pair of cows here, a cow and calf there, maybe a young bull. Somewhere behind them, more buffalo are grunting. You look over your shoulder and flash a palms down signal to your tracker. He is moving up and may frighten the herd. You resolve to bring a pair of handcuffs on the next hunt, so you can handcuff the tracker to a tree while you do the final stalk.

Now what should you do? The wind is good. Best wait. Maybe a bull will step into view. You reach up to pluck a leaf that obstructs your view. A cow raises its head and stares holes through you. You freeze, arm extended, then remember the tracker. Does he see that you've been seen? You pray that he doesn't move. Your extended arm is getting heavy but you dare not relax. An eternity later, the cow loses interest and lowers its head and you drop your aching arm.

You've been watching for fifteen minutes and decide that further waiting is not likely to produce a big bull. You retreat at a low crawl for fifty yards and stand to stretch the kinks out of your muscles. The tracker leads you ninety degrees to the left and points you toward the herd. Another low crawl puts you on your belly on an eroded anthill. Ease up the binoculars. There's a good bull but a calf is blocking the shot to the shoulder. Palms down to the tracker.

You bring the .458 to your shoulder and wait. If either the bull or the calf moves, you will have a clear shot. Now the muscles in your neck begin to cramp. You wonder if a .458, fired from the prone position, will break your shoulder. There! You touch the trigger but never feel the recoil.

Hooves pound, branches crackle, and you are left staring into a cloud of dust, wondering what you've done. Two times out of three, your bull leaves with the herd. It probably is dead on its feet, but sixty-seven percent of the time its last dash carries it out of sight.

"Where's that tracker? Doesn't he know he's supposed to be at my side so he can watch the hit and know exactly where to take up the spoor?"

Solo Safari

Other times you are not so lucky. An unseen cow sees you and spooks the herd. Don't fret. All is not lost. Buffalo are not like elk. Buffalo do not like to run. They take off in a mad rush but they pull up after only one to five hundred yards. Give them ten minutes to settle down, then take up the spoor. Sometimes they will stop so close you can hear them grunting. Circle into the wind and try again.

So they run again and you sneak up on them again. Now you are scurrying along about seventy-five yards behind the herd hoping to get a shot into the buffalo, but all you see are the backs of buffalo fading into the bush. Now, if it is a large herd, if the bush is thick, and if you have a good set of legs, you can enjoy one of the greatest thrills in the world of hunting.

You push the herd into a gallop, then you gallop after them. You crash through the bush, but your noise is lost in the greater noise of the herd. You skirt to the downwind side of the herd to give yourself a possible advantage in subsequent stalking, but this puts you in the cloud of dust. By August, half of Africa has burned and 200 hooves are churning up the ash. Your throat burns, but you keep running.

You run with your eyes open because fifty buffalo are running alongside, fifty yards to your right. You notice two cows running beside you twenty-five yards to your left. Better to fall back and let them rejoin the herd. Visibility through the dust and ash is down to thirty yards. You hear the ghost herd more than see it.

Now various segments of the herd are alternately running and walking. They're tired, but you've been running consecutive seven-minute miles back home and you can take it. You sprint ahead and pass half the herd. You will never let the leaders see you. They would turn away and you would be chasing a lagging buffalo again. The followers see you, but they are physically and mentally weary. They follow the leaders.

There's a small opening, so you dash across it straight into the herd, splitting it in half. The leaders run on, but you've cut off the followers. They see you dash into their path, so they stop. You stop. A couple of bulls step forward, noses outstretched. Your weary arms lift the big gun and the foresight wobbles like a drunken sailor but, at forty yards, a bull's chest is a big target and the bullet slams home. Two times out of three, your bull runs off with the herd. You wilt into the sand, your heart pounding, your arms bleeding from unfelt thorns.

How an Adrenaline Junkie Hunts Buffalo

Sometimes you can successfully alternate the sneaking and running methods. If you've neglected your seven-minute miles, and are completely exhausted, drop back and rest for five minutes. The herd will run another quarter or half mile then stop. Now you do a slow sneak. These physically and mentally exhausted buffalo are easy to approach. Even if one or two animals spy you, they will not spook the herd.

Shooting may confuse the herd. I once took two cows from one herd. The others stood a hundred yards from the second dead cow and watched me walk around in clear view. I had to shoo them away so the skinners could approach.

I developed the running method late in my Botswana tour of duty and successfully ran down several herds. Had I known of the technique earlier, I would have used it frequently. Next to shooting into a herd of cow elephants, these were my most exciting hunts. Unfortunately, I doubt that many professional hunters would risk this with a client, although the unscrupulous ones sometimes use a vehicle to wear down a herd.

Okay, one way or another you fired your big gun. One time in three the buffalo will drop in its tracks. If it goes straight down, be extremely careful. The bullet may have hit the brain or spine, in which case it is dead. Or the bullet may have narrowly missed the brain or spine, in which case it is only stunned and is about to jump up and come see you. Never neglect the insurance shot on a buffalo that has dropped in its tracks.

There is a sixty-seven percent chance that your bull ran off, showing no sign of being hit. But it must have been hit. How could you miss a three-foot bull's-eye while shooting from a supported position at under one-hundred yards?

Your tracker knows exactly what to do. He crawls into the shade and rolls a cigarette, giving the buffalo plenty of time to die. Even as you wait, you must be alert. The herd ran 300 yards and stopped. You can hear them grunting. If you hear a closer grunt, it's your bull. It is alive and quite angry. If you hear a mournful bellow, it is surely dying from a lung shot. If you see a sapling shaking, the bull is dead and making its last, reflexive kicks. More often, there is only calm and silence.

The tracker crushes his cigarette and you approach the spot where the bull stood. Even a .458 does not produce a fist-sized exit hole, so don't expect to find blood. What you find are tracks, about twenty

119

sets, one on top another. It is impossible to sort out the tracks from your bull.

Tracking wounded buffalo shot from herds is the most frustrating aspect of African hunting. I wish I had some professional secret, some gimmick I could share with you. I have none. Well, we're in it for the adrenaline.

Rifle ready, you follow the tangled spoor of the herd for a quarter mile, hoping to find the dead bull. Nothing. You figure a wounded animal is likely to leave the herd, so you search back along the side of the main spoor, to the left or right, wherever the cover is heaviest.

According to the books and magazines, the trackers work ahead, followed by the riflemen. The trackers I've worked with would have none of this. They weren't about to put themselves between a dangerous buffalo and a more dangerous rifle. I don't blame them. I always led, watching ahead for the buffalo, and glanced over my shoulder for directional hand signals from my trackers. An alternative is to wait in the hunting car and let a professional hunter sort things out.

However you handle it, good luck!

BACK TO THE KWANDO

Things had gone pretty well for me on my safari trips in Africa, with one exception. There remained the unfinished business with the lion. My first lion hunt on the Kwando was a flop. Now my two-year contract was nearly up and I still had no lion. Maybe it was just as well. I had killed sixteen buffalo, two elephants, and a leopard without serious mishap, but I had a feeling that my luck was running thin. By now I'd read Ted Gorsline's article in the November 1988 issue of *Safari Magazine*. In West Africa, he concluded in his article, one man is injured or killed for every ten lions killed. That's the injury rate for Himalayan mountaineering, the most dangerous of all sports, one in ten. That's on the thin edge between adventure and suicide. Well, that's West Africa. I was in southern Africa and things were different here.

I asked a professional hunter whether animals differed from region to region. He had hunted in Kenya before it was turned over to poachers and preservationists, then he shifted to Botswana. "Yeah, there are differences. The Kenyan buffalo were bigger and more aggressive. I thought that buffalo were the most dangerous animals in Kenya. But the southern lions are more aggressive than the Kenyan lions. Watch out for the lions here."

So my sixteen buffalo were a bunch of pantywaists. The two elephants were luck, and leopards are no problem if you get the marksmanship right.

Solo Safari

Word came from Zimbabwe that an acquaintance, an experienced professional hunter, had been killed by a cow elephant. This wasn't a character from a Capstick book. I knew this guy. Then another acquaintance, also a professional hunter, and his tracker were both killed in a bizarre firearms accident during a close encounter with a pride of Botswana lions. I began contemplating my mortality, and a lion skin seemed less and less important.

I had tried lions, I really had. No one would fault me for backing off from lions. I'd just slip back home alive and in one piece.

Then one of my colleagues at the Wildlife Training Institute, Eric Molelekwa, came up with a lion permit. He bought the permit knowing full well that I would assist with the hunt. Thanks, pal.

I had done a couple of hunts with Eric for zebra and antelope. He was not the most experienced hunter I had worked with, but he enjoyed the bush as much as any and he had exceptionally good eyes. He was a willing hunter, always ready to leave camp an hour before sunrise, and often he was the one who urged me to go an extra mile. Eric spoke English fluently and he was a good man to share a cool beer with around a warm fire.

Eric's lion permit was for Area 5 on the Kwando River, the same area in which Freeman and I had hunted lion a year earlier. We recruited a northern Bushman as a tracker. This chap had begun life as a poacher. The Regional Game Warden tried for years to catch the Bushman before admitting failure. In a final attempt to end the illegal hunting, the game warden hired the Bushman and put him on the game department's payroll. The arrangement has been mutually agreeable for over a dozen years.

So we began the 200-mile journey to the Kwando. I had the Mean Machine, over a hundred gallons of fuel, a good companion, a reformed poacher for a tracker, and a lion permit. In short, I had the world by the tail.

We ticked off the villages—Matlapaneng, Sakapane, Shorobe, and other settlements. I began to have doubts about the Bushman when he put us onto the wrong track to Khwaai. His duty station was Khwaai, so he should have known how to get there. We finally arrived at Khwaai, thirty minutes late, and bought cigarettes and other essentials. There were no more villages ahead, only sand, trees, sky, and with luck, a lion.

Back to the Kwando

The tracks deteriorated from bad to atrocious. The Mean Machine groaned through the heavy sand, mostly in low or second gear, but it could not be stopped. I remembered my first hunt in Zimbabwe when I had been apprehensive about driving seventy-five miles into the Zambezi Valley. Now we were pushing 200 miles into the wilderness on far worse roads. The fine-grained Kalahari sands blot up horsepower and find any weakness in a vehicle, but I had no apprehension now. The Mean Machine would pull us through.

It took eleven hours to cover 200 miles. We drove past last year's camp and pitched our tents on the Kwando River on the frontier with Caprivi, an extension of Namibia. There is no government here, no law. The northern Kwando is ruled over by Caprivian poachers, and even the heavily armed Anti-Poaching Unit refuses to patrol here.

We lay in our tents and listened to the hyenas and hippos and, yes, there were the roars of lions. At dawn we found lion spoor on the road, less than a mile from camp. We tried to follow the spoor, but I knew immediately it wasn't going to work. The Bushman was supposed to watch the spoor while I watched ahead for the lion, but he kept losing the track, and more often than not, it was I who pointed it out to him. We gave up after 300 yards.

The lion situation was not good. First, I was limited by Botswana's prohibition on the use of bait, and now I had a tracker who couldn't follow a herd of elephants through a foot of new snow. With seven days to hunt, maybe we could get a lion anyway.

We shot a tsessebe for camp meat and tried to track several other lions, but without any luck. I hoped we might get onto lions by listening for their roars in the predawn, then moving in on them, but the lions became silent. Apparently they had made a big kill, probably a buffalo, and they weren't roaring to organize hunts.

Then, on the fifth morning, they cut loose a half hour before dawn. The roaring came from upriver, so we drove a mile upriver, stopped, and listened. They were farther north. Three times we stopped to listen and three times we drove further north. Then we saw a cloud of dust hanging over the bush, a cloud that could be raised by a herd of buffalo being excited by lions. We listened. Buffalo grunted. A lion roared 300 yards away, behind the buffalo. It shook the windows in the Mean Machine, it was so loud. I fumbled some soft points into the .375 and the Bushman and I tumbled into the bush.

Solo Safari

The tiniest crescent of sun broke the horizon as we skirted around the herd of buffalo. They could see us now, but they ignored us, as they were more concerned with the lions behind them than the humans beside them.

A lion roared again and I could hear every overtone. I swear, I could hear the fillings in its teeth rattling. With this new fix on the lion's position, we scurried forward. I could feel the surge of adrenaline hitting my body. I hadn't felt such euphoria since my first buffalo or my first elephant. Fear, I told myself, must not be confused with that quickening of the pulse, that euphoria that reminds us that we are living life fully.

We were past the buffalo, but could still hear them grunting through the cloud of dust. Another roar ripped through the bush. God, I should have known better . . . lions don't have fillings in their teeth. It was the fillings in my teeth that were rattling. Another roar crashed down on us from a different direction. We were smack between a herd of fifty buffalo and a minimum of two lions. We moved up and the lion roared again, it had to be less than fifty yards away. I thought about Ted Gorsline and his one man injured or killed for every ten lions killed. Nuts to Ted Gorsline. Why doesn't he write about cricket scores or some such and stay out of my life. One in ten, fifty yards, not euphoria. I was scared.

But I wasn't too scared to think. Okay, if the buffalo are behind us, and the lions are in front of us, and the lions are hunting the buffalo, and the lions don't know we're here, then all we have to do is hide and wait for the lions to come to us. I tried to whisper all this into the ear of the Bushman. He either did not understand or did not agree and he waved me forward. My first mistake was to follow his advice.

I crept forward, thumb on safety, another five yards. There was the patter of heavy feet and I raised up to glimpse the tail end of a lion disappearing into the bush. By its size, it surely was a male. If only we had hidden and waited.

Then another lion roared a hundred yards ahead. We would have a second chance. We moved ahead fifty yards and listened for an exact fix. Now two lions engaged in a vocal duel 200 yards behind us. The Bushman was overwhelmed with excitement. Two lions! He waved me back toward the duo.

"No," I whispered. "The one ahead is closer and it doesn't know we are here." One of the duet surely was the one we had spooked.

Back to the Kwando

"This way," the Bushman, the ex-poacher who could not be caught, said as he turned back toward the two lions. Well, why pay an expert tracker if you're not going to follow him? I took his advice the second time. It was my second mistake. No lion.

How can two experienced hunters position themselves squarely in the middle of a minimum of three lions and not connect? Oh, how I would love to relive those twenty minutes. Hindsight!

Our failed hunt also caused the lions' hunt to fail. We predicted they would vocalize again that evening as they organized another hunt. We were right. The next morning they were silent, indicating that they had killed. We watched for vultures, which would reveal their location, but saw none. The lions wouldn't hunt again for at least two days, so they would remain silent. By then, we would be out of time and there was nothing to do in the meanwhile but read dime novels and scratch tsetse fly bites. We gave up on lions, abandoned Area 5, and dropped down to Area 20 where we took a buffalo and a zebra.

I was asleep in my tent when Eric yelled. A lion had entered camp and was eating the zebra. I could hear flesh tearing only fifteen yards away. Eric intended to sell the meat, not feed it to a lion, and he yelled at me to do something. Problem was, I didn't have the slightest idea of what to do.

I had the .375 in the tent and I jacked a round into the chamber. The Mean Machine was parked about five steps from the tent and the door was unlocked. It just might work. I very slowly unzipped the tent, silently, so the zipper noise wouldn't attract the lion's attention. Eric and the Bushman were still yelling, which would help cover my activity.

Six steps in a half second, probably a new world's record for barefoot, short distance sprinting. The door slammed shut. I flicked on the headlights to reveal a huge male lion. It had so much hair on its neck you couldn't see its ears. It hung to the ground and covered its ribs. This was the biggest lion I have ever seen. Too bad it was a hundred miles from Area 5 where my lion tag was valid.

The lion didn't bolt and run. It just stood there, ten yards away, and stared at me. A blast on the horn failed to dislodge it. Finally, I started the engine and used the Mean Machine to haze it out of camp. Lions! When you want one. . . .

We returned to Maun, but I had a problem. I still needed a lion. I was writing this book and I needed a lion story, a grand finale for the last chapter. Not that I needed a lion personally, you understand, but for the sake of my readers, I needed to round out the book. This lion was a literary necessity, my obligation to the sports fans of America.

I wondered what it would take to entice Eric Molelekwa to spend another week fighting tsetse flies on the Kwando, but he needed no more than the mere suggestion. We would spend the workweek in Maun and return to lion country the next Saturday.

I spent five busy days in Maun. Since my contract was nearly finished, I contacted several people who might buy the Mean Machine and called HQ to explain for the fourth time how they had messed up my leave records. The mail had the usual stuff, a quotation from Lloyds of London to insure my trigger finger and another offer from the photo editor of *Playgirl Magazine*. I caught up on the news. Iraq had invaded Kuwait and a local fellow had somehow shot and killed himself while trying to dodge a herd of stampeding buffalo.

We had resolved to recruit a better tracker but every tracker in Maun was employed. So on Friday I drove eighty miles to Puduhudu and picked up a Bushman who was highly recommended. He was supposed to work miracles on big kudu, but could he find and track lions on the Kwando? He agreed to go for ten dollars per day plus food, tobacco, and beer.

Bushmen love tobacco and booze. I always carried a supply of factory-rolled cigarettes in the Mean Machine and the Bushman immediately lit up. He smoked the cigarette down to the filter, let the last ash cool, ate the ash, lit up another, and so on until we reached Maun.

The Bushman could not speak a word of English, so that afternoon Eric helped him purchase food, more tobacco, and a half case of beer. By sunrise, only two beers remained. What a way to begin an eleven-hour journey. At 8:30 A.M. we stopped at Shorobe and bought more beer. The Bushman immediately opened one. At 10:30, we stopped at Khwaai Village. The Bushman borrowed a half dollar and bought a huge mug of locally brewed beer, declaring it far superior to the Puduhudu brand.

Sunday morning, while cruising for tracks, we jumped a huge male lion, but it immediately disappeared into tall grass. The Bushman followed the spoor for seventy-five yards, then lost it. A hundred yards farther on, I found the track, but the Bushman could not make it go. This was not a good omen.

The next morning, we found tracks of females and cubs at three locations, plus a pair of tracks from very large females or small males.

Back to the Kwando

The Bushman insisted they were from the grandfathers of all lions, and I wanted to further test his tracking skills so we took up the trail. It stuck to open grass and loose sand, easy tracking. After a mile, we jumped two females with size eleven feet.

We hunted the remainder of the week without finding a single fresh track from a male lion. We rose every morning well before dawn and listened for lion roars. An epidemic of laryngitis had swept through the Kwando lion population. Two lions (or lionesses) roared one morning but their last roar sounded fifteen minutes before shooting light. Not good enough.

Then on the last day of hunting, we spotted three lions sitting on the shoulder of an anthill. Two were cubs and one was a young male with a fuzzy neck. Eric urged me to shoot, but I decided to hold fire. I was in the back of the Mean Machine and Eric was driving. "Drive on," I instructed.

We'd gone only sixty yards into thick bush when I spotted something that might be a lion's ear about forty yards away. I tapped on the roof and Eric stopped the truck. Magnified ten times, the potential ear looked more like a stump. I watched for thirty seconds and was about to tell Eric to drive on, then the potential stump moved. Stumps don't move. Lion ears move. Was it a lion ear or a lioness ear? I tiptoed to the back of the truck bed and looked again. Now I could see between the ears. There was only the short hair of a lioness.

"It is better to shoot a female than to go home with empty hands," Eric reasoned. "You had better shoot it."

Well, a female would provide a lion hunting experience. Females are more dangerous than males, therefore more sporting. In Zimbabwe, they issue female-only permits and I had considered bidding for one. Wouldn't it be foolish to pass up this lioness, then pay ten thousand dollars to hunt a lioness in Zimbabwe? Eric was right.

But I wanted a male. "There could be a male hidden in the bush," I whispered. "I'll just go have a look." I loaded the .375, eased out of the Mean Machine, and began to tiptoe forward. At twenty yards, the lioness bolted. I baby-stepped another five yards and another lion crashed away, probably the fuzzy-necked male who had joined its mother. I could still hear the faint murmurs that lions make when they are excited. There were more lions ahead. More baby steps and more lions crashed away, probably the cubs, but I could not tell how many. Then all was silent.

127

Solo Safari

I returned to the Mean Machine to fetch the Bushman tracker. Possibly one of the departing lions was a male, and I wanted the Bushman to help examine the spoor. He had a different view of the situation. The Bushman wanted nothing to do with lady lions and he refused to leave the safety of the Mean Machine. So I went back into the bush and counted the tracks. We had seen four lions and I found at least five sets of tracks, but none large enough to be a trophy male.

So, that's it sport fans. No lion, no grand finale for the last chapter and no lies, just a disappointed hunter. But shed no tears for me. In my disappointment, I have obeyed the cardinal rule of every African hunter: Never leave Africa without a solid reason for returning.

My first safari to the Zambezi Valley wasn't fancy: a beat-up Land Rover, a trailer full of camping supplies, and a crew of three, James, Mathias, and Ceeasi.

We hunted impala for the pot and to bolster our confidence.

My apprehensions about do-it-yourself safaris were laid to rest with my first buffalo bull. Though not a world-class bull, it was a world-class experience.

My first camp in the Zambezi Valley consisted of a trailer, which served as a hyena-proof pantry, two folding tables, and two backpacker tents.

Mathias, Ceeasi, and James with the fruits of their labor.

Wiro, the Tonka tracker, who knows what elephants will do before the elephants know.

Andy Kockott, safari outfitter and professional hunter who abided my wildest fantasies. (Photo by John Tautin)

That's me with the largest trophy I have ever taken or will ever take.

Ivory is coveted for many reasons. This tusk evokes memories of a day in a faraway place when a life-long dream came true.

Lions aren't always this docile. Statistics show that the lion is the most dangerous animal in Africa.

This East African buffalo is larger and, some say, more dangerous than the buffalo I hunted in southern Africa.

I hope I never meet a man who can sneak this close to an elephant without feeling at least a twinge of anxiety.

You'd better zip up the door of your tent or this guy may walk in and walk out with a piece of your face in his jaws.

I suspect that Jason Mosonto has a secret addiction to adrenaline. (Photo by John Tautin)

My most exciting thrill came from this cow elephant. Because too many hunters have been killed when hunting aggressive cow elephants, Zimbabwe has stopped issuing licenses for them. From left, Pearson, myself, Wiro, and Jason. (Photo by John Tautin)

This tree is ideal for a leopard bait. The heavy brush provides good concealment so a cautious leopard can sneak in during daylight. The sloping branch will be easy for the cat to climb. (Photo by John Tautin)

We didn't plan to hang this bait, so we failed to bring a rope, but it later brought success. Wiro, above, and Pearson, below, managed anyway.
(Photo by John Tautin)

That's not a very large leopard, but I don't care. The quality of the experience was absolute tops. (Photo by John Tautin)

John Tautin and I collaborated on this cow buffalo, which came within a few feet of nailing me. Contemplate for a moment, as I have, the possibility of having one of those horns implanted into your chest. (Photo by John Tautin)

Pearson is a mechanical genius who doesn't understand that vehicles cannot be repaired without spare parts.

This is the suburbs of Maun, Botswana, as seen from the air.

The Okavango River spreads across the Kalahari sands, which blot it dry.
The Okavango Delta is the largest inland delta in the world.

Leslie Reid wrestles with cow buffalo and equally stubborn trucks.

This bull was taken on a ration permit and used to feed my students on a field trip. Victor Kgampi is behind me in the coveralls. (Photo by Janet Bishop)

Victor Kgampi, one of my students, who gave me a lesson in buffalo hunting.

This elephant was shot repeatedly by poachers. Unfortunately for them, it died within view of a tourist track so they could not recover the tusks. Their loss was equivalent to many months of wages.

You learn to pay attention to vultures, as they often indicate that predator kills are nearby. If they are in the trees, the predator is probably at the kill.

These are long, slow, hot kilometers.

Freeman Sewadimo Malebogo was an entepreneur, hunter, and friend who taught me much about Africa.

Our lion camp near the Kwando River, in northern Botswana.

The marauder bit me, wrenched free, and flew off into the blue African sky.

This is Third Bridge, in Moremi Game Reserve, during the dry season when it is above water.

This male baboon tried repeatedly to break into my food box.

This is a bull at full charge. It was a lot more scary at the time.

I tried a dozen times to photograph the saddlebilled storks in Moremi Game Reserve before this fellow finally posed for me.

I shot this bull, one of my best, before breakfast in the Zambezi Valley.

I collected the Zambezi's largest trophy and smallest trophy on the same hunt. This grysbok would rank well in the record book.

My friend, John Tautin, took this veteran bull under dangerous conditions.

Hunting springbok is like hunting pronghorns in Wyoming, a bit of a challenge when using a .375 with open sights.

I hunted the beautiful gemsbok on a ration permit. As with kudu, the strain found in southern Africa is larger than its East African cousin.

I scored a couple of doubles on buffalo, two buffalo from one herd. Here we see one in the Mean Machine and one on the ground.

On a scientific collecting trip, I shot the first tsessebe, shown here, and the first lechwe I saw. Both qualified for the record book, which says something about the standards of today's record books.

I became fairly adept at finding my way in featureless bush. We killed this bull miles into the bush, went to fetch the Mean Machine, then I refound the carcass after my trackers became completely lost. Usually, it was I who was lost.

Jerry Weaver with a beautiful roan antelope.

Jerry Weaver with his lion.

Charlie Craver didn't get enough of Africa in Liberia. He later returned to Zimbabwe where he took this warthog.

Alex Alexakos pauses for a rest with Manou and Manou II.

Nick Alexakos with a good hartebeest.

Alex Alexakos and Manou with a hartebeeste taken at 110 yards, offhand, with the .416 Rigby.

Nick and the safari crew with a water-buck.

Nick and Alex Alexakos enjoying the Pendjari. The guncase doubled as a table.

Nick enjoys a quiet moment in camp.

Charlie Puff and an elephant that fulfilled a life-long dream.

Charlie's elephant had just come from water and his enormous tusks were covered with mud.

Even the game department boys brought out their cameras when Charlie turned up with a tusk weighing 106 pounds.

Charlie Puff with a pair of tremendous tusks taken without the assistance of a professional hunter.

Charlie Puff with an impressive display of trophies. The trackers are Towel and Shorty.

Deep in the rain forest lives the Gabon viper. One of the most venomous snakes, but seldom a danger as it is passive, slow to react, and lies curled up in the daytime in dry leaves. Normally they are betrayed by the warning cries of squirrels, "Que, Que, Que", which indicate that one is present nearby. (Photo by Reinald von Meurers)

Forest elephant. It is very small in body size, but has nice tusks. Is it the debated pygmy variety? (Photo by Reinald von Meurers)

Reinald von Meurers and crew fifty miles into the rain forest on a 17-day foot safari . Notable on these medium-sized tusks is the big difference in size. One tusk is 1.44m, and the other is 1.22m. Usually, one tusk is used more often by the elephant, like right or left handed, and is worn down and shorter than its mate. (Photo by Reinald von Meurers)

Beautiful example of a male Cameroon bush pig. Ideal for forest hunting, except for elephant, is a combination gun. Shown here is a drilling with big-bore, .22 Hornet, and shotgun barrel. (Photo by Reinald von Meurers)

Number one Peter's Duiker, called at the end of the day. Note armor-type clothing— ideal for rain-forest hunting. (Photo by Reinald von Meurers)

Old giant forest hog in Cameroon. (Photo by Reinald von Meurers)

Traditional foot safari in Cameroon. The ratio is about five porters and one tracker for one hunter. (Photo by Reinald von Meurers)

Trophy kudu are a major draw for ranch hunting in southern Africa. Trophy bulls are available on relatively inexpensive week-long hunts.

You can hunt wildebeest in the big-game concessions or on ranches. Ranch hunts cost one-third to one-half as much as wilderness hunts.

Most game ranches offer hunting, but Robin McIntosh, near Harare, Zimbabwe, specializes in photography. You just don't get shots like this in the wilderness areas.

Anyone planning a first trip to Africa should schedule time for the national parks. It's relatively inexpensive and a great way to experience African wildlife.

This ranch-hunted sable missed the record books by a country mile and I couldn't care less. It is a classic trophy, an old bull with scimitar-shaped horns and a jet-black coat. I made a spectacular shot under fair-chase conditions.

The steenbok is another animal that can be hunted on ranches. Why pay two thousand dollars a day to hunt this animal?

Robert Ruark believed that impala jump "... just because they feel so good."
My scientific colleagues have other explanations, but I believe Ruark may
have been right.

Many people are surprised to learn
that giraffe are very common in much
of Africa.

Southern Africa offers many diversions, like fishing in Lake Kariba, game viewing in Kruger Park, fine wines from the Cape, and Victoria Falls, shown here.

The three bullets on the left show the monotonous consistency produced by the Nosler partitions. The one on the right penetrated a three-inch mopane tree, then killed a 700-pound antelope.

These 500-grain Hornadys (.458 caliber) were recovered from my first buffalo. The softpoint on the left went through a shoulder and both lungs. The solid on the right penetrated about four feet of soft tissue. Performance, not appearance, is the ultimate test of a bullet.

Small diameter solids are ineffective. A .338 solid failed to drop this impala and others failed on baboons. Even .375 solids are marginal.

Some very experienced writers have recommended a shoulder shot for elephants. After examining this leg bone, John Tautin came to a different conclusion.

This pretty-good kudu is made to look fantastic by photographic smoke and mirrors. The secrets are a wide-angle lens, placement of the horns high and in the foreground, and placement of yours truly low and in the background.

PART II

PREFACE

Self-guided hunting in Africa is not a new idea. Ernest Hemingway did it and James Mellon did it in great style. Mellon purchased a home in Nairobi, which he used as a base for five years. He owned his truck and hired a permanent staff of Africans. Of course, the availability of unlimited funds made all this a bit easier. Mellon's classic book, *African Hunter*, is considered the single best source of information on Africa and African hunting.

The other published account comes from Chris Klineburger. In 1962, Chris flew to Africa, bought a Land Rover, hired three natives, and headed into the wilds of northern Uganda. He successfully hunted leopard, lion, and buffalo. His fascinating story is included in the book *Big Game Hunting Around the World*, by his brother, Bert, and Vernon W. Hurst.

Self-guiding is probably more common among Europeans. With their colonial tradition, they feel closer to Africa, and many of them speak essential languages.

Who knows how many Americans have self-guided in Africa? Many hundreds, I would guess, perhaps thousands. The great majority have been missionaries, foreign-aid workers, military personnel, and employees of international corporations. Residency in Africa is not absolutely essential for self-guided hunting, but it certainly helps.

Flip through the record book of big-game trophies and check the column that indicates the name of the guide. A few will indicate "self" as the guide. The great majority of these self-guided hunters are licensed professional hunters. The next largest category are hunters who lived in Africa.

Of the thousands of hunters named in the record books, probably about a dozen are sportsmen who have traveled to Africa and guided themselves to dangerous game. The following eight chapters are the accounts of five brave men who made their personal dreams come true, men who made their own adventures.

Solo Safari

The accounts of guided African hunters have several common themes, such as fascination with the game, reverence for the professional hunters, total dependence on the safari companies and professional hunters, and the bizarre affliction, trophymania—that peculiar fixation on horn length. You will find relatively little trophymania in the following eight chapters, despite the fact that some superb trophies were taken.

The common themes in these chapters are apprehension about vehicles, fascination with and respect for native Africans, and a great tolerance, perhaps even a love, for uncertainty. I am grateful that these five adventurers have agreed to share their stories with us.

ROUGHING IT

by Jerry Weaver

Jerry Weaver's adult life has been divided into three phases. First, he was an academician, a man of letters. He taught political science at the University of California at Los Angeles and wrote books on the subject. Next, he entered the Foreign Service, culminating with six years as Refugee Affairs Officer in our embassy in the Sudan. Today, he is a cattleman on the land of his birth in Ohio.

In the following three chapters, Jerry relates his self-made adventures in a troubled part of Africa during troubled times. He tells how he punched hundreds of miles into the wilderness and hunted buffalo with a .44 magnum revolver. All this was done without a professional hunter to correct his mistakes. That, my friends, requires real courage.

* * * * * * * * * *

I came to Africa full of the classic literature: Hemingway, Roosevelt, Ruark, and others. Big-game safaris wove through my imagination. Professional hunters in tailored bush jackets, British double rifles, the charge, the kill, camp servants in white coats serving "sundowners." I was quickly put right.

During the late 1970s, it cost a thousand a day to book a hunt with a Sudanese safari company. For this princely sum the client got to ride hot, dusty mile after hot, dusty mile in a hunting car with two or three

Solo Safari

trackers and a Spanish, Portuguese, or Greek hunter wearing shorts and a dirty T-shirt. No double rifles for them. They'd lost too many rifles to bandits, armed poachers, and assorted revolutionaries to chance anything but the least expensive weapons. In the dense rain forests where they hunted elephants, they typically used a bolt-action .458. An old .375 H&H, often held together with electric tape or dried rawhide, served in the savanna.

As often as not the camp was a collection of grass and mud huts, a dining tent, and an open-pit latrine. If the kerosene refrigerator worked, you might get a cool drink, but ice was impossible. Meat and pasta, hot tea and fresh bread, the occasional tinned fruit or canned vegetables—and thank you very much.

The Sudan is Africa's largest country and it holds the continent's greatest variety of game. It was a hunter's paradise in the late 1970s and early 1980s with Barbary sheep and Nubian ibex in the Red Sea Hills, gazelle without number in the western desert, and thirteen thousand or more elephants in the savanna and southern forests. The south teemed with lions, buffalo, leopards, bongo, forest hogs, and dozens of species of plains game. Each spring millions of ducks and geese came north along the Nile and white-winged doves wintered in the grainfields along the great river. Three small safari companies operated in the south and a few foreign hunters sought the Nubian ibex. The Sudanese hunting industry was small compared to those farther south in Africa.

I met Spiros in Juba, the Sudan's southern regional capital, in 1979. The embassy had sent me south to check on a refugee influx from neighboring Uganda. A small chartered plane delivered me, but I had no ground transport. It had been years since anyone visited the south and no one remembered how to arrange local transport. As I walked the mile from the airstrip to town, a safari car passed by. Sure I wanted a ride to the hotel. Well, if there's no hotel, where can I stay? The company's lodge sounded great.

My savior was a fifty-year-old professional hunter who lived six months each year in the southwestern rain forest near the Sudan's border with Zaire. He specialized in forest elephants and bongo. When we met, his company was striking its camps as the rainy season was starting. I convinced the local manager of the safari company to hire Spiros out to me, along with his safari car, a box of food, and a couple of helpers. We spent two weeks driving through the border-

Roughing It

land looking at incoming refugees and talking to Idi Amin's henchmen, who had come north. When I left Juba, Spiros gave me some pineapples and twenty-five pounds of sugar to take to his family in Khartoum.

Spiros's eighteen-year-old son, Dimitri, shared his father's love of hunting, and he soon understood mine. A couple of days after we met, Dimitri introduced me to "Big George," a young Greek sportsman who lived around the corner from my house. George, Spiros, and Dimitri became the driving force that carried me into five years of lion, elephant, and buffalo.

During the 1979-80 wet season, the four of us hunted gazelle and waterfowl around Khartoum. George and I talked constantly about going south to hunt. Spiros shared his experiences with vehicle problems, camping supplies, where to go, and where to avoid. By early February, George and I were ready to go tackle the backcountry.

You don't just drive off anywhere in the Sudan. Only fifty of the nine hundred miles from Khartoum to Juba are paved. There is no fuel beyond the capital. For hundreds of miles there is nothing at all but savanna. We took two hunting cars, a professional mechanic, one lorry carrying twenty-five drums of fuel and another loaded with food, camping equipment, spare parts, and water. We planned to hunt three weeks, then fly home. We could have booked passage on a picturesque Nile steamer but that would have taken another week or so to get home.

I carried a .30-06 and a 12-gauge shotgun. George had the classic double rifle, a thirty-five thousand dollar beauty with one set of barrels in .375 H&H and another set in .470 Nitro Express. He also brought along a .375 H&H bolt action, which he had used in the south on similar outings. Along the way we shot guinea fowl and gazelle for camp meat. My first head of game was a bushbuck I shot one morning before the others had rolled out of their beds. The excitement of my kill was somewhat diminished when a seven-foot black mamba snaked through the camp.

For reasons best explained by a classic Freudian psychiatrist, there is a widespread fixation on African snakes. Yes, they're around and most are extremely dangerous. But like so much of the prevailing myth about safari, they are overrated as a risk. I spent at least a quarter of my time for more than six years in the backcountry of East Africa, but I do not know of a fatal encounter with a snake. Bees killed a German client in one safari camp and an electric fish killed a duck hunter in the White Nile. I'm sure that villagers and herders are fatally bitten, I just never heard about it.

Speaking of myth, I might as well unload on the "killer buffalo." First off, let me disclaim any personal expertise. I've killed maybe forty or fifty, no big deal, but I know several men who have killed a thousand or more. And one, a great old meat hunter named Nicolas Ginnis, has a record book containing receipts for over 4,000 buffalo he delivered to the British military in Juba during the 1930s and 1940s. A buffalo finally got Ginnis, goring him badly. His accident is illustrative, I think, of how buffalo become dangerous.

At the age of seventy, partially blind and nearly stone deaf, Ginnis agreed to a buffalo hunt with a German doctor working in a Juba medical clinic. They found a herd, Ginnis pointed out a good bull, and the German proceeded to gut shoot a cow, which immediately ran into heavy bush. The doc badly wanted his picture taken beside this bovine, so Ginnis began breaking his career-long rules. First he didn't drive upwind and set fire to the buffalo's hiding place. Contrary to myth, professional hunters do not often follow fresh buffalo blood. They know the animal can kill them at close quarters, so they either burn or wait.

Next Ginnis didn't go back to the car for his .465 Nitro double—he took the German's .375 H&H. Professional hunters like both the push of the big bores and that quick second shot. To further load the scales in favor of tragedy, Ginnis didn't check the game scout's weapon. It turned out that the man who was to be his backup was carrying an empty .303. In other words, Ginnis didn't have any backup.

The wounded cow came from the side. Ginnis neither saw nor heard it until it was literally on top of him and his snapshot didn't stop the cow. Its horns tore him from knee to groin, a wound that took 400 stitches to close. He was knocked on his back and the buffalo came down on him. Ginnis survived by grabbing the animal's nose. Every time the cow raised its head to pound him into the earth, his body came up with it. The buffalo didn't deliver the trip hammer blows that break bones. After what probably seemed an eternity to Ginnis but was actually less than a minute, the scout managed to kill the buffalo with the .375 without also hitting Ginnis.

Buffalo hunting reminds me of driving on a two-lane highway. Approaching vehicles can, and sometimes do, simply come across the line and there's nothing you can do. But following common sense and driving defensively allow us to make trip after trip safely with little or no apprehension of pending destruction.

As George and I proceeded south to Juba, we stopped below the town of Bor and camped near a Dinka village. At sundown a dozen or so villagers came around and told us they had an elephant problem. A herd was staying in the nearby swamp and a particular bull would charge the village women coming for water. It had killed five or six women and the villagers were in mortal terror. Could we help?

At first light George and I were led to the place where the elephants usually emerged. We hid behind some bushes and waited. After a few minutes one of villagers touched my arm and pointed. There came a line of elephants, silhouetted against the gray dawn sky about thirty yards away. George had seen them and was moving slowly to intercept. Cows, calves, no bull. Then at the end of the procession, a big fellow.

Two thoughts flashed through my mind: how big they were and how silently they moved. I stood transfixed as step-by-step George closed on the bull. Slowly he raised his .470 double rifle and then came the blast. The bull dropped like a tree and the ground shook. The herd scattered, screaming in fright. Pandemonium.

I took my eyes off the downed elephant just long enough to reach into my shoulder bag for my camera. Suddenly, I heard a different scream, one of rage more than fear. I glanced up to see the bull scrambling to its feet. George fired again without apparent effect. He grabbed his .375 from the tracker and began firing at the running bull. George, tracker, and elephant disappeared into the bush. I heard trees crumbling and George shouting. The .470 went off twice followed by a .375 or two.

As this uproar surrounded me, I wondered what I should be doing. The villagers had vanished and I was armed only with a .30-06 carrying 180-grain spitzers. I wasn't the least reassured when I heard, "It's coming!" The .470 blasted again then there was a dead silence. Ever so gingerly I moved forward. Finally, the tension broke when I heard the tracker and George laughing and saw the drivers and helpers from our lorries running toward George. There, lying on its side was the bull, a gray hill rising from the red earth.

Shooting at twenty yards, George had missed the brain by four inches. An elephant's brain is surprisingly small and is housed in a mass of spongy gristlelike tissue. If you misjudge the angle of your bullet or jerk the trigger, you'll miss. And because of the spongy helmet, a bullet's shocking power, even one from a big double, may not knock out the elephant.

Once the big fellow was on its feet, George didn't have many options. He shot at the base of the tail, trying to break the spine. His second or third shot did break a hip joint, slowing the elephant down. This bull didn't run away from its attacker. It tried to find him. It was, as the Spanish say, a *toro malo* or bad bull.

Two hours later there remained only a bloodstain. The villagers butchered and carried off everything. The gut must have been fifty yards long, requiring twenty or thirty women to carry it strung across their shoulders. It contained partially digested vegetation that seemed to be the local equivalent of Caesar salad.

The bull had two septic wounds in its left hip. The skinner recovered two .30-caliber, full-metal jacket bullets about eighteen inches deep. These were exactly the type of bullets carried by many poachers. This bull didn't carry heavy tusks, about forty pounds apiece, but this would be enough to make it a target for poachers. It had an earlier encounter with a human that had hurt it, and the village women paid for it with their lives.

That night we were honored guests at a joyous celebration. Fortified with home brew made from *dura* (sorghum), feasting on roast elephant, and freed at least briefly from the threat of sudden destruction, the villagers danced, leaped, and pranced. Drums, a roaring fire, a full moon overhead, whatever tomorrow might bring, tonight we celebrated life.

My first big-game hunt ended safely and successfully. George had his elephant, I had a good lion, a couple of buffalo, a greater kudu, two really impressive pairs of warthog tusks, and a cross section of grass eaters, all taken with the .30-06.

Contemporary African elephant hunting is probably much more dangerous than previously. The traditional practices of spearing or shooting with poisoned arrows have given way to shooting with any and all available firearms.

A couple of years after my first safari, I was hunting buffalo near Rumbek, a provincial town in the center of Dinka country. Guns of all sorts had been coming into this area with increasing frequency as the tribesmen armed themselves to protect their traditional cattle ranges from encroachment by neighboring tribes. There was also suspicion that a local Dinka security-force commander had organized a large ivory poaching ring in the province.

In the distance we saw three local tribesmen trotting along. They stopped as we approached and we had a very good look at their armament. One carried the traditional three spears, one a vintage .303 Enfield, and one an RPG, that's Rocket Propelled Grenade. We shared our water and tobacco. My driver spoke their language and I learned that they were hunting elephant from a camp four or five miles away. Other hunting parties were also in the vicinity. We wanted nothing more to do with these fellows, so we made a wide swing and hunted twenty miles away.

Now an RPG is just about the final word as far as elephants are concerned, and hunting cars, too. The .303 isn't, but since it was widely issued to game scouts and local security detachments, it was widely used on elephants, sometimes with tragic results. I'd already seen an example.

As I traveled through elephant country during the early 1980s, I heard many stories of unprovoked charges, not the familiar ears-out bluff charge, but the ears-back combat charge. Some professional hunters I met had worked in Angola, Rhodesia, or Mozambique. They reported that as poachers and civil strife brought AK-47s and other military weapons into their hunting areas, the number of elephant attacks increased. It makes sense—cause and effect.

The 1980s was a bad decade for hunting in much of Africa. Heavily armed poachers, operating with the connivance of local authorities, drove hunters out of Ethiopia, Uganda, the Sudan, the Central African Republic, Chad, Somalia, and probably other areas where I have no personal knowledge. Civil, tribal, and communal combat led to mining of roads, robbing and murder of travelers, and even the shooting down of small safari company planes. Perhaps things will improve during the 1990s, but I'm not optimistic about any place north of the equator. There are too many modern weapons in the bush, and few African governments possess the military strength or political will to impose law and order beyond city limits.

My assignments changed and I was spending more time in the bush on business. Now I had a vehicle in Juba and an excellent local driver and mechanic, named Andrew. I traveled extensively, so the embassy and Washington could keep up-to-date on regional developments. Weeks in Uganda, Somalia, and Ethiopia offered opportunities

Solo Safari

to sharpen professional and outdoor skills. I was trading my desk for a four-wheel-drive vehicle and that suited me just fine. A typical adventure arose after the embassy heard about a nasty little scuffle between two tribes in southeastern Sudan. Were the Ethiopians arming one or both sides? Might the fighting close the Sudan's only road link with Kenya? I flew south to find out.

Andrew met me at the Juba airport. He had the food box packed, the spares and fuel stowed. We were ready to go, but first I had to make a call on some officials of the Southern Regional Government. We would leave the next morning.

While walking through an office building, I happened upon a senior official of the Ministry of Tourism and Wildlife. Over a glass of tea he mentioned a problem: There was a report of an outbreak of rinderpest among buffalo east of Juba. Since this disease could have a devastating impact on local domestic cattle, the ministry was worried. As usual, the game department lacked fuel and could not send out a patrol. Could I go out for a few days to take a look and maybe cull the sick buffalo? I told the official that in order to reinforce the excellent relations between the United States and Sudanese governments, I would be delighted to help with the buffalo problem.

Two weeks later I was back in Juba, my embassy assignment completed, ready to look for sick buffalo. I didn't radio my ambassador for instructions. He was a busy man and foreign service officers are expected to exercise their own good judgment in promoting national interests in remote places. The remoter the better, I always thought.

At dawn Andrew and I crossed the bridge to the east bank of the Nile. The soldiers waved us through. It wasn't the official plates on the Rover, but the anticipation of a share of the meat I often brought back that greased the wheels. We were off and running again. An hour into the bush, we stopped at the hut of a game scout I knew from previous hunts. He had heard of the sick herd and was eager to accompany us. Next we drove to a nearby safari camp. The resident hunter had seen the diseased animals a couple of weeks earlier and was now hunting from fly camps well away from the contaminated herd.

Next morning we accepted the loan of a local tracker, and the four of us took off. We drove all day and saw several herds but found no sick animals. The savanna was in the grip of the dry season, so the herds were gathering around the remaining water holes. On the second morning the tracker headed us toward a water hole he thought should still be wet.

We found our first buffalo near the water. It was a female under a tree a hundred yards off, head down, bone thin. It didn't even look up when the car stopped. I put a 200-grain Nosler from my .300 Winchester Magnum behind its ear. Within thirty minutes we found and shot eight more buffalo, all very much like the first. The game scout and tracker looked them over and confirmed that they suffered from rinderpest. We spotted the herd about noon, about twenty animals resting under trees. Watching the wind, we worked close enough to get a good look. Several showed signs of sickness, a couple as bad as the ones we'd shot previously. The scout shot one with his .303 and I another with my .300 Magnum. The remainder scattered.

Andrew was carrying my .375 H&H and .44 magnum revolver. I'd used the scope-mounted handgun on small game and wanted to get in close enough to try it on a buffalo. I handed my rifle to the tracker, took the Smith and Wesson, and went after a young bull.

After walking about 300 yards, we saw the buffalo go behind a cluster of bushes growing out of a large anthill. We swung out to the right, circling. I stepped around the anthill and there it stood, about twenty yards away. It didn't look the least bit sick but I knew it was because it didn't run. Our eyes locked, I moved backward, very slowly. Bracing my left arm on the hill, I carefully slid the revolver into a two-handed grip, then inched sideways until I could see its head and neck. The crosshairs finally steadied on the place where the spine joins the skull. The 240-grain jacketed Hornady poleaxed the animal.

We followed the herd the rest of day, killing twelve more sick animals. In retrospect, I'm not sure we contributed anything to disease control. Many animals who carried the virus but weren't terminally ill probably escaped. At best, we saved some animals from death by fang and claw, their certain fate if we hadn't come along. Nevertheless it wasn't hunting—merely execution.

Working in close to sick animals was not a good test of bush craft. Yet it gave me a unique opportunity to study bullet placement and performance, lessons that were valuable later. In heart or neck shots 200-grain Nosler "Partitions" from the .300 Winchester were devastating. So were 285-grain Speer "Grand Slams" from the .375 H&H. We used a second shot only once. The scout hit a little low with my .300 Winchester and I finished the running buffalo with a "Grand Slam."

Solo Safari

I used no solids then or afterward on buffalo. I kept some 350-grain Barnes solids handy and used them on elephant, but never had a situation where I thought them necessary for buffalo. On two different occasions I shot a buffalo, perhaps previously wounded by poachers, that charged my hunting car as we followed its herd across open ground. Both were dropped by "Grand Slams," although one required three to knock it off its feet. Had I needed to enter heavy cover, I would have loaded up with the big Barnes solids since only broken bones or a brain shot will stop a running buffalo in less than ten yards.

Some professional hunters used only solids in their backup rifles while others used heavy softpoints. Several began using the 350-grain Barnes softies in their .375s after I passed out samples. One or two hunters chambered a softy and kept two or three solids in the magazine.

Stopping guns were much discussed at safari camps and hunters' lodges. The .458 Winchester was not popular among the dozen or so hunters I knew. Only one or two carried it. One Spaniard claimed that he had put ten factory-loaded solids into a standing buffalo before it went down. He said that they hadn't penetrated more than four or five inches. A retired Kenyan professional hunter told me that after Joyce Hornady used his solids on a safari, he had them redesigned to strengthen the jackets.

Franz Sodia, the Austrian gunsmith, built a .458 double rifle for me, but I left Africa before using it. One day recently I plunked an old plowshare here on my farm to see what kind of hole the .458 would make in hard steel. The Barnes solids did a hell of a job. If I hunt Africa again, I'll carry this combination for backup.

A few forest hunters carried big doubles in .470, .450, or .465. Two I knew carried .460 Weatherbys and there were a couple of .458s around. These fellows work in very close quarters, often ten yards or so, and want effective stoppers. I think the prevailing theory that bigger is better reflects their distrust of their clients' shooting abilities. From the stories they told, they seemed to have good reason. Spiros, ever the practical man, took stopping power to the logical conclusion. When a client lined up on an elephant, so did he, then two rifles cracked a millisecond apart. Most clients never heard Spiros' shot, and most of those that heard it didn't really care.

Africa is behind me now. Instead of buffalo, I look out upon Black Angus. My crosshairs center on groundhogs, not warthogs. What stays in my memory are the nights around the campfire, listening to Africa. My driver Andrew telling of growing up in the Nuba Mountains, going to a mission school, being the first in his family to go beyond the mountains. I remember the old game scout who got his job from "veteran's preference" because he'd fought with the southern insurgents against the national army in the 1956-72 civil war. The peace agreement brought local rule to the southern region, and old fighters were given government jobs. It wasn't a very good job, he allowed, pay was small and always late. But he had his Enfield and the game department gave him twenty rounds per year. He used them judiciously.

These campfires were repeated again and again, in the Sudan, Chad, Uganda, and Ethiopia. I came away from Africa convinced that it wasn't the killing that mattered, it was having been there, having experienced a different dimension of life, having known Africa. Those campfires still burn in my heart and warm the Ohio winter.

HUNTING WITH MOHAMMED

by Jerry Weaver

"**I**s it true that you Americans sent a man to the moon?" There was a curious glint in Mohammed's eyes across the campfire. The old man's question was polite but serious.

"Yes," I replied, "we put a man on the moon."

My interlocutor reflected a moment. "How did you get him there?"

"We built a giant shotgun, pointed it just right, put the man in a cartridge with plenty of food and water, and fired."

Mohammed worked this over a couple of seconds, then asked, "But how did you get him back?"

"We put him on the moon, Mohammed, but Allah brought him back."

Mohammed studied the fire for a heartbeat or two, looked up and murmured, "Yes, God is great."

Thus did this sixty-year-old desert Arab resolve the conflict between western technology and eastern theology.

Over a hundred years ago, Mohammed Abuzeid's grandfather fought the Anglo-Egyptian army at Omdurman and helped destroy the British general, "China" Gordon, at Khartoum. His father was born in a nomad camp in the Kordofan desert sometime around the beginning of the current century. Like his father and countless generations of Kababish herdsmen, Mohammed's face is scarred in the traditional tribal pattern. His desert craft led him to a lifetime of hunting—sometimes working for the British colonial administration as a game scout, more often as a poacher.   When I met him in 1979, Mohammed lived with his three sons and as many wives in a small compound twenty minutes beyond the western outskirts of Omdurman. He divided his time between his goats and guiding friends in search of dorcas gazelle.

Dorcas gazelle move in herds of three or four to forty or more. Typically males and females run together, with emphasis on run. In more than a hundred desert hunts, I found standing gazelle perhaps three or four times. Driving skill and eyesight are the *sine qua non* of desert gazelle hunting. In many situations, hunting from cars is unsporting and often illegal, but there is no other way to find and pursue desert gazelle. Gazelles move over hundreds of miles of territory at a brisk trot. They must be spotted at distances of up to half a mile and then followed slowly until they see the car. Sometimes this signals a mad dash over the horizon. Occasionally, they trot up on a hill crest or sand dune, stop, and look back at their pursuer.   With experience and coaching, you learn to "read" the animals and to get the car in position for the shooter.   The typical shot is a three or four second opportunity at a forty-pound animal at 200 yards. The driver is at least seventy-five percent of a successful hunt.

I owned a new short-wheel-base Toyota Land Cruiser. I soon found that this vehicle, once modified with extra fuel and water tanks, could transport three or four into the desert, allow us to hunt gazelles, and bring us back despite minor mishaps. On a couple of occasions, when I made the mistake of depending on less suitable transportation, I wished for the rugged Toyota.

I saw everything from .22 Hornets to .375 H&H Magnums used on gazelles and I soon learned that my .30-06 was less than optimal. Among the five or six serious gazelle hunters, three used .243 Winchesters carrying 6X glasses. A big gazelle weighs forty or fifty pounds, so they don't need a lot of rifle and the .243 bullets damaged little meat. The 100-grain spitzers went out fast and flat and proved reasonably wind resistant. The .243 also had the advantage of being available locally, an important factor, because ammunition commonly used in North America is generally unavailable in Africa.

Mohammed was our key to success in gazelle hunting. The guy had uncanny senses of direction and location. As near as I could tell,

Hunting with Mohammed

he navigated by dead reckoning. When traveling at night, Mohammed would occasionally ask me to stop and turn off the headlights. In the dim starlight, he could make out the outline of distant mountains and determine his location.

After a few trips, I began to recognize particular wadis, ridges, and wide plains. I might even go an hour or two without Mohammed's gentle correction and redirection. But I also noticed that neither George nor his cousins, who also were desert hunters, ever went out alone. They had grown up in the desert and had spent twenty years hunting with Mohammed, but they know that the desert, like the ocean, is neutral and is completely unforgiving. Make a mistake in the desert and there is no AAA to tow you in.

My first big mistake was very instructive. One hot, dusty afternoon found me hunting with Nicolas, George's cousin and a man given to hunting and fishing with the passion most men reserve for hunting and fishing.

I was driving Nicolas's old Land Rover when Mohammed spotted five gazelle running about a half mile away. I swung into an intercept line just as they went over a low ridge. "Go, go!" Nicolas shouted. We needed to cut the distance while they were out of sight. I have no idea how fast we were going when we topped the ridge, perhaps twenty-five or thirty miles per hour. It seemed very fast. The first thing I saw when we topped the ridge was a twenty-foot wide, rock strewn, six-foot deep wadi. The Land Rover, plus four people, seventy-five gallons of gasoline, fifty gallons of water, plus food, bedding, assorted spare parts, and two spare tires, never even considered stopping.

I don't remember hearing anyone shout. Nicolas later reported that he had, while briefly disconnected from Mother Earth, questioned why the Almighty had seen fit to place him in my proximity at that particular moment. Perhaps he did, I don't know. I do recall seeing Mohammed fly over the hood while Ahmed, our mechanic, grabbed the Greek's head to keep from following the guide.

We didn't quite make it. Most of the Land Rover cleared the wadi, but the rear wheels, still attached to the axle, rested in the ditch. Somehow the vehicle had remained upright and no one was injured. After gathering our wits, we discovered that both the fuel and water containers were intact, giving us at least a theoretical possibility of exiting the desert alive.

We had planned for most mishaps. We had tube patching kits and two complete mounted tires, extra fuel filters, spark plugs, vee belts, even a carburetor. But a disconnected rear axle?

As I surveyed the wreck and pondered a slow death from thirst, I noticed my companions were behaving very calmly. Nicolas was dragging his bed out of the car and arranging it under a nearby tree. Ahmed was coaxing life into a fire and Mohammed was hanging a gazelle in a tree so he could skin it. Shortly the omnipresent tea was consumed, the gazelle skinned, and Ahmed and Mohammed were down in the ditch looking at the displaced rear wheels. Next they began jacking up the car and placing stones under the sides just ahead of the wheel wells. Then the four of us pulled the axle out of the wadi.

About this time Mohammed, carrying a waterskin, went walking down the wadi. Well, he's going for help, I thought. No, he stopped about fifty yards away and poured some water on a patch of light gray sand. Ahmed soon joined him and in a few minutes they returned with handfuls of mud. After cutting several narrow strips from the fresh gazelle hide, the two Arabs worked the axle under the Rover. Handfuls of mud, strips of rawhide, before long it came to me that they were fashioning rear shackles.

We awoke next morning at daybreak, ate roast gazelle, drank tea, and repacked the Rover. Ahmed announced that the rear drive shaft had been disconnected and stored, and that we were ready to go home. Running on front-wheel drive only, we returned little the worse for it in nine hours, twice the usual driving time. But we returned.

In the following years other mishaps overtook us, but only once did we leave a vehicle in the desert. In the interest of protecting the United States automobile industry, I'll refrain from listing the structural and design failures that doomed this misnamed "off-road vehicle." My Sudanese hunting companions had evolved several sane rules for desert hunting: Take twice as much water as you will ever need; be sure the hunting car is in top condition, then inspect it again yourself; carry spares for the small things that cause problems, such as filters, vee belts, and water pumps, but not motors, which rarely blow up; and tell another hunter where you plan to hunt and then stay in that neighborhood. Above all else, trust your guide's instincts over your own.

I learned this lesson one sunny morning when Mohammed told me to drive several miles north of our previously planned hunting area. About eleven o'clock he said it was time to head home. Instead

Hunting with Mohammed

of driving southeast to our usual lorry track, Mohammed directed me north and east.

"What's wrong?" I asked George.

"Rain far to the north, maybe fifty miles away."

"Then why go north?" I asked. "Let's run south and get ahead of the flood."

"No, Mohammed knows the desert. We'd better follow his direction."

Three hours and fifty miles later, we encountered a previously dry wadi now running fifty yards wide. "Well, here we stay for a day or two until the water drops," I thought.

Mohammed bid me drive into the water, slowly. Finally he got out of the car and waded ahead. I've lived in desert country a third of my life and I know that running water can be a death trap and Mohammed knew that, too. So I eased the clutch out and we crossed without further adventure. Mohammed knew that the sand at that particular crossing was hard, that it didn't wash early in a flood, and that the southern crossing which we normally used was by now impassable.

Hunting small game such as desert gazelle is often overlooked when considering an African safari. Yet there are far more opportunities, at less expense, then most of us realize. National regulations prohibit self-guided big-game hunts in the Sudan, but hunting small game such as gazelle, Barbary sheep, Nubian ibex, and birds can be arranged privately and financed for a fraction of the cost of a traditional safari.

Officials of the national game department know the local hunters, and a letter to the director might turn up a couple of names to contact. Another starting place is the local car rental firms. Their addresses are available through the commercial attaché of the Sudanese embassy in Washington, D.C. These businesses hire four-wheel vehicles and drivers and can find local hunters to act as guides.

One visiting Spanish businessman asked an airport custom's inspector, "Where can I find a local to take me hunting?" The official, knowledgeable about the contents of my incoming baggage, replied, "Well, there's this crazy American. . . ."

FOR THE BIRDS

by Jerry Weaver

I've never shot waterfowl in New Zealand or southern Argentina, nor white wing doves in Colombia. A Spaniard whose elephant camp I shared, a gentleman who spends "about 300 days every year" hunting somewhere in the world, waxed poetic about wing shooting in these distant places. Maybe he's right, but after six years gunning along the Nile, I probably haven't missed a whole lot.

That's not literally true, I've missed a ton of white wings. The first time I tried these feathered Stealth fliers occurred along a county road somewhere below the Salten Sea in Southern California. My neighbor and I had driven down from Huntington Beach the night before opening day. He had a special spot, one he visited every year. We parked about 2 A.M. and slept.

Looking out the camper window at first light, I found a line of vehicles ahead and behind us as far as I could see. Hundreds of nimrods were lining up along the road. Dubious of my safety but not wanting to appear weak willed, I dutifully took a place in the ditch. I was about three feet from my host and an equal distance from a stranger who cheerfully informed me that he and his six companions had driven all night from north of Los Angeles. I've seen combat on three or four continents, but I've never heard a volley of shot equal to that which greeted the first flight. Having a low pain threshold and seeing a distinct possibility of not surviving the next ten minutes, I retreated to the camper.

Ten years later I tried again. This time the venue was an island in the middle of the Blue Nile, a couple of miles below Omdurman where the Blue and White Nile join to form the great north-flowing ribbon of life. Three of us had been rowed over by a local fisherman accompanied by two of his young sons who agreed to remain and collect our bag. Nicolas and Costas, two gazelle-hunting companions, had finally bullied me into dove shooting. It took much persuasion on their part because I had grave doubts about wasting my precious shotgun shells on such small targets. I had brought 500 rounds to the Sudan and wasn't prepared to buy any more from the local suppliers.

With no ammunition being imported legally, the black market prices were fifty cents for Egyptian, a dollar for Polish and $1.50 and up for American, that's per round. My priorities were duck and geese, not doves. Nicolas offered a hundred of his carefully collected stash of shells with the proviso that if I didn't enjoy myself I didn't have to repay. Such a deal I couldn't refuse.

We faced west to get the birds coming from the grainfields to roost in the island's thorn trees. The afternoon March sun was bright, but the breeze across the water cut the temperature to a comfortable eighty-five degrees. My youthful collector tugged my shirt and pointed to incoming birds. About ten were heading straight at me. When they crossed the sand thirty yards in front, I rose from behind my bush. Three quick shots from my 870 Remington 12-gauge and two birds were down.

Twenty yards to my left, Nicolas roared with laughter, "Not those, you fool, they're `gumbre!'" I had shot a pair of mourning doves. Reloading and trying to regain my dignity, I heard Costas shout, "They're coming!"

Dozens, hundreds, thousands of birds filled the air. For a moment I didn't know what to do. Finally I just pointed at the middle of a flight of a dozen or so and fired. And again, and again. None fell. Out of the corner of my eye I saw Costas drop bird after bird. Well, if I

For the Birds

couldn't kill them en masse I'd pick a target. I fired. The bird dodged, climbed, and disappeared safely into the trees.

By sunset the birds had been collected and we were on the west bank. My collector looked sour. We had agreed to pay them one piaster, about a penny, per bird and my boy wasn't going to earn the price of a Pepsi. Nicolas's Benelli 12-gauge had downed about seventy birds, Costas's over-under Merkel slightly more. Both had expended their hundred rounds. I still had fifty shells and about half my bag was *gumbre*. Seemed that the bigger, slower mourning doves were all I could hit. It didn't take me long to realize that I was woefully unprepared for shooting white wings. Nevertheless, it was a far better experience than I'd had in California.

That night we dined at the Recreation Club on Costas's birds. They were delicious and white wing shooting certainly was challenging. By midnight two decisions had been made. We had to find a way to get more shells, and I should find a suitable gun. My 28-inch, modified 870 wasn't going to do.

A MEC 600 reloader and suitable supplies were obtained, and I bought a Browning Superposed skeet gun. Over the next five years twenty-five thousand rounds went through our guns, mostly in the general direction of the little feathered Stealth fliers. My collectors grew, if not fat, more contented.

White wings arrive in the Nile Valley in the fall and can be shot anytime before they returned to Europe in the spring. We waited until they were on the return leg of their migration. Thirty minutes beyond the Khartoum urban sprawl you encounter birds. A half hour or so before sunset brings the best shooting. Two or three evenings a week, a hundred shells, good-natured competition, and you can have an excellent meal of grilled dove. We shot for sport and shared our take with a wide range of friends who hadn't the good fortune to afford gasoline or ammunition. Whether elephant, gazelle, or birds, no meat was wasted.

With such wing shooting available only four air hours from Europe, it is surprising that so few hunters come up the Nile. I knew only one, but he was a dandy. A Greek millionaire came down from Athens each spring as the birds were preparing to migrate back to Europe. The first time I saw him, he was loaded down with ten thousand shells, four Benellis, and great determination. I never asked

Solo Safari

him what it cost to get the necessary importation documents, but I'm sure it was a considerable expense.

My friend Nicolas took him to hot spots each dawn and afternoon. Two of Nicolas's houseboys went along and there were three collectors. Firing as fast as he could, the Athenian would empty one gun, throw it to one boy who reloaded while the other handed him a second fully loaded weapon. After a few minutes the third and fourth Benelli entered the rotation. One morning a gun barrel split from the heat. The next year he arrived with six Benellis.

The millionaire shared his bag with local farmers and herdsmen on whose land he shot and gave hundreds to the local Greek club. After a week of shooting, the sunburned and exhausted sportsman returned to Athens. He always took home three to five thousand frozen birds nesting in the 707's cargo hold. I'm told that he threw a party for a couple of hundred special friends on his private island— lots of birds, no doubt.

* * * * * * * * * *

The White Nile rises in Uganda and comes racing down across the southern Sudanese frontier. Six hundred miles below Khartoum, the river loses itself in the world's largest freshwater swamp, the Sudd. From June through November, this Ohio-sized floodplain is home to millions of ducks and geese. The onset of the dry season moves many of them north into the bean and grainfields along the river. Early December brings the shooting season around Khartoum that lasts through March.

Nicolas and his friend Vasilis were the serious duck hunters. They owned several dozen decoys and knew where to place them. Mostly they shot "near the tree." They shot often and they were good.

The beginning of the dry season in November marked the opening of the dam at Jebel Aliah to pass water down the Nile to the dry fields of lower Egypt. After a week or two, a small island appeared below the dam, about fifty yards from a particular tree along the west bank of the river. The place was just "the tree" and we all knew where it was and what it meant.

We shot there morning and evening, but daybreak was always my favorite time. Dressed in warm clothes and encased in waist-high waders, we humped guns, ammo, and decoys out to the fifty-foot-long

For the Birds

mud bar. One of us always carried a load of buckshot up the spout in case a crocodile happened to be in the immediate area. Arranging the decoys was a tricky business.

For about ninety minutes after first light, flight after flight of ducks came. It was like the rice fields of California or Louisiana, only there were no other hunters. Herders brought their animals to the river before taking them out to distant pastures. Fishermen cast their nets from boats whose design hadn't changed in 500 years. Flights of geese passed by on their way to the large midriver islands where they spent the day.

For a few precious moments I was one of the early explorers seeing this unspoiled vista for the first time. The Nile was like that for me, a window into a different world. I couldn't go through this opening, but the glimpses it offered penetrated deeply and powerfully. I was alone but not lonely, armed to kill but somehow at peace. These pictures registered somewhere. They produced a strong emotion then and still do today.

After the first shots, boys would appear to collect the downed birds. One of Nicolas's servants stayed with the cars to choose a collector for each shooter and they would wade out to us.

Wading around the White Nile was something I didn't look forward to. Besides the odd crocodile, the river was home to a fish that produces a violent electric shock. I once hooked a four-inch specimen, and not knowing its high voltage disposition, grabbed the wet line about four feet above it. The resulting shock left a burn across the palm of my hand. One less-fortunate hunter apparently touched a much bigger specimen while going out to retrieve a duck. The victim's cousin, sitting in a car fifty yards away, saw him suddenly jerk forward into waist-high water and then disappear. By the time he reached his cousin, the fellow was gone. His body was discovered next day with a large burn mark below one knee.

By local standards, our waterfowl bags weren't large, but this became my favorite sport anyway. It wasn't just the furious shooting or the red eyes of crocodile a few yards out in the water or the fear of getting hit by an electric fish. It was all this and something more. It was the sunrise over the Nile and the ribbing over missed shots. It was the roast duck suppers in the garden of the club, sitting with friends, discussing the upcoming hunt and reliving previous adventures. It was being part of something very special and knowing that it would not last.

Solo Safari

* * * * * * * * * *

Some mornings, when the ducks weren't cooperating, we'd move a mile or so to a gritting ground and shoot sand grouse. Coming from their morning drink, these little birds are almost as hard to hit as white wing doves. A colleague of mine at the embassy and his wife liked grouse shooting and argued that these birds tasted better than doves. I disagreed, but we agreed that they were challenging to hit. Unlike doves, the grouse were year-round companions.

There weren't many places within two hours of Khartoum where we found guinea fowl, bustards, or francolin. We hunted birds on the great grass plain east of the river that stretches almost to the Red Sea Hills, the *butanna*. We also found them on the savanna in the middle third of the country. I shot guinea fowl and francolin for a break from red meat during big-game hunts. I enjoyed bird hunting but never organized an outing on the scale practiced by another of the Sudan's "guest hunters."

While I lived in Khartoum, a Saudi prince and his entourage made several visits and Mohammed Abuzeid took them bustard hunting. Twelve air-conditioned Range Rovers, two cooks, Waterford crystal, bone china, Persian carpets, bottled water, the finest tinned food from Jeddah, and four or five hunting falcons.

A couple of the prince's falcons had been captured and trained by a Sudanese I knew. He was very secretive about where he got the birds, but a mutual friend told me the Saudi had paid twenty-five thousand dollars for a particular falcon. The prince liked his birds. While in Khartoum they were kept in an air-conditioned room in the Hilton with an armed guard at the door. Tidbits were flown in each day on Saudi Airlines.

Mohammed never took us gazelle hunting in areas where the Saudis hunted bustard. It made sense, because the prince rewarded him handsomely for a good hunt. Anything over twenty birds was a success. Nevertheless, Mohammed didn't like the prince because he wasted the birds, rabbits, and gazelles they killed. Mohammed hated to waste meat. Like all desert Arabs, he knew what starvation was and that, while Allah is generous, He disapproves of waste. I think the profligate prince deeply offended the pious hunter.

For the Birds

I prize dining on bustard above all wildfowl. It is rich, moist, and sweet, like good turkey. Mohammed told me that the British liked bustard for Christmas dinner. During World War II, he supplied gazelle and other game for a British army officers' mess. In 1942 he was asked to provide bustard for an unusually large feast, but try as he would, he couldn't locate any. Seeing a valuable contract going down the tubes, he hit on an alternative.

Early, the morning before Christmas, Mohammed delivered a dozen nicely cleaned birds to the camp's Sudanese cook. Returning a couple of days later, the mess officer complimented him on the birds, saying they had been delicious. Mohammed took his pay with thanks, thankful that the British couldn't tell a bustard from a buzzard.

LIBERIA—MY WAY

by Charles Craver

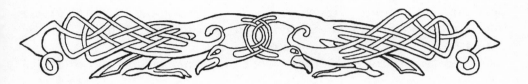

I was leafing through the record books, looking for the names of hunters who listed "self" as their guide. The name Charles E. Craver appeared, again and again. This guy not only had guided himself to numerous record-book animals, his western sitatunga was Number 1 in the book. I tracked Charlie Craver to the Hunters' Den, a sporting goods store which he owns and runs in North Little Rock, Arkansas, and convinced the adventurer and ex-soldier to share some of his stories.

Many sportsmen have hunted bongo, the most elusive of the spiral-horned antelope, and many have failed. Some have spent weeks watching salt licks, waiting for a bongo that never came. Others followed tracks day after day but never saw more than the glint of red as the bongo disappeared into the jungle. Charlie Craver discovered a new way to hunt bongo and describes it here in detail.

* * * * * * * * * *

I was sitting at my desk at the Military Language School at Monterey, California. My boss thought I was working on a new language course but I was daydreaming about the exciting places I had been and the adventures yet to come. The language school wasn't a bad assignment, by stateside standards, but after six years in Korea and two tours of Vietnam, it was rather ho-hum. Then my boss dropped an envelope on my desk. From the return address I knew it contained my new orders and I fumbled to tear it open.

Solo Safari

Africa, this was it! Finally after all those years I was going to Africa. After all those hopes, desires, and promises, Africa was within my grasp. Africa, land of elephant, lion, and buffalo, was finally going to be mine.

Korea had been interesting, because in addition to the friendly people and enchantment of the Far East, there had been no shortage of ducks, doves, pheasants, and deer. There was also plenty of land without "no hunting" signs. The seasons were long, bag limits were generous, and the terrain varied. The two three-year tours flew by and I never regretted one minute.

The two tours in Vietnam were different because hunting of a sporting nature was nonexistent. There was plenty of dangerous game though, and I soon learned what it was like to be the hunted. Vietnam was a very beautiful country and it was a shame that a war had to destroy so much of it.

That was all behind me now and the only thing I could think of at the moment was that I would soon be in Africa. The land of Ruark, Hemingway, Bell, Selous, and Hunter was soon to become the land of Charlie Craver as well. Well, this would not be the fabled East Africa that these men had hunted and written about. This would be Liberia, in West Africa, the land of jungle and unbelievable rainfall.

You might ask, who ever hunted in Liberia? What great hunting books have been written about Liberia? In all my years of searching and reading, I found references in only two books. One was in W.D.M. Bell's book, *Bell of Africa*, and that was only a chapter. The other mention is a chapter of Mellon's excellent book, *African Hunter*. Other than these brief chapters, I had no references to indicate what one might encounter on a trip into the interior of Liberia. This did not deter me in the least because uncertainty is an essential ingredient of adventure.

I immediately began planning my battery of guns. For a shotgun I had a Remington Model 1100 in 12-gauge with a 26-inch ventilated rib and modified choke. It later caused some problems due to substandard ammunition that was not American-made. A good double-barrel or pump shotgun might have been a better choice. Not knowing what I would come up against in Liberia, I took along a variety of ammunition ranging from #6 birdshot to #4 buckshot and even some rifled slugs.

My light rifle was a Mossberg bolt action in .30-06 with a Weaver K4 scope. Here again I took as much ammunition as I could, including

Liberia—My Way

both 180-grain and 220-grain softpoints. I later learned that ammunition for the .30-06 could be augmented from local sources as there were plenty of military solids in Liberia, not the best, but better than nothing.

The big-bore rifle was to become my favorite and I developed full confidence in it. It was a pre-1964 Winchester 70 Super Grade in .375 Holland & Holland caliber. This was a rifle that I had great hopes for and a rifle that came close to doing it all. The .375 had gained a very well-deserved reputation in the African game fields for reliability.

Weeks later, my wife and two daughters and I arrived in Monrovia, the capital of Liberia. The family had to adjust to a culture that was unlike anything they had ever experienced before. All drinking water had to be boiled and all clothes that were washed and hung outside had to be ironed before wearing. This was necessary because of a certain mango fly that laid its eggs on clothing put outside to dry. It was impossible to see the tiny eggs and the hot iron was the only way to kill them. Any carelessness here resulted in welts appearing on any part of the body touched by the affected clothing. The swelling erupted and maggots appeared. This caused great alarm from my wife when she saw it for the first time on the faces of the children. Had there been a passenger plane returning to the United States the first time this happened, she and the girls would have left the country without a backward glance. Later, the country came to grow on them and they all broke down in tears when we left Liberia.

Finally everything fell into place, the girls entered school and my wife learned to accept minor inconveniences, such as electrical and water interruptions and lizards in the bathroom. The American embassy posted security personnel at our house each night to guard against local thugs who would break in and steal everything in sight.

We learned to accept the arrival every evening of the door-to-door salesmen, or "Charlies" as we called them. These fellows peddled local wares, including carvings, fish, lobsters, artifacts, and wild animals, both dead or alive. The animals included duikers, genets, and civet cats. Some Americans kept live chimpanzees, monkeys, parrots, and even a baby leopard or two. The Charlies had leopard skins for sale on occasions. When pressed to find out how or where they had been taken, they were vague and unresponsive. These skins only tended to whet my appetite for big-game hunting.

I could hunt big game in the interior only after the rainy season had passed. To while away the time, I often hunted birds in the area surrounding Monrovia. The variety of birds was enormous and the populations of some species were mind-boggling.

A certain dove known locally as the green pigeon appeared in numbers that would rival the passenger pigeons of early American history. They would literally darken the sky and we would shoot them in the mornings as they came for water. The sight was beautiful beyond belief. We took them on the beaches along the Atlantic Ocean where the fresh-water streams emptied into the sea. The shooting was fast, and if the shotgun jammed, you would literally tear it apart in rage while the other hunters were banging away and laughing at you.

The local children served as retrievers and they rarely lost a bird. Our bags were never large because it was difficult to concentrate on single birds when the sky was full of them. The birds were never wasted, since those we did not eat were given to the locals.

When the season on the green pigeons ended, we went after francolin or guinea fowl as the locals incorrectly called them. Due to a quirk in Liberian history, many animals and people have Americanized names. Although Liberia had a native population, it was selected as the country where freed American slaves were returned. President Monroe was very active in this relocation, so the capital was named Monrovia in his honor.

The returned former slaves, not being familiar with the local fauna, gave them names for animals that they knew from their days in America. Thus the various duikers were known as deer, crocodiles as alligators, dwarf buffalo as bush cows, and francolin as guinea fowl. It is a sad commentary that one of the first things the newly freed slaves did upon their return to Africa was enslave the local population, with slavery continuing well into the twentieth century in Liberia.

The pursuit of francolin led me to the fringes of the jungle or rain forest. There were certain things you had to watch for, snakes being the most important. Liberia had two of the deadliest snakes known anywhere, the Gaboon viper and the green mamba, and they frequented the areas where francolin were abundant. The viper was particularly deadly because it was a sluggish snake and was not fast enough to move out of the way before you stepped on it. Then it struck like lightening. This meant almost certain death because you were too far from proper medical attention. Even if you could get to a doctor, there was little he could do anyway, except sign your death warrant.

Liberia—My Way

The green mamba was thin and lithe and its venom was almost as deadly as that of the Gaboon viper. Its color blended in perfectly with the surrounding greenery and it was also found in the same type of bushes as the francolin. I soon learned to part the bush with the barrel of the shotgun, not my hand, when reaching for downed birds.

As the weeks passed, I learned more about the local hunters. They did not have a wide choice of firearms and everything had to be taken with a shotgun, and a single-barrel, single shot at that. The biggest shot available on the local market was #4 birdshot, the type we normally use to take ducks and squirrels. The Africans used this gun and load for everything from pigeons to antelope. They also used shotguns for elephant, demonstrating levels of ingenuity and courage unknown in Western civilization.

For elephants, they removed the shot and wads from a shotgun shell. The shot and wads were then removed from a second shotgun shell and all of the powder transferred to the first shell. Then grass, yes grass, was tamped down on top of the powder charge to create a seal or wad. The shell was loaded into the chamber and a twenty-four-inch spear with a hand-forged steel point was pushed down the barrel.

Then they would sneak to within five feet of an elephant and fire the spear into its heart or lungs. The spear was not poisoned, but at a range of five feet, shot placement and penetration usually were pretty good and the elephant died within an hour. You must admire the ability and courage of the local hunters who can get so close to an elephant.

I had hunted birds with a United States Navy chap named Jim. He seemed both likable and reliable, so we began preparations for the interior and big game. We also recruited Sergeant Green of the Liberian army, who would serve as an interpreter and help with the driving. We then approached the ministry of defense, our local counterpart, for a letter to enable us to ask the minister of the interior for hunting permits. Nothing happens easily in Africa.

Quickly, we got our food and gasoline rations together, along with a tent and camping gear. You have to remember, this was all up to Jim and me, as there was no professional hunter to organize these minute details. We had to plan for every situation from medical problems to trading with the locals for anything we might need.

Food was the least of our problems and we took all canned goods and military rations that were well suited for field operations. We gave much thought to what to do about snakes and concluded that a standard snakebite kit would not work against the more poisonous ones. We took one along anyway, just for peace of mind.

Finally the big day arrived and we loaded all the gear into a suburban-type vehicle, with the rear seat removed. Liberia has an adequate road network that serves the mining and timber industries. They are not four-lane, paved highways, but they do beat driving across country on game trails.

We traveled for hours through rolling country with large trees and an occasional clearing where small food plots were maintained by subsistence farmers. We finally arrived in a small village, where Sergeant Green negotiated with the village elders. His knowledge of the local dialect was barely adequate, but with lots of gesturing and repetition, he lined up a couple of local hunters to act as guides.

Jim and I pitched a little two-man tent and stored our gear in another one. Then we prepared and ate a light supper. All this was carefully overseen by the villagers. While they were friendly, some had never seen a white person and they couldn't stop looking at us.

We prepared our gear for the next day, our first day of big-game hunting in Africa. Wow, how do you organize your ammunition when you haven't the slightest idea what to expect? I counted out some #4s for the jackrabbit-sized royal antelope, some .30-06 180s for the larger antelope and some .375 solids in case we ran into bigger game.

We had just about finished our plans for the next morning when we were approached by the village chief and several of the elders, followed by several women. One woman appeared very upset and under much stress. After a vigorous exchange of words, Sergeant Green explained that the woman had recently given birth to a baby boy who was having trouble keeping food in his stomach. He needed medical attention and the villagers clearly expected us to provide it. The fact that we were not doctors and had no stomach medicine was of no concern to the villagers. They had heard of the white man's powers and they wanted help.

We had a problem. We wanted to help the boy, but we dared not jeopardize relations with the villagers because we needed their help as hunting guides. If we gave the baby the wrong remedy, we might have a bunch of angry Africans to deal with. After much soul-searching and a quick check of our limited supplies, the only thing we could come up with was some canned applesauce. American babies eat applesauce, so what harm could it do? It might actually help. The villagers took the cans and left.

Our canned food found little favor with Sergeant Green. He had been unable to buy any chickens locally, so he jumped into the vehicle and headed for the next village with the assurance that it produced the biggest, fattest chickens in all Africa. He apparently found entertainment, as well as chickens, because he did not return that night.

About three o'clock in the morning, a loud hue and cry came from the village. Here we were in the middle of nowhere, without any help or assistance for hundreds of miles, and a riot was breaking out. Our only interpreter, who knew better than we what was going on, had abandoned us. We had no idea what had happened and the wildest thoughts raced through our minds.

Liberia was not the most civilized country in Africa and we had even heard rumors that cannibalism was still practiced. The country also had a Leopard Society, whose members killed their human victims and ate their hearts. Some high government officials had been convicted of this just prior to our departure from Monrovia. I know you must think this is just foolish thinking and that we were letting our minds run away from us, but this was not the case here. This country was run by Africans and the color of your white skin granted you no special privileges.

The cries from the village increased in volume. We were sure the baby had died of acute applesauce poisoning and the villagers were working themselves into a frenzy, preparing to take their revenge on us. Jim was stuffing buckshot into the shotgun and I loaded the .375. We really did not know what else to do. There was no way we could have shot our way out of a situation like this, and with no vehicle, there was no place to go even if we could have gotten out of the village.

The noise and crying continued throughout the night as the whole village gathered outside their huts and started dancing around a large fire. Dawn came and no threat had been made on our lives. Hindsight reveals there was no real danger, only very real fear.

Again and again, in Vietnam, Korea, and Africa, I had found myself in situations where I didn't know what was going on around me. The experience with the sick child, in a remote village on a remote continent, was as new and frightening to me as the adventures of Livingstone a century and a half ago. If you travel with a touring company or professional hunter, you simply do not encounter these situations. If you find your own way, and survive those tense moments, you will have lived life to its fullest.

The natives gathered to watch us eat breakfast and they acted as if nothing had happened the night before. The baby was not mentioned and we got down to organizing the hunt into the rain forest. Sergeant Green returned with the vehicle, a couple of live chickens, and bloodshot eyes. He tried to explain to the guides which antelope we wanted to hunt, but the guides only understood that we were after "meats" as they called all animals that could be eaten. Sergeant Green shouldered a pack containing food, extra ammunition, and the totally worthless snakebite kit, and we struck out on foot. The rain forest is too thick to allow the use of vehicles for hunting.

We had been told that the natives could call the antelopes no matter what shape or size. They grasped the nose between the first and second fingers with a slightly clinched fist and made a mewing sound. This sound imitates the noise made by a young antelope or duiker in distress. Both the male and female antelope would respond to this sound and so would leopards. How a leopard would react when it found out the noise wasn't real left a whole lot of doubt in my mind.

We followed the network of game trails away from the village and after several miles the chief hunter, a chap named James, got us to spread out in a straight line about forty yards apart. We then kneeled down and kept quiet for about ten minutes. After the forest had returned to normal and the birds and animals had resumed their activities, James made the mewing sound several times and we waited in silence for several minutes.

At first there was nothing, and then as if by magic, without a sound or movement, the black-backed duiker appeared. At first I thought it was an accident, just an incidental occurrence, but James repeated this performance several times throughout the day. Once he called in two duikers at the same time. On another attempt we had to shoot in self-defense to stop a duiker from running right over the top of us. The duiker came on a dead run, and if we had not shot, the outcome might have been disastrous.

The locals called five different times and brought in a total of six animals. The action was fast-paced and more duikers got away than were bagged. It was like no other hunting that I had ever done before. Sure, we had tried predator-calling back in the States, but had experienced nothing like the success and fast action we had in the rain forests of Liberia.

We could have made it a slaughter, but that would not have been right nor was that what we wanted. To hunt, to experience new country and a novel and successful method of hunting, that is what it is all about. The company of a good group of guys who enjoy the same things you do makes it all the better.

After arriving back in camp later that evening, we turned in and enjoyed a good night's rest. The next morning we took it easy and planned for a later start. We were relaxing in camp, enjoying the local sights, when Jim noticed a couple of young fellows climbing high into the palm trees. We summoned Sergeant Green for an explanation.

When the people want to celebrate, he explained, they brew palm wine. The "makings" are available right outside their huts and the process requires a lot of agility but not much labor. They just select the right type of palm tree, scale to the top, and chop off the last foot or two from the top of the tree. They then scoop out a hollow in the remaining top. The sap collects in the hollow and ferments for several days. This brew has tremendous potency, as it continues to ferment in the stomach. It also brought about some terrific hangovers that last for several days. Thank goodness we had better sense than to experiment with this personally.

These remote villagers seemed content in their jungle home. They raised a few crops and some chickens that they supplemented with wild meat. Their fuel, building materials, and other essentials were easily harvested from the rain forest.

Later in the day we moved out again and this time we were looking for the larger animals, such as the bongo and sitatunga. Other sportsmen have returned to Africa again and again in search of bongo, the big, spiral-horned antelope of the deep forest. Bongo are never plentiful and are so secretive that hunters have pursued them for weeks without seeing even a hair. I amused myself with the thought of bagging one on a self-guided hunt. It wasn't a realistic expectation, but we were here, so why not try?

We moved into another area along the border between Liberia and the Ivory Coast. This area was lower in altitude but still had a few hills. A canopy of overhead trees obscured the skyline and made the atmosphere thick with humidity. If we left the game trails, we had to cut our way through the steaming vegetation with machetes. This slowed progress considerably and the noise made it impossible to approach animals.

Fortunately, game trails led in every direction and James always knew which way to turn. The temperature was high, we were hitting the water canteens regularly, and we had to stop at the river often to replenish our water supply. It had to be sterilized with iodine tablets, a time-consuming process, so we tried to ration the water. The more water we drank, the less good it seemed to do. The water just didn't satisfy and we drank more and more while the locals went all day without taking a drink.

James began picking up signs of bongo and we moved quietly, trying not to disturb the birds and monkeys. This was not an easy task since they were everywhere. We finally came to the area James was looking for. We concealed ourselves in the bush and James repeated the calling sequence that had proven so successful. He tried calling at several locations, but to no avail. Duikers appeared but we could not risk a shot that would ruin our chance for a bongo. This was becoming more frustrating. We had just about given up since it was getting late in the day and we were many miles from camp. We were tired and the water supply was getting low. James called one more time and a bongo suddenly materialized from nowhere.

It showed chestnut-red in the afternoon light. The thin vertical stripes accented the brilliance of its coat. Its horns were big and black and beautiful. It bounded in much like the duikers. But with ten times their weight, it made more noise as it slipped through the bush. It stood alert, trying to find the source of the calling. It turned to take another step before vanishing into the jungle, but a shot from the .375 Holland & Holland brought it to the ground, and with a slight kick or two, it was mine. The quest for the "Holy Grail" of African hunting was over.

Up close, its coat showed brilliant red and those beautiful, ivory-tipped horns spiraled to more than twenty-nine inches with bases thicker than a man's arm. The trackers were excited too, not about the horns, but about the hundreds of pounds of meat that would be distributed around the village upon our return. Regrettably we could not save the cape and hide since we had no salt.

The pressure was now off and our next attempt would be for buffalo, not the big burley Cape buffalo of Kenya, but the smaller and more feisty dwarf buffalo (*Syncerus nanus*). What they lack in size they more than make up for in nasty disposition. Young animals are reddish in color but they tend to darken later in life, until finally they are black all over. They do not travel in large herds like the other buffalo, but in small groups of three or four. Like their brethren, they can soak up a lot of lead if the first shot is not fatal.

At first, James and the other trackers wanted nothing to do with these bush cows. But with promises of all the meat and a little "dash," as money tips and bribes were called, they finally agreed to a buffalo hunt. We started out with high expectations and more than a little apprehension. The foremost authority on dwarf buffalo, a Dr. Christy, had been killed by one as had many native hunters who had tackled them with single-barrel shotguns.

There was not a cloud in the sky and there wouldn't be until the rainy season came again in a few months. It wasn't long until the heat and high humidity began to work their treachery. Again we tried to keep from drinking for as long as we could and even tried the old French Foreign Legion trick of sucking on a clean, round pebble. It wasn't too many miles until even this trick failed and thirst forced us to hit the canteens for water.

The trackers finally found a fresh spoor. It was a small group of buffalo composed of one large bull and what appeared to be two cows and a yearling calf. After a quick conference, the local hunters determined the course the buffalo would follow and we took a big loop downwind to intercept them.

After what seemed like several hours, we moved over a slight rise and saw the smallest of the buffalo grazing in a small valley. We slowly eased back into the bush to avoid alerting it and the rest of the buffalo. The local hunters had a quick conference in muted tones and we then scattered out in a quickly laid ambush. We waited in silence for what seemed like an eternity, our apprehensions growing with every minute. I heard a noise coming through the bush and I eased the safety forward. It was a cow feeding on the move, always alert. Soon all the cows were in partial view and I held my breath, hoping the bull would show.

And suddenly there was the bull, trailing behind the cows, also feeding as it went but always alert. I slowly raised the .375 and put the iron sights on its shoulder. At that angle, the bullet should catch both the shoulder and the lungs. I squeezed the trigger and the .375 fired. The bull stumbled and righted itself, and the whole group ran off into the bush.

Solo Safari

Jim and I speculated about the shot, but we didn't know whether to be thrilled or scared. James and the other trackers didn't seem too anxious to go looking for blood, and we didn't push them. Finally they carefully moved to where the bull had taken the hit. There was some blood but not a whole lot. The blood showed a little froth and James indicated the bull had been struck in both the shoulder and the lungs.

We set off in single file with the best tracker in the lead, followed by Jim and me with rifles at the ready. We had given the locals slugs for their shotguns, but I didn't have much confidence in their ability to stop a charge. Jim had his .30-06, but I knew its limitations as a stopping rifle against a wounded buffalo. That left me with the .375 H&H. I knew the rifle was up to the challenge, but I wasn't so sure about myself.

We moved slowly, taking a step or two at a time as if walking on eggs. The bush wasn't too thick now, but the sun and wet air were oppressive. The sweat poured from our faces and made our hands slick. The birds continued to sing and the monkeys moved about overhead. We surprised a small duiker and as it crashed into the bush, it sent a jolt through my overly taut nervous system. We continued to find traces of blood but not enough to suggest a quick end to this misery.

The bull split off from the cows and we found larger spots of blood where it had lain down several times. We knew that the bull was feeling very sick and that it would soon loose its patience with us. The tension was so thick that you could have reached out and grabbed it. The bush was now getting thicker and our pace slowed even more. Everyone was on the alert and, although no words were spoken, each gained strength through the group. There were no supermen here, no one wanted to steal the show. I hadn't felt this sense of comradeship since Vietnam.

With my senses working at full capacity, I noticed every detail of this beautiful place. I glimpsed the magnificent Diana monkey with its black and white mane that made it appear larger than it really was. Numerous birds flitted about and we did our best to keep from alarming them. The last thing we needed now was to alert the wounded bull.

We gained some more time when we gambled with a shortcut and picked up the spoor once more. At times I could read the tracks as well as James. On other occasions, I was completely befuddled, while he read the forest floor like an open book. The blood trail finally gave out and the trackers were looking for nothing more than footprints and disturbed vegetation. Several times we thought the bull was just ahead, only to hear a crash as it moved off into the bush. We kept dogging it, expecting at any second to see a ton of angry black buffalo explode into our faces. The pucker factor was off the top of the scale.

There was no talking, only pointing at each newly found track. Every step was like taking one in a minefield, with the stakes just as high. I hoped I would have the intestinal fortitude to stand and keep on shooting when the time came. I also hoped that I would not get shot from behind by one of the locals. I glanced to the rear to see a lineup of shotgun barrels being gripped by nervous hands. It was not a reassuring sight.

An explosion came out of the bush, followed by a volley of gunfire that brought me a flashback to Vietnam. The buffalo came in a blur with what looked like fire in its eyes. Every rifle and shotgun greeted its charge and the shear might of those many gunshots staggered it. With that, the locals departed through the bush like a bunch of rabbits, throwing away their guns, clothing, and anything else that would impede their hasty departure.

I quickly bolted another round into the .375 H&H. My first shot, like everyone else's, had been into the biggest part of the bull. This time I took a more careful aim and busted it between the eyes. If anyone ever tells you that the skull of a dwarf buffalo will turn a .375 H&H bullet, don't believe him.

The bull took another step and went down in a cloud of dust, or at least it looked like dust to me. It could have been snow because at the moment, I would have believed anything. I'd been holding my breath and now I gasped for air. I also had to sit down for a few minutes to keep my knees from buckling.

There was much back-slapping and hand-shaking and a few sheepish faces as the recently departed natives drifted back from the bush. Jim was standing a few feet away and he had a big grin on his face. I got up and we both let out a big shout of sheer joy. We had met the buffalo on its ground, taken everything it had to give out, and had defeated it.

A sign hangs in my store that explains my outlook on my days in the field with a gun. It reads, "Most of my life has been spent hunting, the rest I've just wasted." I often feel that truer words were never spoken and I have tried hard not to waste many days.

Solo Safari

* * * * * * * * * * *

The current political situation in Liberia isn't favorable and hunting is not feasible, but this situation could reverse itself within a few years. If I wanted to hunt in Liberia or elsewhere in West Africa, I would try it this way.

I would begin by seeking out missionaries in the field. The Baptist Church has more missionaries in Liberia than any other group and they might give you a list of field personnel. Other possibilities include Peace Corps volunteers, but they tend to turn over very rapidly. U.S. embassy personnel also might be helpful, but they often lack knowledge of the remote areas. Missionaries offer both stability and knowledge of the rural areas.

Expect to exchange a long series of letters and possibly try to meet with the missionaries during a home visit. Remember, the best way to get a favor is to give one. All overseas personnel need and appreciate food and equipment that are not available in Africa. Send them whatever they want, at your expense, and offer to bring along anything they need if you finally get to visit Africa.

You also might try writing to the American embassy in Liberia. A good contact person might be the Noncommissioned Officer in Charge (NCOIC) of the U.S. Marine Contingent. With all contacts, ask for their suggestions about others in the country who might be interested in hunting. At some point, you will need to ask your local contacts to explore the laws and regulations governing noncitizen hunting licenses and permits for importing firearms. There may be only a dozen officials in the entire country who know these regulations. If your local contact fails to locate the right official, your hunt probably will never happen.

All this will take much time and effort. You probably will come to several dead-ends, but if you persist it will work out and the rewards are so great that these minor problems will seem of little consequence. Keep the following tips in mind when you start packing.

Clothing should be washable and mostly of cotton. Footgear should be of the canvas tennis shoe type with a lug sole. L.L. Bean of Freeport, Maine, has a French canvas boot that is the best I've ever seen for this type of hunting. It is called the Palladium.

Firearms and ammunition will likely be a major problem. Just before I left Liberia, the importation of rifles and handguns was prohibited. Only shotguns are now allowed. If this rule persists, you will have to borrow rifles once you are in the country.

If you can take weapons, take something that is reliable and inexpensive. A good used pump or double-barrel shotgun with short barrels would be ideal. A 12-gauge gun with three-inch chambers will handle any locally made ammunition. I would take along some #1 or #4 buckshot. These smaller sizes offer a better pellet count and they probably will not be available locally. You might even include some of the new sabot type of slugs. These reportedly will shoot through an automobile body and in a pinch they might even handle a dwarf buffalo.

When I returned to the United States, I brought back what I felt was a pretty impressive group of animals. Six went into the *Safari Club International Record Book* and five went into the *Rowland Ward Record Book*. They include the Number 1 Jentink's duiker, Number 1 western sitatunga, gold medal yellow-back duiker, silver medal western bongo, silver medal dwarf buffalo, and bronze medal harnessed bushbuck.

These and other fascinating animals are native to Liberia. It is up to you to seek them out. Good hunting!

TO BENIN AND BACK

by T.N. "Alex" Alexakos

I had begun to think that my first self-guided buffalo hunt in Zimbabwe was the hunt of the century. Then I read the story of a guy who had pulled off the same stunt in Benin, a country with no tourism infrastructure. That guy was T.N. "Alex" Alexakos.

As a Marine Corps pilot, he spent World War II over the Caribbean, and once spent seven days on the sea in a rubber life raft, finally rowing to a beach on Grenada Island. He later served in the Pacific at Guam, Iwo Jima, and Okinawa.

Alex then tried a variety of adventures. He was an avocado grower in Florida, a revolutionary in Haiti, a commercial airline pilot, a columnist in a dozen newspapers, and a published book author. Today, Alex lives with his wife in the California Sierras, not far from Lake Tahoe. Alex's favorite hunting partner is his son, Nick. A world-class competitive shooter, Nick lives in Canada where he is a rare coin and precious metals dealer.

I want to thank the editors of *Guns Magazine* for letting me reprint Alex's story.

Solo Safari

* * * * * * * * * *

In the predawn darkness of my tent, I rolled over on my pad and listened to the rumbling engine of the Peugeot 505 SR warming up. I couldn't help thinking how this hunt began and I blame it all on Hemingway.

It was years ago, in the pre-Castro days when I last visited Papa in his Finca Vega outside Havana. We had talked the hunting talk and he had told me how he had assembled his own safari in Nairobi. Ever since, the idea of organizing my own African hunt, doing it without benefit of outfitters and professional hunters, has wormed around within me and I couldn't let go. Then one day it festered. To hell with it, I thought, I'm going to do it.

I telephoned my son, Nick, who lives in Canada, and told him of my plan. "I guess it's crazy," I said.

"It sure is," he agreed, "but let's do it."

Finding a country that had the game we wanted and also permitted do-it-yourself safaris does not come easy. In Africa some places permit hunting and others don't, and those that do, have large "blocks" or "concessions" on which only safari companies have the hunting rights. Many other countries are embroiled in border wars, uprisings, revolutions, and other bloodletting.

After months of corresponding with numerous African countries and their embassies in Washington, D.C., I was getting nowhere. I had heard that hunting was closed in Benin and did not write until I had exhausted my research. Benin replied and included a booklet that said hunting had opened for the first time in ten years and characterized its game as being an "abundance of antelopes, both large and small." It also said that it had African buffalo (of the northwestern variety, a subspecies of the great Cape buffalo of southern Africa).

Where is this place called Benin? Well, it's east of Togo, west of Nigeria, and south of Burkina Faso. Let's put it another way. Benin is a small country tucked under the west shoulder of Africa above the equator.

Hunting, the book said, is permitted in the great Parc National de la Pendjari, two million acres in the northern part of the country. French is the official language, although various tribal languages, Fon, Yoruba, Mina, Bariba, and Dendi, are also spoken. Because letters written in English tended to take longer to bring replies, I drafted the

214

letters and faxed them to Nick, who is fluent in French. He then translated them into French and faxed them on.

Attempting to organize your own safari by long distance communications is a frustrating task. Conflicting reports came from a variety of sources that provide hunting information on a worldwide scale.

Since we were spinning our wheels and hard-pressed for time, we made a desperate decision. We decided to go and "play it by ear." The worst that could happen, we reasoned, would be that we'd end up on the beach in Benin vacationing.

My battery included a .416 Rigby which was made for me and I had labeled, because of its all black appearance, the Midnight Express. This trip, I hoped, would be its first test in the hunting field. Benin's variety of buffalo, I felt, would be a proper test for the Midnight Express. I also wanted a hartebeest, a curious creature that has an extremely long and narrow skull and sports grotesquely twisted horns that give the trophy the appearance of a work of art designed by Picasso.

For the Rigby, I took a box of 400-grain Barnes monolithic solids and a box of 400-grain Swift A Frame softpoints. For the other rifle, my .375 H&H Magnum, I took one box of Hornady solids and one of Nosler partitions, both 300 grains. I was all set.

Nick wanted to collect a hartebeest and a harnessed bushbuck. He packed his .375 H&H Magnum, along with his Remington model 1100 12-gauge shotgun, a box of #4's and a couple packets of 00 buck and a box of 300-grain Power Points for his .375.

With me flying from San Francisco and Nick from Toronto, we met in Paris.

"Are we nuts?" he asked.

"Well, we will just take it one step at a time," I said.

"Even Stanley would never have done it like this."

When UTA's 747 touched down in Contonou, the largest city in Benin, we were met at the gate by one Monsieur Kenneth Johnson, who was holding up a sign with our name on it. A smiling black African, he introduced himself and said in English that the minister of tourism of Benin had sent him to greet us and be of assistance.

"After all," he said, "you are the first Americans to hunt in our country since hunting opened. We welcome you!"

We were in good hands. We slipped through customs, our rifles were cleared with efficiency and even Nick's 9mm Glock went through without a hitch, although one official asked what it was for. Apparently he had never seen a pistol.

"*Pour le coup de grâce,*" Nick said. That satisfied the official.

"Can we buy camping equipment?" I asked.

"Not necessary, Papa," Monsieur Johnson said. "There is a hunting camp on the Pendjari that you can use. It has everything. All you'll need is food." From the moment Johnson knew that Nick and I were father and son, he called me Papa and it stuck. Everywhere we went it was the same. It was not familiarity, but a mark of respect.

"We'll be wanting to hire trackers, porters. . . ."

"No problem. You can get them in the village, Batia."

"How about at the camp? Cook? Others?"

"No problem, Papa. They are waiting for you."

The 4x4 was, however, a problem. None were available, and furthermore, if we were to drive there were insurance complications. Johnson suggested that the best way would be to hire a car and driver. Having a driver got us around the insurance problem. That's how the Peugeot 505 SR came into the picture, complete with driver.

Exactly a day and a half after our arrival, our Peugeot, loaded with bags, rifle cases, gear, and supplies, roared out of Contonou, heading north to the Pendjari, 580 kilometers away. Our driver, a garrulous fellow named Paul, whom we later renamed "Reloader," was heavy on the gas pedal and on the horn but light on the brakes. Somehow he managed to miss colliding with any of the hundreds of bicycles, motorbikes, motor scooters, and motorcycles that crowded the main street going out of the city.

We slipped by coconut groves and pineapple plantings, bananas and papayas, and mango trees heavy with green and golden fruit. In a little while the asphalt became dirt, and the ride to Natitingou, where we spent the night, was hot and dusty and took seven-and-a-half hours.

The next morning the ride from Natitingou to the camp took one hour and twenty minutes on the dirt trail through the savanna forest. Our camp was located by a small stream that came from a natural pool below a waterfall. We were greeted by the owner, Sabegote Salifou, a Muslim, whom we addressed as "Patron," and who was offended when we asked if our rifles and cameras would be safe if left in or around our tents.

"Absolutely," he replied with great dignity.

To Benin and Back

We apologized for our bad manners, which reflected our experiences in the urban jungles of our country.

Batia is where the Pendjari begins, eight miles from camp. The village, Waama, is there too. It is also the place where the *chef brigade* (chief game warden), a Monsieur Sebastian Agonnoude, holds his office. We drove over to meet him, and after exchanging pleasantries, Monsieur Agonnoude got down to the business of hunting licenses. And then with handshakes all around, he welcomed the first American hunters to the great Pendjari.

We told him we wanted to sight our rifles, and he said he would take us. Our rifles were right on. No problems. Then Nick let the chef brigade shoot the 9mm. It was the first time he had ever seen a pistol and was delighted with the experience.

Back at camp, Reloader asked me if he could have my empty .416 brass cases. Puzzled, I asked him what he was going to do with them.

"I'm going to reload them," he said.

"We'd like to know how that's done," Nick said.

"It's easy," Reloader grinned, and showed us how he removed the primer. "Then I bore out the primer pocket and insert a small firecracker in there. Then I pour powder up to here, and fill the case to the top with ball bearings."

"But how do you shoot it?" I asked. "Do you have a .416?"

"A friend in the village will make me one."

"Holy Toledo! A .416 zipgun!"

And that's why we named him Reloader.

The next morning, Monsieur Agonnoude, as promised, had a tracker and a porter waiting for us at six o'clock. Fleming, an old weathered and wiry man, was the tracker. We all piled into the Peugeot and drove into the Pendjari several miles before we stopped and got out to walk. By the time the sun was well up, we came to a pan that had a small pool of water in the center.

Coming up to the pan stealthily, we counted six different species taking their morning sip: warthog, roan, hartebeest, waterbuck, a nice ram cob, and a forest pig. Fleming became excited and urged us to shoot. He seemed extremely agitated that we were simply looking at the animals through our binoculars and not preparing to shoot.

When later we came on a large herd of buffalo that was about 300 yards across another large pan, Fleming once again agitatedly urged us to shoot. Nick questioned him and it turned out that he didn't have the foggiest notion about trophy hunting. It became apparent to us that he had been a poacher, and to him, game meant meat on the table.

No amount of discussion, however, could change him, and hunting for horns was a concept beyond his understanding. He would bring us to animals and be put off because we wouldn't shoot. The idea that horns had to be at least a certain length was altogether foreign to him.

Nor did he understand about shooting distances. To him, if you could see it, you could shoot it, no matter how far it might be. And as for brush, to him, any rifle could easily shoot through brush and even trees.

The following day it was more of the same. We cut our hunting short and returned to Batia and told Monsieur Agonnoude that Fleming didn't seem to get with the program. We were promised another tracker. The next morning we began walking at first light with our new tracker and porter. They were brothers and each had the same name, Manou. To escape confusion, we called the tall, thin, younger lad Manou Two.

Both of them turned out to be most satisfactory. Manou not only was an accomplished tracker, but he had the most incredible eyes I've ever seen. He could see animals at enormous distances across the pans and be able to tell whether there was a good trophy among them or not, even better than we could, looking through binoculars.

Through the trees at a distance of approximately 200 yards, Manou pointed out a hartebeest. After a careful stalk, I was able to move closer and line myself up for a clear shot without any intervening brush. The hartebeest, a handsome bull, presented himself for a picture-perfect broadside shot at a distance that was later paced to be 110 yards. The .416 roared and the bull went wobble-legged for about twenty yards, then dropped dead.

The 400-grain Swift had entered just behind the right shoulder and exited near the opposite shoulder, leaving a hole of about 1.5 inches. It was an offhand shot, a position that I'm most reluctant to take, preferring a rest if possible. In this instance, there were no trees readily available, no termite hills, and the hartebeest was staring at me and about ready to head south. When your heart is pounding and the adrenaline is surging, 100 yards offhand is just about the maximum shot that I'll attempt.

By late that afternoon, clouds gathered and by the time we were back at camp, the rain came. And a welcome rain it was, too, for it had been hot during the day with the temperature estimated to be at least 100 degrees. In the evening, under the thatched canopy, we had dinner of rice and hartebeest steak, washing it all down with EKU beer that had been cooled in the stream.

"It doesn't get any better than this," Nick said.

Every day we saw plenty of game. To say that we were selective in our shooting is an understatement. Although neither of us think of ourselves as avid trophy hunters, we, nonetheless, like to look our quarry over with great care to see that it is indeed worthy of taking, that it is an old bull and if possible, beyond its reproductive years. We'll pass up many before we'll knuckle down for a shot.

We got into the swing of things and settled on a routine: up before dawn and out in the field waiting for morning light, hunt hard until noon or close to it, then back to camp for lunch. I would write in my journal, shower, stretch out in the hammock by the stream, and then be back hunting by three or three-thirty, and back in camp again after dark.

We'd sit under the stars and enjoy a hot scotch toddy, a couple fingers of scotch with a splash of water, both at room temperature. Dinner was guinea fowl, which Nick had shot and rice covered with Felix's special sauce and then in the pad by nine o'clock.

This is Africa in every sense of the word. It is Africa without fences, Africa without electricity, Africa that's about as close to Stanley and Livingstone as one is likely to find today. It's the first time I've seen men with teeth filed to points, painted faces, and tribal scars on their faces or foreheads.

And it is hunting unlike that of other African hunting, where you drive until you see game and get out and shoot. Here, it's walk, walk, walk, till you see game, then stalk, stalk, stalk, and hope, if your stalk is successful, to shoot.

Then one morning, I think it was the fifth day, I saw lions. It was a lioness with two yearling cubs. We knew they were up among the large boulders on the side of a small hill. Manou Two had seen them. I started up the hill and about halfway up I peered through my glasses and looked right into the eyes of the largest lioness I had ever seen anywhere, including the San Diego Zoo. Lazily, it rose from the flat boulder on which it was lying and slipped away with its two nearly mature cubs following.

Solo Safari

You learn a great deal about Africa when you're in the Pendjari. But more importantly, you'll learn a great deal more about yourself when you're in the Pendjari looking into the eyes of a lioness just thirty-five yards away. It could have taken you, you say to yourself. You were an idiot, climbing that hill with your head down. The old girl could have taken you. From where it was watching you, it could have made it to you in less than two seconds.

In the afternoon we came upon a large, hard pan. A variety of species was sprinkled over it. Standing by a splash of water near the center was a fine bull waterbuck. From the edge of the pan, Nick took the prone position and shot. The distance was about 325 yards.

When the power point whacked the waterbuck, it spun as if it hadn't taken the bullet and, splashing water, it ran to the nearest edge of the pan, going for cover. We found it thoroughly dead just before it was able to reach the trees. It was a lovely bull with horns that roughly measured twenty-five inches.

The next afternoon we went to a small water hole we'd seen before. Earlier I had sat by that same hole and had noticed that duikers came down to it. Approaching the water hole, Nick flushed out a bushbuck. It scampered out from a bush almost at his feet and raced away clattering rocks as it went. Manou yelled excitedly and Nick knew from Manou's reaction that it had to be a fine trophy, although in the shadows he couldn't tell. Quartering away from Nick, and going behind him, the bushbuck made a run for it. Nick made a twisting turn to his left and got off a fast shot. The bushbuck tumbled but got up and ran. Nick's glasses fell off with the shot and he had difficulty picking the bushbuck up in his scope. I yelled and pointed to where it had come to a stop by a bush about a hundred yards away. Nick shot and it dropped. Manou was right. It was an old bushbuck with an exceptional set of horns.

The next morning we came on a small herd of buffalo. There were a couple of good bulls in it, so we played hide-and-seek for several hours and were unable to close in on it without exciting it. At one point, close to noon, after making a long and circuitous trek around the herd so that we could be in good position to intercept it, we squatted in the long grass, waiting for the buffalo to come by.

The lead cow came directly abeam of me, just twenty-five yards away, and just then the wind made a change that sent our scent directly to it and that was it. Its head instantly snapped directly at us and it whirled and trundled off in the direction from which it had come, taking the herd with it. I creaked into an upright position.

"That does it for this morning," I said. "Let's get back to the car."

That afternoon, Nick shot a hartebeest that sported an enormous set of horns. He and his .375 made an excellent shot across the open pan of about 200 to 225 yards and the hartebeest was his.

That night the tent was like a steam bath. I got up at four and dressed, then sat outside waiting for a breeze to come up. This is the day of the buffalo, I said to myself. I could feel it in my bones. Today is the day.

Breakfast, as usual, was coffee and half of a well-ripened mango. Then we were off. The car stopped in the dark about a half mile from one of the large pans where Manou had said there would be buffalo. And there they were. In the thin, dawn light, the hulking black forms could barely be seen, like black ghosts on the open pan. Already they were moving slowly toward the forest.

In a crouched position and under cover of the forest brush, we crept quickly and silently to get nearer to where we expected the herd to enter the trees. Although the wind was in our favor, the herd seemed nervous and began moving faster toward cover. Crouching and walking rapidly, we moved to close the gap. Then the wind shifted, favoring the buffalo.

We retreated and went into a strategy session, kneeling, huddled together, whispering. Manou said that the wind would change soon, swinging toward us, into our faces. We waited, and it did. Again we began moving toward where the herd had gone. We came closer and began the crouching walk again. Several times I had to stop to wipe my glasses clear of sweat.

A full two hours after we had begun this exercise, we pulled to about sixty yards of the passing herd. Two buffalo became suspicious and stopped to stare in the direction where we crouched in the long grass. We remained motionless, hoping the wind would not shift again. Manou whispered excitedly in my ear. It was the excitement in his voice that made me raise my rifle.

The buffalo were in the morning shadows. The one on the left was looking straight at me. The crosshairs of the 1.5X5 Leupold settled on the black shoulder and the trigger snapped. The heavy, humid stillness shattered with the sound of the Rigby introducing itself into the scene. I heard the thud of the 400-grain Swift. It was a solid hit.

Solo Safari

The buffalo went rodeo. It made one spectacular, Brahmalike twisting leap and collapsed in a heap with the rest of the herd stampeding out of there. Then silence. I reloaded, this time slamming a solid into the chamber and ran to the buffalo, which was lying on its side, and from six feet away I delivered the *coup de grâce* to the back of the head. Then all was still.

Nick, Manou, and Manou Two ran up. Congratulations, handshaking and all that. Then Nick told me that Manou said that I should have shot the other one. The other buffalo was bigger, larger.

"That's all right," I said. "They were in the shadows and I took my best shot."

"He says you are not happy," Nick said, translating.

"It's all right. Tell him I'm happy. Tell him I'm coming back next year for the big one."

Manou is a serious tracker and he does not take his work lightly. He works hard at his trade.

"It is not the big one," he said, muttering.

"Tell him he worked hard and is a true tracker. Tell him that!"

Again Nick translated.

"*Merci*, Papa," Manou said, smiling.

That night, our last night in camp, we had a farewell party. The *patron* brought out a sealed, wax carton of Spanish wine for us and a Coke for himself. We brought out what was left of our Jack Daniels for the staff. We toasted each other and laughed loudly and long and warmly with a camaraderie that is found only among hunters in the field and soldiers in war.

The next morning Reloader warmed up the Peugeot again, only this time it was not in the dark, for we only had about an hour-and twenty-minute drive to Natitingou. We all shook hands and saddened, I got into the car.

"*Au revoir*, Papa," the *patron* said, waving. "May Allah be with you."

It was fine and good and I think Hemingway would have approved.

TESTING THE METTLE

by Charles J. Puff

Charlie Puff is the kind of guy that gets things done. By the age of twelve, he decided on the three things he wanted to accomplish in life, and he completed the last one before reaching middle age. Along the way he traveled the world and established an international booking agency for hunters and fisherman. When told by the government that it was impossible to establish a big-game farm in Missouri, he did it anyway. He is a man that other men envy. Not bad for a guy who never finished high school.

Charlie Puff hunted in Zimbabwe's Zambezi Valley in 1983, back when bags were generous and prices were low. This was a self-guided hunt, one of the most extraordinary safaris ever organized by an American. Oh, to have those bag limits and prices again. I hunted the same area in 1985, but prices had doubled and bags were cut in half. Prices doubled again each year for the next several years and are still climbing. With today's prices, I doubt that Charlie's feat will ever be repeated.

Why did Charlie Puff self-guide his way to danger? Despite his accomplishments in life, did he still have doubts about the inner man? Did Africa offer a chance to test the mettle? I don't know his motives, but the following chapter reveals that Africa put the man to the test, and the mettle was strong.

* * * * * * * * * *

Solo Safari

When I was twelve years of age, I had three things I wanted to accomplish in life: learn to swim, learn to dance, and bag a hundred-pound elephant. Strange wish for a boy of twelve, an elephant! I had started hunting at an early age and had bagged my first deer at the age of ten. I read all the hunting magazines I could get my hands on and the dream was kept alive.

Later in life, I started International Adventure, a booking agency for hunters and fishermen, which led me to far-away places and experiences which cannot be covered in this brief chapter. I have been an explorer since my early youth, so that opening new areas for hunting seemed easy.

I made several trips to Africa in the 1970s. These were traditional safaris, fully guided and outfitted. One might think that a couple of trips to Africa would satiate the desire, but that rarely is the case. Those early trips only deepened my fascination with that great hunting ground. I learned a lot on those hunts about the game, the country, and the people. I learned from the native trackers and professional hunters and came to greatly respect their abilities. Nevertheless, it began to occur to me that I could do anything they could do. It's just not my nature to follow another man's lead. I lead when I dance and I prefer to lead when I hunt. Would it be possible to hunt dangerous game without a professional hunter?

After considerable research, I learned about the hunts in the Zambezi Valley of Rhodesia, now called Zimbabwe. The Department of Wildlife and National Parks annually sold several dozen "camps" to the highest bidders. Bids were accepted from around the world and hunters were not required to hire professionals. Each "camp" authorized the use of an unimproved campsite and nearly exclusive use of a hunting block of many thousands of acres for fourteen days. The camp also included a basic bag, which typically included one bull buffalo, one cow buffalo, a half dozen or more impala, and several other animals. Permits for additional animals could be purchased separately. All this was available for a fraction of the cost of a fully guided hunt.

The Zambezi Valley, I learned, was not the greatest place in Africa to hunt a variety of antelope, but it offered the best hunting in the world for dangerous game. Ivory was not large by East African standards, but the tusks taken throughout the 1970s averaged a respectable fifty-two pounds. Elephants were numerous, enabling the hunter to

Testing the Mettle

look over dozens of animals before selecting a bull. Buffalo existed in astonishing numbers, and lions and leopards got fat and lazy feeding on the thousands of impala.

I first contacted the Department of Wildlife and National Parks. The department sent me a packet of information and rules and regulations. I recruited a friend, Joe, who had been a client for years but had never hunted Africa. Together, we weighed our finances against the cost of a hunt. Rhodesia had just settled a bloody civil war which resulted in the creation of Zimbabwe and scared off most travelers. Well, adventure without risk isn't really adventure. If the security problems in Zimbabwe were keeping lily-livered hunters away and depressing prices, Joe and I would just take advantage of the situation.

We purchased two fourteen-day camps, back to back, in the 360,000-acre Nyakasanga region. That gave us twenty-eight days of hunting with a three-day period between camps to rest and resupply. Our bag allowed two trophy bull elephants with ivory over twenty-two kilos and two nontrophy bulls under twenty kilos. Also included were four Cape buffalo, two lions, one leopard, one kudu, twenty-four impala, sixteen baboons for leopard bait, one warthog, and a variety of birds.

During my negotiations with the parks department, they recommended a fellow in Koroi who owned a motel and bar and who had set up camps in the valley. Rufus Snyman, a South African, loved the bush and the booze. He was the only man I knew who was put to bed every night by his staff by means of a wheelbarrow. Rufus was not a hunter, nor did he care to be one, but he knew how to put a camp together. We had three vehicles, two to hunt with and one to fetch supplies 200 miles away, if necessary. Rufus provided tents, generators, a hot shower, and all the other essentials for a comfortable camp. There was one cook, two waiters, and eight skinners. Two of the very best trackers, Shorty and Towel, were provided by the parks department and included in the price of the camps.

Joe and I were totally spoiled by camp life. We woke up to hot tea at bedside, our underwear laid out freshly ironed with a hot rock, our dirtiest clothing looking new. (Why we can't get service like that in the U.S. is still a mystery to me.) Rufus presided over nightly banquets of buffalo steak, eggs, impala stew, fresh fruit, breads, juice, and don't forget the ice cream.

What more could you want? The thrill of lions roaring in camp? No problem. The crazy whoops and whines of hyenas as they trip

Solo Safari

over your tent ropes? Well, those buggers are a continual pain. If they can't eat it or carry it off, they mess it up. But this is what makes camp life so exciting and so very unforgettable.

Each day began at 5:30 A.M. We would awaken to a huge breakfast and climb aboard the Land Rover with Towel, our senior tracker, on the hood. This gave the best view of the road ahead so he could watch for elephant tracks large enough and fresh enough to warrant a stalk. A typical stalk consisted of a fast walk for four to six hours, checking piles of elephant dung by sticking our hands inside the bowling-ball-sized heaps. If it was cool, we increased our pace. If it was hot, the bull was just ahead, relaxing in a shady grove, fanning itself with those huge ears.

Towel looked for tusk marks in the earth or the unusually large footprints which are signs of a big bull. Trackers describe animals in three categories: big, big big, and big big big. It was easy to know what they meant. However, disappointment was the rule. We could be stalking for eight hours only to find the bull of the day was only forty pounds per side. One fellow that we followed had trash-can-lid-sized feet and left an occasional tusk mark in the ground. We knew it was good, and we stayed with it all day only to find that it had one enormous tusk of ninety pounds but the other tusk was broken short.

I've been in on four elephants. By American standards, that's a lot of elephant-hunting experience. There are so many things that make elephant hunting the greatest sport on earth. Elephants are not shot at the distances one should shoot at a deer, bear, moose, kudu, or any other game animal. They are stalked close and shot at a few paces. Many times we came upon large bulls in the *jess*, the tangled, thorny vine approximately eighteen feet in height. *Jess* is so thick a human would have trouble running through it, if the need arose. Only Jumbo can maneuver in this and maneuver it does. How can a five-ton animal standing only ten yards away disappear and never make a sound?

The trick is to get as close as possible. Why? Because the bush is so thick you can't see the elephant, let alone the tusks. So you are at twenty-five yards and trying to get closer for a peek at the tusks or a clear shot and the cows catch your scent. Towel and Shorty were always checking the wind with their dust bags, tobacco sacks filled with fine ashes from the campfire.

Your blood races, your stomach does flip-flops, and your brain is in overdrive. The bull has taken two steps forward and you com-

Testing the Mettle

pletely lost sight of it in the *jess*. You can hear that low rumble, but where is it coming from? Then you hear another low rumble behind you and you are right in the middle of the beasts. Your escape plan, now five seconds out of date, is totally worthless. The cows are getting nervous and you don't have a professional hunter to tell you what to do. Out of the corner of your eye your see your buddy trying to separate his jacket from a thornbush and there isn't a ghost of a chance that he can get off a backup shot. Then the sudden truth hits home, there will be no escape in the event of a charge, none.

Well, things could get worse. Sometimes it's your jacket that's tangled up in the thornbush. Now, readers, you are getting an idea what elephant hunting is about. It's about tradition, campfires, heavy ivory, good companions, sore feet, and disappointment. But mostly its about fear and danger. And in the end, there are the memories. Who in his right mind would risk his life just to shoot an elephant? Me, for one, and I could do it every day until my number gets drawn.

Joe and I had an agreement that was etched in stone. When I was hunting, I would be the one to shoot first. Unless an elephant was crippled, no shots would be fired by him. When he was hunting, the same restrictions applied to me. Today, in Africa, that rule is not followed by most professional hunters. They will give you first shot on an elephant, then they fire their gun. It sounds like " bang, bang." Did you kill the beast or did the professional? It's a question you will ask yourself the rest of your life and that's one reason I guide myself.

I certainly understand the professional hunter's reasoning. Most clients can shoot paper targets well, but they may become nervous when it comes to dangerous game. The professional knows this and he is just protecting the client, his reputation, and his license. If he looses a client, they pull his professional hunter's permit.

Our no-shoot rule was broken only once, by me, when a young bull decided to trample Joe. I put a .458 solid into the bull's brain at fifteen yards and he fell at Joe's feet. Every day there were those split-second decisions to make. Shoot! Don't shoot! Get out while we can, cows and calves in this herd. Walk out, don't run, don't panic, don't give away our location. God, help us. This is elephant hunting.

I would like to tell you we tracked Mr. Big Big Big for days, or that several of our entourage died of fever or thirst, but that was not the case. We were out looking for baboons as we were setting out leopard baits that evening. We had just rounded a bend in the road when

Solo Safari

Towel spotted tracks in the dust. He turned and looked up at me and said, "Boss, Big Big Big." His eyes were wide with excitement.

We took off at a run for 200 to 300 yards and there it was just leaving a water hole and heading into the bush. Ivory was sticking out of its head, six feet of absolutely perfect tusks. The childhood dream, a 100-pound elephant, was before my eyes. The bulls walked into a grove and stopped. Towel tested the wind while we discussed the stalk.

We circled into the wind and moved close, very close. I could make out its ten-foot height and its tusks, but could not see its head. I personally favor the brain shot, because it is merciful and, if done properly, leaves little doubt about whether you will leave a crippled elephant in the bush. The big fellow offered only a heart shot, an area about the size of a basketball, but a very big target when the range is measured in feet. My decision was made. I raised the .458 Winchester, took a deep breath, and fired. The mighty beast fell dead on its stomach. I ran around the trees to the front and put a round into its brain for insurance.

The size of the beast overwhelmed me. I had a touch of melancholy, tears were running down my face, not because my lifetime dream had just come true, but because I had just put an end to a sixty-year-old mammoth.

I found out later that Mr. Big Big Big was to have been radio-collared by the parks department, which would have marked it off limits to all hunters. They were months behind in their work, and I stumbled into the bull first. It normally hung out in Mana Pools National Park. Perhaps illness caused the disorientation that led it out of the park.

Word traveled quickly by African methods to the park offices at Marongora. Within two days the district warden, Mr. Willie De Beers, stopped by our camp to admire the ivory. Willie is famous for having survived three lion maulings and having cropped over 5,000 elephants, but he told me that he had never bagged a 100-pound elephant. Willie weighed the tusks on the official scale: One was 106 and the other 94. One tusk measured eight feet, four inches and the other one was eight feet. Mr. Big Big Big places Number 176 in the *Rowland Ward Record Book* and Number 15 in the *Safari Club International Book*. I was given a Third Place Trophy for Hunter of the Year Award by Safari Club International. A lion took first place, as the king of beasts. A leopard took second and my elephant was third.

Testing the Mettle

Twenty-eight days is a lot of hunting, but we had a large number of permits, and we hunted every day from dawn to dusk. The meat cutters worked well into the night and Rufus Snyman shuttled many truckloads of biltong out of the valley. Everything went well, except for the elephant charge described earlier. I was repeatedly impressed, though, with the tenacity of African game.

A lion roared about a hundred yards from my tent, not a bad substitute for an alarm clock. I rubbed the sleep from my eyes and swung my bare feet to the floor. A waiter entered with a lighted lantern and a tray of hot tea. I noticed a bug crawling across the tent floor, so I grabbed a shoe by the toe and whacked the bug with the heel. While reaching for the tea, I noticed the bug was still crawling, so I whacked him again. And again. It just kept going.

"Now enlarge that bug to the size of a lion or buffalo," I thought, "and what would it take to stop it?"

* * * * * * * * * *

Joe had just brained a fifty-two pounder, not bad for the Zambezi, and the trackers removed the tail. Towel said it lets all who come upon the elephant know it belongs to someone and not to touch it. As big as our concession was, I doubted that anyone would stumble onto the behemoth. I was reluctant to depart without the ivory, but we didn't have the time or the axes needed for the job. Our plan was to come back the next morning, and if any lions had come to feed on the elephant, Joe would pop a good male. Then the trackers would remove the tusks and the meat cutting crew would tackle the elephant.

The next morning we parked the truck a mile from the elephant carcass and instructed the meat cutters to stay behind. Towel, Shorty, Joe, and I walked quietly to within 200 yards of the elephant. Towel explained that no vultures were sitting in the trees. This meant that they were feeding on the carcass, indicating that no lions were present to hold them at bay. If lions were present, the birds would be waiting in the trees. This sounded logical, so we dropped our guard and waltzed in. At twenty yards we started talking and damned if a big maneless lion didn't jump out of the stomach cavity of the elephant. It didn't make a sound, just disappeared into the bush. We stood around dumbfounded. This lion had been inside the elephant having breakfast and had not heard us until we were on it. I'm glad Joe didn't chance a shot at a running lion. Who knows how that would have turned out.

We removed the ivory and a truckload of meat and returned to camp. The elephant skeleton still held enough meat to make an effective bait, so we decided to return the next day and try again for the maneless lion. That night around the fire, Shorty and Towel planned a stalk from a different direction that they felt would take Joe's lion by surprise.

The next morning we stopped a mile from the carcass again and began a careful stalk. For the last few hundred yards, Towel was using his dust bag, checking the wind. It was okay. All four of us moved ahead slowly. Joe was in the lead, inching along with me at one side and the trackers with their full auto rifles on the other side. Towel whispered to us that he felt the lion should be approximately fifty meters ahead. Joe's eyes were enlarged, my hair was standing up on the back of my neck, the adrenaline was really running, everything was dead quiet. That's when it happened.

A blur of yellow bolted toward us, roaring and growing larger and larger. The beast was really angry. We had invaded its space and spoiled its breakfast. It would just run out, kill us all, salvage its self-respect, and then return to dine.

I stepped to Joe's right, the two trackers to the left. The growl of a charging lion will never be forgotten. The yellow blur was getting larger and larger but no one was doing a thing. I could stand it no longer. I raised the .458 and filled the scope with yellow at a distance of approximately twenty feet. There was another roar, this time from the Winchester, and the lion crashed down. I rammed another shell up the breach and let fly again, and bolted a third shell into the chamber, but never fired. The lion was still. I opened the breach and tried to replace the fired rounds, but I was having a difficult time due to a nervous condition I had just developed.

I looked over at Towel and Shorty, who were still at port arms. Why were they carrying those full autos? Joe looked like death warmed over. He was petrified. No one else had fired a shot. No one ran, but no one fired a shot.

This is Africa. It has been said that a hunter could take on a hundred charges by dangerous animals, stand his ground ninety-nine times and kill the beasts, freeze the one-hundredth time and be eaten alive. Your mettle is always tested in Africa, that's what makes us insane hunters come back again and again. How I would handle the same situation again, I don't know, but I will go back and find out.

* * * * * * * * * *

Would I recommend a self-guided hunt for dangerous African game? Answer these questions. Are you a good judge of African game that is running at a distance? Are you a good to excellent shot offhand on running game with a .30-06? Can you shoot a bone cruncher like the .458 as well as you shoot a .30-06? Do you know how to skin heads and preserve hides? Do you get excited easily? How do you react when under tension? Do you have time restraints or commitments back home that would jeopardize the hunt? Are you prepared to spend a lot of money and be defeated? You can answer no to some of these questions and self-guide in the States, but not in Africa.

Remember the parks department expects you to adhere to their regulations with no exceptions. What will you do when a lion is in your camp, circling your tent, and roaring its head off? When a cow elephant defends its calf and is about to trample you flat, can you refrain from shooting? If you shoot in either of these instances, there will be a thorough investigation and if there was evidence that the situation was not life-threatening, you might face a large fine and a possible jail sentence.

If you have any doubt about your answers to any of these questions, hire a professional. He will handle all these situations and also will become a good friend. I highly recommend that, before trying a safari on your own, you hunt several times with professional hunters. Learn all you can from them and their African staffs. Spend a couple of extra days in the country getting acquainted and checking on logistical services. Then you be the judge.

HUNTING WITH THE PYGMIES

by Reinald von Meurers

Reinald von Meurers is a physician who practices in Florstadt, Germany, and he is also possibly the most accomplished self-guided safari hunter in the world. His specialty is the pursuit of elephants, dwarf buffalo, sitatunga and the diminutive duikers in the rain forests of Cameroon in West Africa; otherwise, he is a dedicated mountain hunter.

When other hunters boast that they hunt on foot, they mean that they abandon their vehicles for several hours to stalk game. Dr. von Meurers abandons his vehicle for weeks at a time as he and a string of porters plunge into the jungle in pursuit of dangerous and difficult game, putting up fly camps here and there, wherever the hunt leads him. Von Meurers moves easily between the world of high-tech, Western medicine and the primitive society of African Pygmies.

* * * * * * * * * *

Tired from a hot day, we slog silently, Indian file, through the forest. Two German friends, one a hunter and the other a photographer, sixteen porters, and I are returning to the village after a tough

Solo Safari

fortnight hunting in the rain forest of southern Cameroon. My trouser belt is tightened to the last hole, a desirable side effect of this rigorous life, but for now I feel only fatigue.

The odors from my tracker, walking in front of me at the head of our group, are appalling. The foul odors are coming from a dozen pieces of blackened, smoke-dried elephant meat that are bound in a backpack improvised from twigs and reinforced by strips of bark. In addition to the fifty pounds of meat in the rucksack, the tracker carries my 11-pound .460 Weatherby. Despite the burden and the wet heat, he does not complain. I walk closely behind him in case I need to suddenly seize my weapon. Following his steady pace, I have the time to muse about the adventures of the last weeks.

We had entered the rain forest by following game trails, but we still had to hack our way through with machetes since these trails had not been traversed by anyone for two years. Our return trip should be easier because we are returning on the same paths.

Five years have passed since the last European had visited this area. The lure of the pristine forest and the promise of adventure was irresistible. It would prove to be a treasure, although somewhat disappointing for big game. The soil is poor, consisting mainly of laterite. The hilly structure of the landscape does not add much to its fertility. The undergrowth is sparse at the tops of the ridges because there is no water during the dry season. This is helpful for walking long distances in a short time, but the ridges offer little food for the bigger game.

During four strenuous days we cut our way through the forest, finding only gorillas, chimpanzees, duikers, and small game. There were plenty of fresh elephant trails but all were made by the small pygmy elephants that live side by side with the larger bush elephants.

Between the ridges we had to cross small creeks with denser vegetation, but the habitat was still not good enough for larger game. Many hunters prize the beautiful spiral-horned antelopes, like the huge bongo or the smaller night ghost, the sitatunga, but both were very rare. Only the occasional hoofprints in the wet clay of a muddy creek suggested their presence. The long, fine prints of the sitatunga caused the greatest excitement among us. Their remote ranges, nocturnal habits, and impenetrable habitats make sitatunga invulnerable to sport hunting, so very few Westerners have taken them.

On the evening of the second day, we had come upon a clearing with lush green grass and muddy swamps, an ideal location for the large animals that like to roll in the mud to get rid of parasites. We found several fresh elephant tracks, including some that were quite large.

We set out the next day to follow one of the huge footprints. The tracks showed that the elephant bull was joined by a small herd of pygmy elephants. While crossing a dense thicket of Aframomum plants, which was possible only by crawling through the small tunnels left by the elephants, we suddenly found ourselves just below the animals.

Slowly, we stalked our way up the steep sides of a forest-covered hill for 300 yards, coming out in the middle of a small herd, three cows with two calves and a young bull. The old bull had vanished. All of these elephants were pygmies, their height not exceeding six feet. They had only small thin tusks of yellow ivory, which was typical of this region. It was fascinating to watch them, but they soon got our wind and fled. We ran too, in the opposite direction. It is no fun being charged by elephant mothers, even if they are pygmies.

Fifty yards farther on my tracker and I stopped in a rocky place at the edge of the clearing and squatted down to wait for the porters left behind in the valley. We sat comfortably on stones shaped like chairs that hid most of our bodies. To bring the porters up to us without alerting the game, I asked my tracker to make the call of the duiker. After several calls we saw movement to our right.

Two big chimpanzees were sneaking toward us to investigate the noise. They came close, within forty yards, then hid behind several fallen logs to watch us. They were curious and moved their heads from left to right to change their angle of vision to get a better look at us. They may never have seen human beings, or was it the white skin that intrigued them? As the porters arrived, the chimpanzees disappeared as silently as they had come. Probably they were hunters too, looking for fruits, nuts, and possibly an injured duiker.

We had seen few tracks of larger antelope and buffalo on this excursion, so we decided to change location. My tracker had a dim memory of a game-rich swamp he had visited eight years before. He was uncertain of its location but led us along a small river that he thought might take us to the big swamp. We proceeded for several hours and the vegetation became more and more lush. The soil was sandy, small herbs were growing, game food was more abundant, and the number of animal tracks sharply increased. Still, we saw only duiker tracks.

Finally, after four days of slow, easterly progress, we arrived at the swamp. Suddenly fresh elephant and buffalo tracks were everywhere. Large piles of fresh and old droppings indicated the abundance of game. Here on a promising, beautiful green swamp that was in front of a large salt lick and next to a clear, running creek, I left one of my German friends and slowly continued along the creek. He and a small crew would still hunt elephant and other game for several days while I explored more of the swamp.

Just fifty yards farther, a Peter's duiker was feeding on the lush grass. It continued for a few minutes without realizing our presence, then moved into cover. As we moved forward, the presence of big game was almost perceptible. This was an undisturbed paradise.

We sneaked along the large game trails on the creek's banks for another mile, when suddenly two buffalo jumped up from the creek. We froze and watched them through the bushes, standing just fifty feet away between several small trees. One was a fine old bull with good horns for a dwarf buffalo. Both had a bright reddish color, which is unusual for older bulls, and on their backs sat a half-dozen ox peckers. When the bulls moved on, the birds remained on their perches, swaying back and forth with the movement of their hosts' bodies.

I signalled my photographer friend to be ready to take pictures. The bull carried a worthy trophy, but I had shot so many buffalo previously that I was unwilling to disturb this beautiful area by shooting game that I did not need or really want. Nevertheless, I gripped my rifle the moment they jumped up on the bank and I was ready, just in case.

Then the bulls moved toward us. The game trail led to our right through the small trees. We were situated nicely behind a mound of earth with small trees growing from it. The bulls started trotting toward us, presenting my friend with a marvelous photographic opportunity, but he froze. He did not have the security of a cocked big-bore rifle in his hands and he was awestruck.

"He is charging," my friend hissed into my ear. That was too much noise for this short distance. With an indignant snort, the bull turned away and I relaxed the grip on my .460.

A hundred yards farther to our right was an open spot with three cow buffalo grazing in a swamp. This time, to be sure of a good photograph, I left my crew behind and grabbed my camera, having the rifle ready for self-defense. Slowly I crawled forward through the waist-high grass. I managed to approach to within fifty yards before the buffalo became wary and I was able to fire several shots rapidly with the camera.

After this we moved carefully for another two miles and came to a beautiful clearing. Between thirty and sixty yards wide and about one hundred yards long, the ground around the river was barely covered by green grass. The knee-deep creek broadened to ten yards. At the far end water was cascading over a rocky bank.

It was just past noon, so I decided to stop and wait. There were too many elephants in this area and the risk of running into a dozing giant in dense cover was too great. I did not want to shoot a nontrophy elephant in self-defense because the shot would frighten other game from the area. Elephants rest from around 11:30 A.M. until 3:30 P.M., so this was the time to stop and wait. We squatted under some bushes and relaxed. We had both shade and cover and an undisturbed view of the opening.

But our paradise was not perfect. Big black horseflies attacked us, trying from every direction to get to our blood. They were especially vicious as they would get under the garments or sting through the clothes. Most of the Pygmies retreated into the dense forest to avoid the pests.

I decided to lie down and sleep, covering my head with freshly cut branches of big green leaves. This was perfect protection since the horseflies did not crawl through the leaves, and I was quite comfortable. My tracker kept watch while I napped. After fifteen minutes I woke up and looked into the opening and in just a few minutes it miraculously filled with a herd of red buffalo. Quickly they headed into the water. It was a wonderful and exciting picture, sixteen forest buffalo splashing in the water under a blue sky, completely unaware of any human presence.

We studied the forest buffalos' behavior for a half hour before a trace of our scent reached them. Suddenly they became uneasy and slowly moved into cover in the typical alerted buffalo posture, their heads pointed upward.

I dozed some more until my back began to ache, and then I sat up again. As I was gazing over the empty opening, which was shimmering from the afternoon heat, I suddenly believed in a *Fata Morgana*, a vision caused by the air. I saw a huge gray animal moving with quick, ground-covering strides into the open. From the same place the buffalo had appeared, a huge bull elephant was advancing toward the water.

Solo Safari

A single, old, bull elephant in the full sunlight in the rain forest is a rare sight. Its wrinkled skin sagged from its body, its whole configuration showing its advanced age. Its tusks were thick for a forest elephant, but not very long, probably around sixty inches and weighed about eighty-five pounds together, which is very good for the Cameroon. The Pygmies became excited and urged me to move closer and shoot.

Kamba, Kamba, was their name for this one, which means good bull, but I wanted *Seme*, as they call the biggest bulls. I had shot an elephant with sixty-five inch tusks two years before, so I was not very interested in hunting this one. The noise of a rifle shot at this time of the day would scare all the big game in the area and might spoil my friend's hunt. Then all the Pygmies would want to participate in cutting up and smoking the elephant meat and none would want to continue to hunt. The Pygmies could not understand my decision.

We watched the big bull walk into the creek and splash water with his trunk. After fifteen minutes, the elephant's trunk suddenly behaved like a snake, its tip curling upwards and swinging from left to right. I knew the signs. The bull had gotten a hint of our scent. With one turn the elephant was running back to the forest.

The Pygmies were completely dispirited and probably they were right. I was not sure of my decision, but I had shot enough elephants and only wanted long tusks for decoration, regardless of their total weight. My friends placed great value on that huge amount of venison. For Africans, the value of the meat is determined by the power of the animal because they believe the power and magic of the animal transfers to those who consume the meat. So they prefer elephant, gorilla, python, and buffalo meat, even though the small antelopes are much tastier.

Different tribes have taboos on certain animals. The Baya and Baboute tribes of middle Cameroon are not allowed by tradition to eat the juicy meat of hippopotamus and they cannot even touch dead venomous snakes. They fear that the partner of the dead snake will come at night and throw poisoned ribs at the person who touched the snake. But they avidly hunt the nonvenomous python, which can be up to seven yards long. One part of it must be given by the lucky hunter to the local chief, otherwise he might be cursed.

Black magic is feared by both uneducated and educated Africans. Even the three wives of one of my best friends, an Alhadji based in the

Hunting with the Pygmies

capital of Cameroon, ask me what kind of magic I use. They could not understand that I came each year from civilized Europe to the dreadful bush, hunted successfully each time, and then came out unharmed after several weeks. It was impossible to convince them that my only magic was my rifle. They just giggled and said, "Oh, you do not want to tell us your secret."

After this climax of exciting animal sights, we continued our search for a trophy elephant for several days. We came across several large footprints indicating large tuskers. Nevertheless, it had not rained for several months, the ground was hard, and it was impossible to follow the tracks.

Each day brought long hours of stalking through the rain forest, fresh explorations of small rivers and swamps, beautiful views of shy forest animals, hunting duikers for the daily supply of camp food, and the thrilling pursuit of big game. I enjoyed every minute of it, even though we found only young bulls or old pygmy bulls with small tusks. After four days it was time to return to base camp, where we had left my young German friend.

This was new territory for the Pygmies, so on the final day we had to stay close to a small river that led toward our base camp. Suddenly the tracker stopped and scanned the forest intensively. He was always looking at the trees, but was interested only in a specific type of tree. These trees had cracks and fine splits allowing honey bees sufficient shelter to construct their honey combs. By watching the flights of the bees, he zeroed on a particular tree. As he approached the tree, he started to grin and immediately handed me the heavy rifle. A steady stream of bees entering and leaving a thin slit in the bark promised honey.

Everyone put down his load and started making preparations. It was a smooth operation, requiring few orders. Everyone knew his task and went off to collect the wood of dead palm trees to make torches and twigs, bark, and large leaves for weaving baskets.

My tracker made a large ring of lianas that he knotted around the tree and tucked behind his back. By leaning back in the ring and putting his feet firmly against the tree, he walked up ten feet to the entrance of the bees' nest. Then he held a blazing torch under the entrance and blew smoke into the hollow tree to calm the bees. The bees were buzzing all around him, but that did not stop him from hacking big chips of wood out of the tree with his heavy machete.

Solo Safari

Gradually he enlarged the opening of the dark brown cavity. Repeatedly he had to calm the defending bees, who were becoming more and more aggressive, with the smoke from the torch. Then he was able to reach inside the tree with his arm, pull out one honeycomb after another, and throw them toward the Pygmies waiting under the tree. Occasionally he paused to lick the golden honey that dripped from his fingers and to flash a contented smile.

The pile of honeycombs grew and grew, making this by far the most successful operation of the last four days. After twenty minutes all the honeycombs had been removed and about sixty pounds lay under the tree. Now the tracker distributed it evenly among the other members of our safari and also kept a good portion for my share. Everybody was sitting under the bushes, well away from the tree with the buzzing bees, eating incredible amounts of honey, wax and all. The light became dim and we camped in the area.

The next day found us back in base camp and my native friends were soon busy cutting elephant meat. The young white hunter had been lucky and shot a very good bull elephant. He was extremely happy about the short but very beautiful yellow ivory tusks, measuring only fifty-eight inches in length, but weighing seventy-five pounds together.

In the evening the camp was lit by many fires. Each man built a meat-cutting table from freshly cut timber. The meat was sliced into two-foot lengths of about thigh thickness and smoked all night long by blazing fires. By morning the slices were black and dry and had shrunk to two-thirds of their original size and weight.

After another day we were back on our trail to the village. The long file of sixteen natives was an impressive sight, each carrying a heavy load, two carrying shiny elephant tusks. By ten o'clock the long file was spread out along the path. They moved slowly to ease their tasks and possibly to bring another day's pay. My entreaties to hurry in order to arrive at the big river in two days were not successful. The heat and exhaustion caused by two weeks of tough hunting had taken their toll and I gave up trying to get them to walk faster.

Suddenly I received help from an unexpected source. A shrill cry cut through the forest, accompanied by the loud noises of game charging through dense cover. We were under attack by several gorillas.

Of course the natives love to hunt and eat gorillas. Due to the Pygmies' primitive weapons and the intelligence of the gorillas, the number of serious maulings by wounded gorillas is quite high. Gorillas hate man for hunting them and can easily attack in the deep forest.

For our safari it was beneficial—at least for me. The gorillas realized that we were standing our ground, so they stopped their charge and retreated with lots of noise. But all my porters were suddenly very eager to join me and to walk close to the protection of the heavy rifle. As my pace was fast, we now were covering greater distances.

The day was hot and the air heavy. We had come the same way a fortnight ago and had not encountered any gorillas in this area, but now it was different. Another two attacks followed, one at noon and then again in the early afternoon. Each time everybody became horrified as the gorillas rushed up to us with appalling cries accompanied by the loud noise of breaking bushes and slashing of twigs and leaves. The foliage was so dense we could barely catch a glimpse of the black hairy skin at distances as short as ten feet.

My friend remarked dryly, "It looks as if they came by appointment to keep the porters going. What did you promise them?"

We covered much ground that day and arrived in the evening at the same clearing we had passed on the second day on our way into the virgin rain forest. The dense forest opened into a 200-by-300-yard area with a muddy, meandering creek. In an elevated clay bank there was a hole almost as deep as a man. Apparently the soil contained some minerals or salt because it attracted many animals. There were tiny tracks from the hooves of the water chevrotain and enormous impressions left by the tusks of elephants as they dug into the soil. We proceeded cautiously into the open hoping to spot any game that might be present, but the clearing was empty. We walked toward the salt lick to check the trails in the soft earth.

When we were about twenty yards away, a huge gorilla suddenly bolted from the hole and charged us. I automatically grabbed my rifle from the shoulder of my tracker who was walking in front of me. With one movement I cocked the rifle and started to aim. The beast was dangerously close and there was no cover or shelter within reach. Fortunately, the gorilla relieved me of the decision whether or not to shoot in self-defense when it turned and fled. In a panic-stricken flight it tried to reach the far-off cover of the forest, but between it and the foliage lay the muddy creek. Suddenly it caught its foot and fell flat with its entire length almost totally immersed in the soft mud.

Solo Safari

My men, who were initially very frightened by the unexpected attack, had recovered from their shock and began yelling and laughing, throwing sticks after their enemy. The poor gorilla paddled frantically and eventually managed to get free of the mud. It disappeared into the forest, caked with mud and dripping with black water, accompanied by the roaring laughter of the entire safari crew.

Everybody was recapping the last few minutes, talking and laughing with his neighbor. All the strain of the day was forgotten and the men were filled with fresh energy. It was, I thought, a fine way to end our safari. We had come to the forest with reverence. We had tread lightly, taking only that which nature would quickly replace. But it had been an intense experience, filled with wonder, excitement, and fear. The comic relief eased our transition back to the civilized world.

SMALL HORNS DON'T COME EASY

by Reinald von Meurers

I am sitting quietly, contemplating the green rain forest, listening only to the birds. The soggy, hot air and the rising excitement are taking their toll. Slowly, small pearls of sweat appear on my exposed skin, form bigger drops, and roll down here and there. That would be no problem, but my eyeglasses are fogging and impairing my already poor vision. Suddenly a short complaining noise, like a hare in distress, cuts the silence. It is repeated several times. On my left, in the same shade of the planklike root of a giant tree crouches my Pygmy tracker, Daniel, imitating the noise of a duiker.

These small slender antelope cry to attract mates, to call their fawns, or to alert others of danger. For these reasons other duikers, both male and female, come running to the noise. Duikers do not have fixed rutting seasons and can rut several times a year, but the does are receptive for only one day. Maybe that is why duikers come running from almost everywhere to the call.

Daniel makes the duiker call by compressing the front end of his nose with his first and middle fingers and using his nasal sinuses for resonance. The silence after his calling sequence is astonishing. All the birds are now quiet and appear to listen attentively.

Then pandemonium breaks loose. A family of chimpanzees starts yelling and crying like madmen, excited by the duiker call. The chimpanzees are 500 yards away, but their noise is deafening. They were probably searching for food and fear that their enemy, the leopard, was the cause of the duiker call. After some minutes they calm down.

My nerves are tense now, I expect a duiker to run up any moment. I focus on the foliage and the image becomes sharp. I distinguish in the mass of green foliage the climbing and twining lianas, small and large trees, huge leaves, and the openings between them. I can see parts of several small game trails tunneling through the forest. Daniel chose the densest vegetation where the game hides during the daytime.

Then a reddish flash dashes through the forest. Like a vision, a duiker, sometimes hidden, sometimes partly shining through the leaves, is running from left to right. My gun is instantly up and I try to set the red dot of the scope on its shoulder, but it is a dancing dervish, whirling through my field of vision. I cannot aim properly.

I regret not having a shotgun because a thrown shot, like one aimed on a hare, would be perfect. Aiming through sights takes too much time for this game. Although the red point is much better than open sights or crosshairs of a scope in this dark light, it is still not fast enough. In an instant it vanishes, leaving me full of adrenaline, my heart pounding.

Moments later Daniel points to the right. Like a ghost, a bright red duiker is clearly visible thirty feet away in the opening of a small game trail. I did not hear anything coming, even though the ground is covered with dry leaves, making walking as audible as stepping on corn flakes. Apparently this Peter's duiker managed to place its small hooves between the leaves, allowing it to sneak in silently.

It stares intently at us with its big, black eyes, its poise showing its readiness to bound to safety. No question of turning the rifle that is pointed to the left on a major game trail. Fortunately, I am wearing woodland tarn camouflage, which I believe is absolutely the best for hunting in the dark environment of the rain forest. It breaks up the human silhouette and allows a see-through effect, like a green mirage. The game is fooled by having a kind of "window" to look through.

I've also covered my treacherous white face and hands with woodland tarn-stained mosquito net, so I melt into the black and green moss and bark of the tree. Daniel is by nature better off, the black-yellow color of the Pygmies, together with his faded brown garments, hides him well among the lianas.

The prized animal is within reach and I feel my heart trying to leap out of my chest. This kind of hunting is many times more

Small Horns Don't Come Easy

interesting than stalking big game, which is my primary goal. I am fixed into my awkward position, any movement of the gun in its direction would be clearly visible and probably result in immediate flight by the duiker into the surrounding cover.

All my nerves are taut, so are those of the Peter's duiker. Suddenly, with a slight movement it is gone. Now we can hear its clumsy, blustering gallop, as it moves into the bush. The sweat is running in pearls down my face and chest, still to be absorbed by my already saturated cotton garment. I regret the missed chance, but finally I am able to move and relieve the tension in my aching muscles.

Rigid, statuelike, Daniel immediately emits his call and now we can hear the duiker coming again. Apparently it did not detect anything wrong on its first visit and it now seems intent on discovering the source of this attractive noise.

This time I knew where to expect the game and my muzzle is pointing in the proper direction. The red dot of the scope plants firmly on its shoulder the instant it becomes visible in a small window in the foliage. The shot breaks. The dull sound of the reduced load does not carry far. We could go forward a hundred yards and call again if necessary. But there is no reason to be anxious. From the point where the duiker vanished, a twenty-yard trail of bright red blood drops leads to the collapsed animal. The 180-grain, half-jacketed .45 bullet passed through both shoulders.

Daniel looks again at the big opening of the muzzle. He admires the big bore of the .460 Weatherby and appreciates its effectiveness with its reduction shells that create just a small sound. I developed these to avoid too much noise and to save the need to carry a second gun into the forest for small game. I even shoot guinea fowl with the .460 Weatherby.

The secret is simple. An exact outer copy of an original .460 case is made of steel. Then it is drilled through so the base accepts a .357 magnum case and the neck accepts a .45-caliber pistol bullet. The .357 magnum case is filled only with powder and sealed with beeswax or a greased felt wad.

The pistol bullets are a bit under caliber but accuracy is acceptable if I hold the velocity to about 1,350 feet per second. Typical shooting distances in the rain forest are around thirty to forty yards, so there is no need to aim differently with the reduction and the heavy load.

245

Solo Safari

The noise reduction was my main reason for developing this small tool and its effectiveness is astounding. A regular cartridge with a reduced-powder charge would produce far more noise. A small powder charge in a big case also carries the risk of a detonation that could burst the chamber.

So I carry a handful of these steel reduction cartridges on the belt and a pouch with spare .357 magnum shells and .45 bullets. I reload the fired cartridges in the field like a muzzleloader, from back to front. This is a fine and elegant solution for shooting smaller game without scaring the big game away with a big bang.

Daniel interrupts my daydreaming and brings my attention back to the daily routine. He wants to leave for camp and asks whether I want to take a photo first, so I have a closer look at my game. Its horns look good, but we are more interested in the venison. I have to feed eight Pygmies, it is late in the evening, and darkness is coming. This was our last chance for meat.

We had been walking all day through thick undergrowth to reach a swamp that contains a lot of big game. The animals are very rarely disturbed because black poachers seldom venture so deeply into the feared forest.

One of my Bantu trackers from middle Cameroon had hunted here some years ago with the Pygmies. My friend was fond of the Pygmies and was enthusiastic about their tracking abilities. I came to the Pygmy village in southeastern Cameroon near the Congolese border in search of Daniel, my friend's head tracker.

I heard the villagers describe the swamp as the "village of the elephants" and the "place where the elephants dance." I decided immediately this was the place I had to go, even if only to explore this pristine area. After days of negotiation, a crew was put together for a three-week foot safari into the primary rain forest.

Now after three days, walking from dawn to dusk, we are only thirty minutes from the swamp and have put up our spike camp. Daniel is very pleased with his *patron*, the traditional French expression for the boss of the safari. In his eyes, the white hunter has proven that he can feed them, which is the most important objective for Pygmies on a hunt. They are confident and will try everything to find bigger game as well.

The tracker slashes with his ever-present machete into a dark-colored tree and pulls down a strip of bark. Then he splits it and tears away the fine inner layer, which he uses as a flexible string to bind the legs of the duiker together. Shouldering this load, he sets out firmly on a game trail, which I hope leads in the right direction.

I have confidence and follow without a word. Darkness is falling, and we have to cover the last mile in near obscurity. I am relieved to hear noises and shouting from our porters who stayed in camp. The crew put down their loads and cleared a ten-by-ten-foot place of leaves and roots for me to erect my mosquito net. Under this I assemble my ultra-light camp bed, the only luxury I carry in the forest. Someone has prepared my shower by hanging a water bag from a tree behind my net. A mass of large leaves is placed underneath to keep my feet from getting dirty. The daily shower is a small luxury after a long and strenuous day of hunting.

The porters cheer our arrival, see the game, and surround us. *Merci, Patron, merci, Patron*, mix their thankful voices. For them it is not the thrill of the hunt. It is just the meat for the evening and morning meals that counts. Maybe they think foreign hunters are crazy to endure the jungle just to have some odd trophies like skin and skulls. Natives imagine there must be some hidden value for Westerners that they do not comprehend.

Once a customs agent at an African airport was intrigued by a helmet-sized termite hill that I carried in my hand luggage. I wanted it for my taxidermist for a natural display of a full-mounted, scaly anteater. Of course the customs agent could not understand why a white man carries in his hand luggage to Europe one of the most commonly available mud structures in Africa. It took me some time to convince him that I was just a crazy German with a quest for souvenirs.

I am exhausted from the long day's walk in the heat, so my first interest is to have a shower, change clothes, clean my rifle, and then relax. Finally I can have a closer look at my trophy. Its horns are long and heavy at the base. My interest perks up when I note that the horn's length exceeds the four-and-one-quarter-inch length of my forefinger. Intrigued, I sort out the tape and measure the horns properly. Despite my fatigue I feel a surge of adrenaline flooding my body. Five-and-three-eighths inches, by far the largest Peter's duiker ever recorded.

Now we have a photo session by flashlight in the dark. A pity, I could have documented this extraordinary trophy better in the daytime. But hungry men were waiting and I need contented people to continue with my expedition, so finally I gave them a sign. In an instant the antelope is skinned and cut up with the machetes into small pieces. The fire is already going, in no time the meat is simmering in an ancient, dented pot and a delicious smell is wafting through our simple camp.

We hunt purely in the traditional African style carrying only rice, plenty of salt, half a gallon of oil and some awfully hot spices. The rest of our food must be provided by nature.

The Pygmies and Bantus prepare their camp for the night. It is a simple camp, reduced to the basic need for warmth and protection from feared, wild animals. Around each fire are formed two beds of large, freshly cut leaves. The Bantus have a bedspread at least, but the Pygmies just sleep in their clothes.

All game trails leading toward the camp are barred with high piles of freshly cut bushes and the tops of small trees. The Pygmies are afraid of the forest leopard. I had several encounters with them during the daytime, each resulting in quick flight by the cat. Sometimes, when the leopards felt safely hidden in the densest bushes, they would continue to growl at us for several minutes.

An hour later dinner is ready and I fetch my share from the big pot. A deliciously prepared sauce is poured over the long rice. The small red stains remind me to be careful, since it is spicy. Fortunately the Pygmies use much less of the red spice, named *pili*, a kind of red cayenne pepper, than the tribes of middle Cameroon. The small pepperoni-shaped, red spice is painfully hot and must be added carefully. But they did it well and dinner is delicious. No three-star restaurant can compete with this simple meal, crowning a peaceful end to a tough day and a passionate hunt. Lying satisfied under my mosquito net and having a long evening before me, I scan my pocket field guide about duikers.

Duikers were named by the Dutch settlers in South Africa. The Boers called them divers or "duikers" because they seem to dive for cover with their high backs and very low-held heads. The head looks much too big for these small antelopes. That's why the French named them *"cephalophe,"* or "head animal," or simply *"biche,"* which means doe. The twenty varieties of duiker vary in size from the tiniest blue duiker, at eight to twenty pounds, up to the yellow-backs which approach 200 pounds. More varieties can be found in the primary rain forest in central and western Africa than anywhere else.

Small Horns Don't Come Easy

Duiker hunting holds the special challenges of calling the game and trying to get a clean shot in these tangled forests. There also is the special appeal of hunting for trophies while at the same time procuring venison to feed your safari crew. The hunter needs his crew and the crew needs the hunter, both sides depending on each other.

Duiker hunting is possible almost everywhere. They are scarce only in areas hunted heavily by leopards or by trappers using snares. Some hunters try to collect all the duikers, which is very difficult due to the isolation of their habitats. Collecting the Big Five is easy, provided you have enough financial means, but duiker hunting requires physical strength, stamina, and skill as a hunter. On a pound-for-pound basis, duiker horns cost the hunter more than elephant ivory.

PART III

Appendices

by Terrance Cacek

PLANNING THE DREAM

Three markets will affect the future of hunting in southern Africa. First is the worldwide market for ivory and rhino horn. Second is the EEC market for disease-free beef. Third is the United States market for sport hunting, and that is you and me. Since we are the market, we can exert some control over production. The ranch-hunting industry is limited in size, not by production capability, but by the size of the market, so we have considerable clout. Allow me to suggest several things we should expect from the hunting industry.

First, most of us should demand fair-chase hunts, meaning wild animals hunted on foot under sporting conditions. A friend of mine took his first African hunt in South Africa. Like many first-timers, he went on a killing spree and loved every minute of it. He shot his wildebeest, for example, over the hood of a Land Rover in a small, fenced pasture.

Two years later he returned, this time to Namibia, to hunt kudu. He hunted a large ranch with no game fences. He and his party tracked a kudu for several hours and many miles before he made the kill. The kudu was average in size but the hunt has become one of his most treasured memories, simply because of the quality of the pursuit. In hindsight, my friend feels cheated by his wildebeest shoot. He will never have the opportunity to take his first wildebeest under fair-chase conditions.

The quality of pursuit has deteriorated as the safari industry has shifted from East Africa to southern Africa. In the old days in Kenya, it was illegal to shoot within 500 yards of a vehicle. This was a fairly good law and a good ethic as well. Vehicles are used far too much in southern Africa, especially on shorter hunts. Nonetheless, I do not believe that the use of vehicles should be a matter of law. The law and the industry should accommodate elderly or handicapped hunters who must depend on vehicles. The other eighty percent of us should forcibly drag our professional hunters out of their vehicles if necessary and set them off on foot.

Game ranchers and safari companies make their money selling animals and they make their reputations on trophy quality. They know that they will sell more animals, and larger ones, if they use the most efficient method of hunting, which is from vehicles. If these motives are not consistent with yours, you should have a heart-to-heart talk with your professional hunter. Many sportsmen will insist that the aesthetic qualities of the hunt are more important than the size of the bag or the length of the horns. We are paying the bills and it is our right.

Second, we should insist on hunting each animal within its original range and in its natural habitat. The South Africans are especially fond of moving animals around. If a rancher in Natal offers you a gemsbok, turn it down. Gemsbok do not belong in Natal. This would be like hunting pronghorn antelope in the woods of Virginia. If you are willing to shoot a gemsbok outside its natural range, shoot it on an exotic game ranch in Texas and save yourself some money.

Third, I believe we should insist on richer experiences with the black staffs. The really successful hunters of old, W.D.M. "Karamojo" Bell, John "Pondoro" Taylor, and others, all loved the native people of Africa. What a shame it is to spend ten days hunting in Zululand without learning the name of that remarkable Zulu tracker who leads you through the bush and finds your game.

On the old-fashioned, thirty-day, tented safaris, sportsmen came to know their black staffs. On today's quick ranch hunts, the sportsmen tend to be socially isolated from the blacks. Most black Africans will not even speak to a visitor, except for curt answers, if a white African is present. Sadly, the very presence of a white African is a major, if unintended, obstacle to communications with the blacks.

Even on short hunts, several things can be done to increase interaction with the blacks. First, book with hunters who are likely to have liberal attitudes toward race. In southern Africa, hunters of British descent are more likely to empathize with their black staffs and understand your interest in learning about black culture. Try to find some excuse to get away from the professional hunter and spend some time with just the trackers. Then, take a break, pass around factory-rolled smokes, ask them about their wives, and brag about your sex life. That breaks the ice anywhere in the world.

Trade your buck knife for your skinner's village-made knife. It will become one of your most prized mementos. Ask to eat some native food and drink some native beer. The only worthwhile hangover I've ever had resulted from a night spent in a bar with two Ndebele chaps. We didn't solve all Zimbabwe's problems, but we surely cemented some international relations.

Most visiting sportsmen will need help in experiencing African culture. Very few white professional hunters can provide this help and most are hindrances. This help must come from blacks. We need more blacks who are comfortable with wealthy Americans and Europeans. A few black tour guides in Kenya and a very few black professional hunters in Tanzania, Botswana, and elsewhere are successfully bridging the gap. They are developing reputations of their own and are in high demand.

Too many American hunters have been swept up in an epidemic of trophymania, that peculiar fixation on horn length. The trophymaniacs always carry a tape measure in their pocket and, upon killing an animal, they reach for the tape before they reach for the camera. The quality of their hunts is measured in inches.

Take two gemsbok and lay them side by side. Both are beautiful animals. The three-inch difference in their horns is indiscernible to my eyes, but to the trophymaniacs, the tape measure shows one to be a fine trophy and the other to be just another disappointment. Such is the tyranny of the tape.

That is not the African hunting I have known, nor the African experience that I would like to share with my friends. The tape measure tells nothing of the quality of the pursuit. The trophy book includes no record of the friendships tempered in the heat of the African sun. No one can measure the quality of pursuit or the bond of friendship, so no one can say mine are second best.

African hunting is changing, but the changes are not all bad. The activity has shifted from East Africa to southern Africa. The emphasis has changed from the Big Five to the antelope. The once-in-a-lifetime, thirty-day hunt is being replaced by a succession of shorter hunts. The dream is alive, but now we must turn the dream into adventures. These are easily purchased, New York to New York, drinks included, as package deals. Are more genuine adventures available? No, they are not available in packages. They must be created.

A hundred years ago, hardy sportsmen landed at Mombasa and spent two weeks outfitting their own safaris. Then, with one good headman, a hundred porters, and plenty of courage, they plunged into the interior of Africa for months at a time. They created their own adventure. I did a modern version of the old adventure when I flew to Harare, rented my equipment and a worn-out truck, hired a crew of blacks, and headed north to the Zambezi Valley. Alex Alexakos did the same thing in Benin (Chapter 24).

Regrettably, opportunities for self-guided hunting are diminishing. In the colonial era before 1962, most of Africa was available to self-guided hunters. Now, about half the countries and most of the land mass are closed to all hunting. Most of what can be hunted is available only through safari companies.

Ten years ago, South Africa, Namibia, and Zimbabwe offered excellent opportunities for self-guided hunts for plains game on private ranches. Now, all these nations will issue trophy export documents only for game taken with professional hunters. This is the work of the safari industry's lobbyists, using arguments as ridiculous as those used to limit self-guided hunting in Alaska and several western states.

The hunts in the Zambezi Valley are perhaps the best opportunity in Africa for self-guided hunting. Information about the hunts and auction are available from the Zimbabwe Department of Wildlife and National Parks, and Zimbabwe has one of the best infrastructures in all of black Africa. The roads are decent, the petrol stations actually have petrol for sale, and with luck, the four-wheel-drive truck you reserved by telephone might actually be there when you arrive to pick it up.

Nevertheless, a Zambezi hunt presents formidable challenges and risks, aside from the four-legged ones in the bush. First, you must place funds on deposit in Zimbabwe before you can participate in the auction, and heaven only knows if you will ever see that money again. Then you must either attend the auction or have someone bid on your behalf. Unless you have a cousin who happens to live in Harare, this could be a problem.

Now let's say you want to hunt an elephant. First you must successfully bid on a camp. This gives you nearly exclusive use of a hunting area and campsite for ten or fourteen days and licenses for a bull buffalo, a cow buffalo, and a number of impala, but no elephant.

Planning the Dream

Having bought a camp for several thousand dollars, you are now allowed to participate in the elephant auction. If the elephant prices exceed the amount of funds you have in the country, you end up with no elephant, but you are still stuck for the price of the camp.

Assuming you are successful in the auction, you have two options: You can hire a professional outfitter to provide your vehicles, equipment, and staff, or you can outfit yourself. If you hire an outfitter, the total cost will exceed the cost of a fully guided and outfitted hunt. If you outfit yourself, the cost of renting a truck and camping equipment, hiring a staff, and purchasing petrol and food will equal the cost of a professional outfitter, and you forgo all the luxury of a professionally outfitted camp.

Self-outfitting carries two big risks. The first is that you will arrive in Harare, but your rifles will not. If you are working with a professional hunter, he will loan or rent you a rifle. If you are on your own, you cannot legally purchase replacement rifles. End of safari.

The second major risk of self-outfitting is the truck. You will reserve a rental truck in advance by telephone, but if the Zimbabwean army decides they need another truck for the weekend, they go to the front of the line. End of safari.

There are a thousand other problems that you would never think of ahead of time. It takes at least two days in Harare to rent all your equipment and purchase food. Leave the gear you've collected in the back of the truck in the hotel parking lot and the thieves will cart it away in about ten minutes. For a case of beer, somebody will let you park your loaded truck in their locked garage, but who? You will need a set of tools and a second spare tire, but the rental company does not provide these. The rental company does offer extra five-gallon petrol cans, but they are too filthy to use, so how do you carry sufficient petrol?

After the safari is over, you must deliver your trophies to a taxidermist. The burden will fall on you to prepare half a pound of paperwork and place it in the hands of the taxidermist. You will need export papers from the Department of Wildlife and National Parks, a veterinary certificate, and import documents from the U.S. Fish and Wildlife Service. The taxidermist figures he will never see you again, so expect the worst possible service. Then you must figure out a way to get your shipment cleared through customs in New York. Some of my shipments have sailed through customs without a moments delay, others required the services of a customs agent. This is totally unpredictable.

Solo Safari

Zimbabweans are wonderful, helpful people. With their help, I somehow worked through these problems and conducted a successful self-outfitted safari. I take great pride in that accomplishment, but I recall suffering the physical symptoms of stress. Is that what you want to experience on your African vacation?

Other African countries offer opportunities for self-guided hunts, and my coauthors offer good advice on how to approach these. Realistically, if you want to self-guide in Africa, the best way to do it is as a resident. Thousands of Americans are in Africa today, employed by private companies, nonprofit organizations, African governments, and the U.S. government. If you are involved in education, medicine, conservation, construction, agriculture, or any of dozens of other fields, you could become one of those thousands of Americans in Africa.

Short of moving to Africa, the best approach is to plan a business trip or conventional photographic or hunting safari. Allow a couple of extra days in the capital city to explore possibilities for self-guided hunts. Take along a list of names of people in your profession. If you are a brain surgeon, I'll bet you can figure out a way to identify the local brain surgeon in Brazzaville, and he might be able to help. Drop by the wildlife department, hang around the bars, get acquainted.

I know of a chap who flew for three days from Wyoming to the Zimbabwe wilderness, spent one day hunting buffalo, then spent another three days flying back to Wyoming. He now has a fine set of horns on his wall and mention in the record book, but he has not experienced Africa. He went to Africa for the wrong reasons.

Africa moves at its own pace. An African once told me, "The white man knows his God well. The white man wears his God on his wrist." To fully experience Africa, you must abandon Western time and adopt Africa's slower pace. However, with the cost of wilderness big-game hunting from $1,000 to $2,000 a day, not many of us can afford to spend a month or two hunting in Africa. Because our booking agents are paid a commission, that's exactly the type of safaris they try to sell. Unless you have unlimited finances, you must resist that pressure.

For the price of one day of wilderness hunting for big game, you can buy two or three days of ranch hunting for antelope or four to six days of photography in the parks. A week of photography will not get your name into the record book, but it may provide something of greater value.

Planning the Dream

If I were planning a first safari to Africa, I would insist on a day or two in the capital city to recover from jet lag and enjoy the flavor of an African city. I would then spend the bulk of my time on a photo safari, learning the animals, their habits, and their habitats. If funds permit, I would spend a short week hunting antelope on a ranch. Finally, I would insist on another couple of days in the capital city. I would explore possibilities for employment and self-guided hunting, drink a couple of beers with an African, and lament the return to America.

I don't need to tell you how to plan your second trip to Africa. You will know how to do that yourself.

CARTRIDGES AND BULLETS

For Plains Game

The day is finished. We have hunted hard and shot well and the skinners will work well into the night. The bathwater won't be warm for another thirty minutes, so let's pour a couple of gin and tonics, lay another log on the fire, and talk about our favorite subject, guns.

Of all shooting in Africa, ninety percent is for "plains game," the antelope, plus zebra and warthog. Calibers used for similar-sized American game are suitable in Africa, but several differences should be considered. First, in America, you typically hunt for one species at a time, so you can use highly specialized rifles and cartridges. In Africa, a dozen species may be on a license, so you must choose a cartridge and bullet suitable for the largest animal. Therefore, my beloved .25-06 has never made the pilgrimage to Africa. It would be perfect for springbok and impala, but what if I encounter a kudu? With a .25-06, I would be undergunned.

Second, we must note that Africa has a lot of big-bodied plains game, requiring a lot of rifle. Most first safaris include wildebeest at 550 pounds and zebra and kudu at 650 pounds each. Any good elk rifle should handle these animals. Okay, you've killed a half-dozen elk with your .270 or .308, but these were mostly yearling (spike) bulls at 350 pounds and cows at 450 pounds. Your kudu will be a trophy-class bull at a full 650 pounds. Will your .270 or .308 handle him?

Solo Safari

For general use in Africa, you should not consider any cartridge or bullet that will not reliably handle trophy-class bull elk. But how should you select from the dozens of combinations that are available? First, consider just what a bullet should accomplish, then select it. From there, it is very simple to select a cartridge and rifle.

Hunters are divided into two schools on the issue of bullet penetration. One school believes that bullets should expend all their energy inside the animals' bodies. They say bullets should not exit and waste their energy on the ground behind the animals. Bullet performance is judged perfect when bullets are found just beneath the skin on the animals' far sides. These hunters tend to prefer light-weight, high-velocity bullets that expand rapidly and retain a small percentage of their weight.

This is an attractive theory. The primary purpose of big-game bullets is to transfer destructive energy to the animals' bodies. Few experienced hunters would argue that lightly built, high-velocity bullets bring a higher percentage of instantaneous kills than heavy, slow-moving bullets.

The other school contends that bullets should exit the animal and create two external wounds, one at entry and one at exit. This causes more blood loss, creating blood trails that are easier to follow. This school places high priorities on dependability, consistency, and high retention of bullet weight.

Advocates acknowledge their heavier bullets will not produce as many instantaneous kills, but they are assured these bullets will kill from any reasonable angle. If necessary, they can slam heavy bullets through the thick shoulder muscles, break the shoulder bones, and still reach the vital internal organs. Or if animals are quartering away, the heavy bullets can penetrate the paunch and liver and still reach the heart or lungs. Lighter bullets, they argue, produce more quick kills, but these fickle bullets also result in more failures, leading to crippled animals. While many American hunters belong to the first school, professional hunters in Africa generally belong to the second, preferring heavy bullets.

Keep in mind that we must choose between short, fat wound channels associated with rapid bullet expansion and longer, narrower wound channels associated with slower bullet expansion. For smaller animals, we want short, fat wound channels. For really large animals,

Cartridges and Bullets

we want longer, narrower channels that extend into the vital organs deep inside the animals.

Listen, hunting fans, I don't really enjoy writing about mangled lungs and I sincerely hope you don't enjoy reading about them. As a professional wildlife manager and sportsman though, I am concerned about the suffering and waste of animals caused by crippling. If more of us would select and use the correct bullets, I believe we could reduce crippling substantially. If we understand what these bullets do inside animals, we can make better choices in bullet selection, so please bear with me.

For a given caliber, the hunter controls expansion and penetration by selecting three variables: bullet weight (length), velocity (energy), and point design. Lighter bullets are short for their length and are said to have low "sectional densities." Suppose it takes 2500 foot-pounds of energy to peel one inch off the front of a .30-caliber bullet of given construction. If the bullet is only seven-eighths of an inch long, you run out of bullet before you run out of energy. The bullet will be destroyed completely and penetration will be limited by the adequacy of the bullet, not by energy. Increase bullet weight until the length exceeds an inch and you will run out of energy before you run out of bullet. Penetration will be limited by the amount of energy, not by adequacy of the bullet. Penetration then could be increased by increasing velocity and energy.

I verified this by firing conventional 140-grain 7mm bullets into stacks of telephone books. Those fired at 7mm-Express velocities produced the greatest penetration. Bullets fired at reduced velocities, 7mm-08 equivalent, lacked sufficient energy for maximum penetration. Bullets fired at higher velocities, 7mm-Remington-Magnum equivalent, expanded too rapidly for maximum penetration. Apparently, the 7mm Express produces about optimum velocity for 140-grain conventional bullets for shooting telephone books. Experience shows it is a well-balanced combination for deer-sized animals. When I repeated the test with 160-grain premium bullets, maximum penetration was achieved at magnum velocities. Penetration can be increased by increasing both bullet weight and velocity, but only if the two variables are kept in reasonable balance.

The other easily controlled variable is point design. Bullets with large holes in the front ends of the jackets expand more rapidly than bullets with smaller holes. Bullets with large holes are said to "have a lot of lead showing." Round-nose bullets generally have larger holes than pointed bullets. All other factors being equal, round noses expand much more rapidly than pointed bullets. The often repeated recommendation that round-nosed bullets be used on very large animals is wrong.

Manufacturers have several options for reducing expansion and increasing penetration. They can thicken the jackets either uniformly or in stages, switch from pure, soft lead to harder alloys, and further reduce the size of the hole in the jacket.

So where does this leave the hunter who is trying to decide what ammunition to use? I reject both dogmatic views: Bullets should always exit or bullets should never exit. On broadside shots through the ribs, I believe bullets should almost always exit, and on all other body shots, bullets generally should not exit. I fear that bullets which fail to exit on rib shots have no reserve of mass and energy which is needed to reach the vital areas from the more difficult angles.

These dual criteria are more important than some traditional standards, such as weight retention and expansion. If bullets consistently break the shoulder bones of animals and devastate the lungs, I care little whether the recovered bullets retain fifty or ninety percent of their original weight or whether they have doubled their diameters.

Most American hunters have experience with small-diameter bullets on deer and they expect bullets to expand to double their original diameters. This is fine for deer, but it is an error to apply this criterion to larger-diameter bullets and larger animals. As an extreme example, a .45-caliber bullet that doubles its diameter would destroy too much meat on a deer or impala but would not provide sufficient penetration on much larger animals, like African buffalo.

The following bullets often meet both criteria for animals in the 400-to-800-pound class and are suitable for most African shooting:

.270	150 grain
.284/7mm	150 or 160 grain
.308	180 grain
.338	225 grain
.358	250 grain
.375	270 grain
.458	400 grain, heavy jackets

Cartridges and Bullets

This list should be used only as a starting point in selecting cartridges and bullets. The .270 Winchester and 7mm Express barely qualify as African rifles, then only with the best bullets. I had a 155-grain .270 bullet of European manufacture fail to exit on a rib shot on a kudu bull. The bullet did not even reach the far side of the rib cage. Other .270 bullets might be totally adequate.

Most hunters worry far too much about selection of cartridges and far too little about selection of bullets. A .270 Winchester loaded with good bullets is a far better kudu rifle than a 7mm or .300 magnum loaded with inadequate bullets.

The bullets listed above often meet my dual criteria for kudu, zebra, and other large plains game. They also will kill impala and other smaller animals reliably, but the results are not instantaneous, as we expect with lighter bullets. Since animals are less likely to show signs of being hit, all shots, even suspected misses, must be carefully investigated. Typically, impala hit with heavy bullets run from twenty-five to a hundred yards before falling.

For mixed species hunts, always base bullet selection on the largest animals. When velocity increases, as with magnum cartridges, bullet weight should be increased also. When in doubt, select the heavier bullets. Always go for reliability, rather than spectacular results.

My comments to this point apply to conventional big-game bullets. The partition bullets allow us to break some rules. The jackets of these bullets include partitions that separate the front halves of the lead cores from the back halves. Upon encountering resistance, the front halves expand quickly, but the back halves are securely locked in place. I have fired dozens of different conventional bullets into sand, soil, clay, and stacks of telephone books. Virtually every bullet tested disintegrated in the more severe test media, unless velocities were reduced greatly. But I cannot make a partition bullet fail. The recovered bullets show superb, if monotonous consistency. I have experimented with some, but not all, of the so-called "premium" bullets on the market. None of the others comes close to the performance of partition bullets.

Nosler partition bullets are available over the counter in .243 through .375 calibers. Several are available in factory ammunition from Federal and Weatherby. Partition bullets in .30 through .45 calibers are available from Swift Bullet Company in Quinter, KS. Several other ammunition manufacturers also include Swift bullets in their catalogs.

Solo Safari

With partition bullets, it is almost impossible to make a mistake in choosing bullet weights. For Alaskan moose or eland, the only suitable conventional bullets in .30 caliber are those weighing 200 or 220 grains. However, with partition bullets, any weight from 165 grains on up will get the job done, the heavier weights providing only slightly more penetration. I always use partition bullets for animals weighing over 400 pounds and for cartridges with muzzle velocities greater than 2,800 feet per second.

Now you must select a cartridge. Regrettably, logistics may weigh more heavily in your decision than ballistics. In the old days, hunters bound for Africa often packed three rifles and a shotgun. Airline regulations have changed all that. At best, you are allowed two weapons, typically two rifles or one rifle and one shotgun. You are limited to five kilograms (eleven pounds) of ammunition, so forget about carrying shotgun ammunition. Further, you must pack your weapons in one case and your ammunition in another, so it is possible that your rifles will arrive on time and your ammunition will arrive a couple of flights after you have disappeared into the bush. Best stick with common cartridges for which you can buy or beg ammunition in places like Maun, Lusaka, or Windhoek. That means 7mm Remington Magnum, .30-06, .375 H&H Magnum, and .458 Winchester Magnum, and for shotgun, 12-gauge only.

I believe that the .30-06 and 7mm Remington Magnum are the smallest cartridges that should be considered for general use in Africa. The .300-magnums or .338-magnums would be even better. These rifles should be equipped with low-power, fixed-power scopes.

Sixteen years ago, when I bought my first powerful magnum, my choice was between the .338 Winchester and the .375 H&H Magnum. Based on reduced recoil, increased velocity, and availability of lightweight rifles, I chose the .338. At that time, the largest partition bullets available were in .338. I figured a .338 with partition bullets would be more reliable than a .375 with standard bullets, a view I still hold. (Now, both Nosler and Swift produce partition bullets for the .375.) For American hunters, the .338 also has the advantage of being more useful in the Rocky Mountains and Alaska. The .338 immediately became my standard meat rifle.

When I began hunting the Zambezi Valley, I needed an impala rifle that could put down a rogue buffalo or elephant in an emergency. This requirement does not exist for sportsmen who are backed up by

Cartridges and Bullets

.458-toting professional hunters. Since I didn't have a backup, my impala rifle had to be capable of doing it all. In a pinch, I figured the absolute minimum was the .338.

Altogether, my .338 has felled several deer, six elk, more than a dozen impala, one leopard, and several larger antelope. A 250-grain Nosler once penetrated a four-inch mopane tree, then killed a 700-pound antelope. Don't try that with a 7mm magnum. With Nosler bullets, the .338 will reliably kill impala from any angle. The only disadvantage of the .338 is that ammunition is not widely available in Africa. Nevertheless, for ninety percent of African shooting, it's the cartridge I prefer.

For Big Game

Let's get serious. Africa is the continent of monstrous animals and monstrous guns. Buffalo, rhino, elephant, and hippo: .375s, .458s, .460s. On bent knee, and in a reverent frame of mind, we dare mention the great British cartridges: .470, .416, .505, and others. A ton or more of beast, a ten-pound rifle, 70-foot-pounds of recoil. This is the stuff that separates the strong from the weak, the brave from the timid.

As with cartridges for plains game, you must first decide which bullets are required, then select a cartridge that will deliver those bullets. Full-metal jacket or "solid" bullets are used for the world's largest game for two reasons. First, they produce maximum penetration needed for large, deep-bodied animals. Second, they offer greater reliability than softpoint bullets. Solids can smash through heavy bones and continue in straight lines to the vital organs hidden behind those bones. Well, sometimes they do and sometimes they don't.

The first solids were made of lead cores surrounded on the sides and over the noses by thick jackets of some tougher metal, usually copper alloys or nickel. These proved inadequate, especially when they hit heavy bones. The jackets deformed and broke open.

The second generation of solids had lead cores, tough steel jackets, and thin coatings of softer metals to prevent rusting and avoid damage to barrels. Many hunters believe that the British firm of Rigby produced the best solids the world has ever known, and the reputation of the .416 Rigby was due in great part to the excellence of the bullets. These bullets are no longer available.

Decades of experience have proven that wound channels of less than .36 caliber are ineffective in soft tissue unless velocities are high enough to cause damage by hydraulically transmitted shock waves. Decades ago, the U.S. Army abandoned .35 caliber handguns in favor of .45 caliber. The smaller caliber would not reliably stop enemy soldiers, even at close range. Police departments have come to the same conclusion. Their solution is to retain the .35 caliber (.38 Special or 9mm) but switch to hollow point bullets that expand rapidly.

The .375 H&H Magnum is the smallest cartridge that has proven successful with solid bullets against African game. Rigby tried to compete with its .350 Magnum, but the diameter was too small and it ultimately was rejected by hunters. In my experience, .338 solids are inadequate for game of any size and .375 solids are only marginally adequate. I don't know why this threshold occurs at .37 caliber but I suspect it may relate to the elastic limits of living tissue.

We have two ways of creating a .37 caliber wound channel. The preferred method is to begin with a bullet of smaller diameter but leave a hole at the front end of the jacket. Upon encountering resistance, the bullet deforms and the tip shortens up and expands, often doubling its original diameter. Therefore, even a 6mm (.243) bullet can exceed the .37 caliber threshold and kill effectively.

The smaller diameter bullets have many advantages. Due to their light weight, they can be fired at high velocities and their streamlined shapes retain velocity over long ranges. Upon impact, they automatically reform into short, fat projectiles that quickly expend their energy by creating large wound channels.

The other way of creating a large-diameter wound channel is to begin with a large diameter bullet. Given the lack of reliability of early expanding bullets, hunters of the very largest animals were forced to adopt this strategy. The manufacturers preexpanded the bullets to .37, .45, or larger calibers and attempted to impart total dependability by encasing the bullets in steel jackets. The flight characteristics of these bullets are poor, but the large beasts they are used on are generally shot at very close range.

Let's compare our expectations for solids, total dependability and deep penetration, with their actual performance. Dependability tradi-

Cartridges and Bullets

tionally is judged by the appearance of the bullets after they are recovered from animals. Solids should show no deformation and should be unmarked, except for the rifling grooves. About two-thirds of the steel-jacketed solids I have recovered meet these criteria. About a third show some deformity, often at the bases where the jackets are weakest. A solid recovered from the shoulder of a friend's hippo was badly deformed. The jacket was intact but the tip had flattened and mushroomed (riveted) like a softpoint bullet. The .375 bullet did not break the bone and did not enter the rib cage. I personally have not seen a solid completely break into fragments, but it occasionally happens. This, of course, is totally unacceptable.

Some hunters claim that even the slightest deformity will cause a bullet to veer off course, to turn a corner, rather than punch through to the internal organs aimed at by the marksman. Therefore, any deformities are thought to indicate unacceptable performance.

I believe, however, that the criterion of recovered flawless bullets is unrealistic and unnecessary. Why do solids deform? Not because they hit skin, muscle and blood. They deform when they hit heavy bone. Why do solids veer off course? Surely not due to deformities alone.

Three things can occur when a solid hits bone. First, there is a great chance that it will deflect and assume a new trajectory. When this happens in air, we say the bullet has ricocheted. Second, the bullet may tumble or "keyhole." I have examined the tiny marks etched on the copper coatings of many recovered solids. Some marks appear to begin at the base of the bullets and range forward, indicating that the bullets were traveling backwards, and others run from left to right or right to left. I am convinced that most solids which hit bone lose stability and tumble. This, I believe, is a major reason solids veer off course. If a solid is traveling through flesh with its long axis rotated forty-five degrees to the left, the bullet will veer left.

I also have noticed that most deformities occur at the bases of solids where the steel jackets are open. The front end of the steel jackets are arches which can withstand tremendous forces. A force applied to the front end would not deform the base of the bullet. The frequent deformities at the base could occur only because the bullets were traveling sideways or backwards, which would expose the bases to greater forces.

Third, the bullet may be deformed by the bone. This could throw the bullet further off course, but the effect generally would be minor compared with the effects of deflection and tumbling.

Now for the second criterion of solid performance, depth of penetration. Solids can penetrate up to two-and-a-half times farther than softpoint bullets, but the penetration of solids is very inconsistent. I once shot a wounded buffalo in the buttocks with a .458 Winchester. The 500-grain solid stopped next to the fifth rib, after penetrating about five feet of muscle, intestines, and lungs. Another solid stopped in less than three feet after chipping a light bone projecting from the spine. Why the difference? Of course the small bone soaked up some energy, but the big difference is that the bullet tumbled off the bone. Traveling sideways, a solid creates a wound channel with a huge cross-sectional area, about equal to a softpoint bullet which has doubled its diameter.

Solids sometimes penetrate far more than softpoints, but sometimes the difference is measured in inches rather than in feet. Solids so frequently fail both criteria, dependability and penetration, that we must seek alternatives.

Solids became popular among African hunters years ago when softpoints were notoriously unreliable, but today's best softpoints have been improved tremendously. I'm referring, of course, to partition bullets I described in detail in the previous chapter. The worst problem with solids, their tendency to tumble, rarely occurs with softpoints. Long bullets tend to be less stable than short bullets because the point of resistance is farther from the center of mass. When a soft-nose bullet hits flesh, it immediately begins to mushroom and shorten up. The point of resistance moves back toward the center of mass and the bullet remains stable and continues to travel point on. Because softpoints remain stable, they tend to penetrate in straight lines. Good softpoint bullets, such as partition bullets, are tops in consistency and reliability.

I once believed that a .45-caliber solid would be more effective than, say, a 7mm bullet which expands to .45 caliber. The bigger slug creates a big wound channel from end to end, while the expanding bullet starts out small and doesn't achieve .45 caliber until it is almost out of energy. Experience in the field does not confirm my earlier hypothesis. Given reasonable matches between the size of the expanding bullets and the size of the animal, the smaller expanding bullets performed better than larger solid bullets. Perhaps the jagged edges of expanding bullets cut or tear the flesh more than smooth, solid bullets.

270

Cartridges and Bullets

Cape buffalo sit on the dividing line. Most hunters use softs for smaller animals and solids for larger animals, but they argue endlessly about buffalo. The growing trend, which I often follow myself, is to initially load a softpoint in the chamber and solids in the magazine. The first shot is well-chosen and well-aimed, so softpoint bullets are appropriate. Follow-up shots must be taken as they come, from any angle, so solids are preferable. When following wounded buffalo, most hunters load solids from the top down. This is the best procedure when only conventional bullets are available. Nevertheless, if partition bullets are available, I would use nothing else on buffalo, wounded or unwounded.

The problem is with hippo, white rhino, and elephant. These animals require more penetration than any expanding bullet can produce, so we must use solids and hope they do not lose stability and tumble. The secret is to shoot for the brain or behind the shoulder, never through the shoulder.

What can designers of solids do to improve their performance? We now have a third generation of solids made of solid masses of bronze or similar metal. These are so hard that they absolutely will not deform. I've shot five .375 caliber, 300-grain bronze bullets into buffalo and recovered four. Every one came out looking perfect.

But deformation is not the problem. The problem is stability. Bronze is lighter than lead, so bronze bullets of equal weight must be longer, therefore less stable. Bronze bullets are more likely to tumble, and when they tumble, their increased length causes excessively large wound channels and reduced penetration. Recall that I recovered four of five bronze solids fired into buffalo. Solids generally should shoot through buffalo. An eighty percent recovery rate indicates lack of penetration. This development is going in the wrong direction.

How could we make solids more stable? We could either reduce their length or increase their rate of spin. The rate of twist of rifle barrels is determined by the requirements for stabilizing bullets during their flights through the atmosphere. Whether or not increasing the rate of spin would have a significant effect on bullet stability in flesh and bone I cannot say.

I am more confident suggesting that some solids are too long and heavy. My hunch is that the .375 caliber, 300-grain bullets; .416 caliber, 400-grain bullets; and .470 caliber, 500-grain bullets have about the right ratio of diameter to weight, that is sectional density. But the .458 caliber, 500-grain bullets; .338 caliber, 250-grain bullets; and 30-caliber, 220-grain bullets are too long and therefore tend toward instability on impact. A better weight for .458-caliber, steel-jacketed solids would be about 460 grains. A lighter, shorter bullet would be a blessing for those who reload the .458 Winchester, because the longer bullets use too much case capacity that is woefully lacking in this cartridge.

The manufacturers of bronze solids recognize the problem of excessive length and instability, so they offer a 400-grain, bronze solid for the .458. Great! But a 400-grain, steel-jacketed solid would be even better.

The minimum standard for the largest game was established in the first half of this century and summarized by John "Pondoro" Taylor in his classic book, *African Rifles & Cartridges*. The prescription is .45 caliber, 500-grain bullets, and 5000 foot-pounds of energy. Anything less is a compromise. Anything more is a macho display. Now that many ordinary citizens own chronographs for measuring bullet velocities, the secret is out. The British cartridges rarely reached their advertised velocities. In truth, energy levels were often closer to 4500 or even 4000 foot-pounds. In reality, the British standard was closer to these figures. The standard was met by a host of rimmed cartridges designed for use in double-barreled rifles. Most common were the .450 with the three-and-a-quarter-inch case, the .465, and the great .470. Exceeding the British standard were the .500, .577, and .600. Surprisingly, the Brits never designed a rimless cartridge for magazine rifles around the standard. The .416 Rigby fell short in diameter while the .505 Gibbs exceeded the standard in every criteria.

The British double-barreled rifles perhaps were and are the best rifles the world will ever see. Now the Brits produce only a few dozen annually and they cost as much as a thirty-day safari. Today most doubles, including the less expensive ones, are made on the Continent.

I recently visited the Bretta showroom located in Alexandria, Virginia, just a few miles from my home. I had the rare opportunity to examine their .470 double and I fell in love. Its eleven pounds rested so perfectly between by hands that it felt no heavier than a 20-gauge shotgun. It was sleek and it had the right curves and it felt like it belonged at my shoulder. I checked my savings account and found that I had just enough money to pay the sales tax.

If you can afford to buy a double and still afford a safari, do it. Due to problems with standardization and availability of ammunition, don't consider anything except the .470.

Cartridges and Bullets

Most of us must use less expensive magazine rifles. The only rimless cartridge designed around the British standard is the .458 Winchester Magnum. It is built on the Winchester short magnum case which functions in the short Model 70 action. This short case has limited powder capacity which has plagued this cartridge.

The history of .458 ammunition is difficult to reconstruct. When Winchester introduced the .458 in 1956, they loaded the ammunition to high velocities and the cartridge and rifle won quick approval. Advertised velocity for the 500-grain bullet was 2130 feet per second (fps) with 5040 foot-pounds of energy. Then Winchester backed off the velocity and the .458 failed to reach the brain on frontal shots at elephants. When fired from the stubby 22-inch barrel on the Model 70, the 500-grain bullet limped along at 1900 fps and energy fell to 4000 foot-pounds. The reputation of the .458 was ruined.

Today, Winchester advertises 2040 fps and 4620 foot-pounds. I've checked the recent ammunition over a chronograph. With a 24-inch barrel, the advertisement is right on. I make my own ammunition using Reloader Number 7 powder. I can reach 2045 fps with a 500-grain bullet with moderate chamber pressure.

Some professional hunters continue to bad-mouth the .458 Winchester, but professional hunters are notorious for their lack of sophistication in ballistics. If a cartridge let them down twenty years ago, they will refuse to use it ever again. To date, I've taken one elephant, four buffalo, and several smaller animals with the .458 Winchester. I have absolutely no doubts about the adequacy of the cartridge.

Mike LaGrange worked for the Zimbabwe Department of Wildlife and National Parks and culled over 6000 elephants, more than any other man who has ever lived. In his book, *Ballistics in Perspective*, he confirms that some earlier ammunition was inferior and failed on frontal brain shots on elephants. Today, LaGrange prefers the .458 over all other cartridges, if he can obtain custom-made ammunition loaded to full velocity.

The Winchester 510-grain, softpoint bullet has contributed to the poor reputation of the .458 Winchester. This bullet has a thin jacket and a big hole in the front end of the jacket. It expands very rapidly, which makes it an excellent bullet for lion, but it will not hold together when thrown against the shoulder bones of buffalo.

The 500-grain Hornady has a thicker jacket and a smaller hole at the front end. I've taken two buffalo with this bullet with excellent results. Mike LaGrange confirms the adequacy of this bullet for buffalo. Fortunately, it is available in factory ammunition. The Remington 510-grain softpoint is, in fact, the 500-grain Hornady. This gives consumers an excellent choice. Use the Winchester softpoint for lion and the Remington brand for buffalo. If you want to simplify your inventory, go with the Hornady/Remington all the way.

Okay, the .458 may be a bit shy on penetration with solid bullets for frontal brain shots on elephants and for raking shots at wounded buffalo. We might solve this problem by taking a giant step to the .460 Weatherby Magnum. This monster hurls a 500-grain bullet at 2700 fps for 8095 foot-pounds of energy. However, both the cartridge and the Weatherby rifles have drawbacks. Noise and recoil are atrocious and very few bullets, whether softpoint or solid, can hold together at this energy level. The Mark V rifle is too light, too long, has too thin a stock, holds only two rounds in the magazine, and is impossible to reload in a hurry.

I took a .460 to Africa in 1988, but I loaded the ammunition to a more reasonable 2300 fps for 5900 foot-pounds. It performed well on elephant and stopped a charging buffalo.

The search for a more effective .458 has led to a host of wildcat cartridges, including one that makes sense. The .458 Lott uses the long .375 H&H case with the sidewalls straightened out to accept .458 bullets. It is a .458 Winchester stretched out, just like the .357 Magnum is a stretched out 38 Special. Ballistics of the .458 Lott are about equal to my downloaded .460. The tremendous advantage of the .458 Lott is that it will accept standard .458 Winchester ammo, just like the .357 Magnum will accept 38 Special ammo. So if your .458 Lott arrives in Dar es Salam and your ammo doesn't, you can pick up a box of standard .458 Winchester ammo and complete your safari. For those wanting more oomph than the .458 Winchester can offer, the .458 Lott is the best alternative.

The latest craze is cartridges in .416 caliber. Several wildcats have received a lot of publicity. Federal and Ruger revived the .416 Rigby by introducing factory-made ammunition and rifles, respectively. Remington then introduced its own .416 cartridge followed, quickly by Weatherby. All are potent cartridges and all exceed the energy level of today's factory .458 Winchester. All will handle buffalo, hippo, rhino, and elephant very nicely. Federal, Remington, and Weatherby all use custom-made bullets, and these superior bullets will enhance the reputations of all three .416 cartridges. These high-energy, smaller-diameter bullets will penetrate well and outperform the .458 on frontal brain shots on elephant and raking shots at buffalo.

A viable alternative is .416, but it cannot be my first choice. Animals are not killed by penetration but by the transfer of destructive energy to vital organs. In ninety percent of all situations involving solid bullets, a .458 transfers energy more efficiently than a .416. For every buffalo you shoot in the buttocks, you will shoot ten in the chest. Both .458 and .416 solids will exit the chest, but the .458 will shed more energy and destroy more vital tissue on the way through. Sure it would be good to reliably reach the lungs of an outbound buffalo. I'm more concerned about the incoming buffalo, those that are about to nail me to a mopane tree. I want bullets that will shed energy in the front half of the animal.

The correct brain shot for elephants is from the side. Bullets of either .416 or .458 caliber will easily exit from the side of the head. John Taylor claimed that, if the brain is missed, the larger-caliber bullet is more likely to stun the elephant, allowing time for a second shot.

Okay, you've really muffed it and now you must take that last desperate shot, the frontal brain shot on a charging elephant, and all you have is a sniveling .458 Winchester. Chances are the bullet will reach the brain. If not, the beast probably will be stunned and fall flat on its nose. Failing that, it probably will turn away. Or maybe your professional hunter, tracker, or buddy will get in a shot. You want absolute guarantees? Then invest in U.S. Government bonds and stay out of Africa. Sure, a .416 would pulverize the brain, unless you short-stroke the action and click on an empty chamber, highly possible with the longer .416 actions. Or you might hiccup just as you press the trigger and put a .416 bullet through your elephant's ear. There are no guarantees. We must play the odds and, in most situations, probability favors the larger caliber.

Anything less than .45 caliber is a compromise, and that is precisely why some will select the .416. Some hunters will top off a .416 with a scope and use it for all game. In chapter 24, Alex Alexakos described the effectiveness of his .416 for buffalo and for a 110-yard, offhand shot at a hartebeest.

For smaller animals, the 400-grain bullets and higher velocities offer some advantage over the slower, heavier .458 bullets. A scope-sighted .458 is ballistically suitable for about eighty percent of all

Solo Safari

African shooting. A scoped .416, due to its flatter trajectory, would be ballistically suitable for about ninety percent of all situations. Big deal! The only reasons I don't use a scoped .458 as an all-around rifle are recoil and weight. Since the .416s recoil as much as the .458, they should weigh as much. Where's the advantage?

The revival for the .416s was spurred by professional hunters. It might be a good compromise for them, but it is not the best compromise for most sportsmen.

If a safari consisted of ten buffalo and one impala, the .416 would be a good compromise for the sportsmen, but safaris aren't like that. A more typical safari involves ten antelope and one buffalo. If you want a compromise cartridge, the .375 H&H Magnum is better suited to most safaris.

With a 300-grain bullet at 2600 fps, the .375 produces far less recoil than the .458 or .416s. With its reduced recoil and flatter trajectory, the .375 is the largest cartridge that can be considered for long-range, precision shooting. I once excised the heart from a sable antelope, with witnesses, at three hundred long paces. With various .375s, I have taken a couple of truckloads of plains game ranging from duiker at thirty pounds to zebra at 650 pounds, as well as thirteen buffalo. I would not hesitate to hunt any animal, anywhere in the world, with a scoped .375. It seldom would be my first choice, but it would get the job done.

There is a growing consensus that the .375 is a bit light for buffalo and larger game. However, most professional hunters would prefer that their clients use .375s rather than larger calibers. The reason is simple. Most clients can't shoot the big boomers well, and a .375 through the lungs is superior to a .458 through the knee. Clients shoot better with the .375 because they have less fear of recoil and because .375s are more frequently equipped with scopes, which greatly improve accuracy. Because .375s hurt less, casual shooters are more likely to practice with them.

I've taken more than fifty animals with the .375, and the more I use the cartridge, the less I like it. Performance on buffalo is marginal. Sometimes it kills as quickly as a .458, and sometimes it fails badly. Four buffalo hit with a .458 ran an average of thirty-five yards before dying. Thirteen buffalo hit with a .375 ran an average of 103 yards before dying, three times farther. This average does not include two buffalo hit with a .375 but never recovered, despite hours of searching. Most interesting

Cartridges and Bullets

buffalo stories begin with reference to a .375. Sure, a .375 to the chest is more effective than a .458 to the knee. So what? I shoot a .458 as well as a .375, so why not use the more effective cartridge?

I believe the .375 is adequate for buffalo provided three conditions are met. First, .375s should be equipped with low-power, fixed-power scopes. Three power is ideal. The .375 just doesn't do the job with marginal bullet placements, and a scope will help you drill the bullets between the sixth and seventh ribs. Second, you should use the very best bullets available, and that means Swift or Nosler partition bullets. Finally, the .375 should be backed up by a heavier gun.

For animals under 700 pounds, and that includes almost everything, the .375 does not kill as quickly as a .300 or .338 magnum. The smaller, higher-velocity bullets cause more hemorrhaging and quicker death. Many professional hunters will disagree with me on this, but these are the same guys who recommend 220-grain, .30-06 bullets for impala. If they have trouble killing zebra with a .30-06, they switch to a .375. If this fails, they try a .458. Within reasonable limits, a better solution for small and medium game is to increase velocity. I've wounded and lost more game with the .375 than with all other cartridges combined.

Why is the .375 a ballistic underachiever? Does it violate some rule of physics? Of course not, but there may be a problem with .375 bullets. For animals under 700 pounds, we need lighter bullets. All my experience with the .375 is with 300-grain bullets, the only weight available in Botswana. Bullets weighing 270 grains are available in the U.S., but I believe even these are a bit heavy. Swift offers a 250-grain partition bullet I would like to try.

In criticizing the .375, I really am arguing for more specialized rifles. A .338 and a .458, in combination, will outperform a .375, but that assumes you have the money to buy two rifles and the means of getting them both to Africa. The dual advantages of the .375, moderate recoil and unequaled versatility, cannot be denied. The .375 is and will always be the most useful single cartridge in Africa.

The Weatherby version of the .375 is called a .378. It fires the same bullets at much higher velocities. Bullet performance is a serious problem with the .378, as is excessive penetration. However, the Weatherby Mark V rifle is the only American-made, left-handed monster masher. A left-handed hunter could buy a factory Mark V in .378

or .416 caliber, then load the ammunition down to velocities a smidgen above those obtained with standard cartridges.

If you take two rifles to Africa, they should be selected to provide flexibility without duplication. Bullets for the lighter rifle should weigh about half as much as bullets for the big gun. If the big gun is a .375, it would balance nicely with a .30-06 or 7mm magnum. The .375 should be used for the big stuff including eland, kudu, and zebra. Take plenty of ammo for the .375. As a matter of practicality, you probably will use it for almost everything.

If the big gun is .45 caliber or larger, it could be matched with a .338 or possibly a .300 magnum. The big gun would be used only for buffalo and larger game and the .338 would be used for all the antelope. I've coupled a .338 with a .458 on two safaris and consider this combination nearly perfect.

BIG RIFLES

Rifles for use in Africa must be built to the highest standards. Heavy recoil can literally tear a rifle apart unless it is strongly reinforced. Most deer hunters don't realize their rifles are only 99 percent dependable. Their rifles jam one time in a hundred, usually during practice. No big deal. When my .458 jams, even on the range, I break out in a cold sweat. If a rifle jams once, it could jam again, perhaps when an angry buffalo is at ten yards and closing. No rifle ever built is 100 percent dependable, but the African rifle must come as close as possible.

The recoil of big-bore rifles causes a special problem that most manufacturers deny but that experienced African hands know well. The problem is split stocks. In bolt-action rifles, recoil is transmitted to the stock by the recoil lug which is located fore of the magazine. As the recoil lug pushes backward, the wood to the left and right of the magazine is forced outward, and the stock splits. The first spilt occurs on the block of wood between the trigger and magazine. The next split occurs at the tang.

The best solution is to add two crossbolts, one fore of the magazine and one between the magazine and the trigger. It also is preferable to add a second recoil lug ahead of the usual one and bed both in fiberglass. For many years, the only American-made .458 with all these features was the Winchester Model 70. All others split. Several years ago, Remington began reinforcing their stocks and I believe they are now adequate. The other possible solution is a synthetic stock.

Solo Safari

My Ruger M77 in .458 split after about eighty rounds. I noticed the split in my Weatherby .460 after three rounds, but I assume the split occurred on the first shot. Both rifles came with one crossbolt, so I've added a second crossbolt to each.

Before shooting a new boomer, it is essential that you tighten all the screws holding the stock to the metal. This will greatly reduce the probability of splitting. Under recoil, the metal presses itself into the wood, causing the screws to loosen. They should be retightened after ten rounds, again after thirty rounds, and periodically thereafter.

As they feed from the magazine into the chamber, the .458 cartridges tend to hang up. Most modern cartridges have a bottleneck design, and the shoulder of the case guides the cartridge into the chamber. The .458 has no shoulder, so the nose of the bullet guides the cartridge. Any slight burr on the feeding ramp will bite into the noses of the bullets, especially into the exposed lead of softpoint bullets, and prevent the cartridges from passing into the chamber.

The entire area around the feeding ramp must be polished. Then feed a hundred cartridges from the magazine into the chamber, feeding from both the left and right sides of the magazine. This test should be done with the Winchester 510-grain, softpoint bullet which has a lot of lead showing at the tip. If this bullet feeds well, the rifle is okay. If even one cartridge in a hundred jams, have the rifle fixed or sell it to someone you don't like.

Let's be realistic about recoil. It hurts and it causes flinching. Anyone who claims to enjoy shooting a .458 is a liar or a masochist or both. Still, many serious shooters can learn to shoot a .458 as well as a .30-06. Even they need relief.

First, any big boomer should be heavy. The Winchester Model 70 in .458, with its twenty-two-inch, buggy-whip barrel, is too light. A .458 should weigh nine-and-a-half to ten pounds. A guy bragged to me about his custom-made, seven-pound .458. He said he has to take a step backward with every shot to keep from being knocked down by the recoil. This is absurd and dangerous. How can you reload quickly if you are walking around backward, especially if you trip on a log, a rock, or your tracker?

If you have trouble carrying a ten-pound rifle for eight hours, the solution is not to reduce the weight of the rifle. The solution is to buy a set of dumbbells and tone up your shoulder, neck, and arm muscles.

Big Rifles

Even a ten-pound .458 or .416 hurts. First, it should be fitted with a soft recoil pad. The next possible step is a recoil arrester at the muzzle, but these devices have both advantages and disadvantages. They reduce felt recoil noticeably. Nonetheless, because they divert escaping gas back toward the shooter, they increase muzzle blast. Those standing beside the rifle, such as your professional hunter and tracker, can suffer a severe auditory beating. Some muzzle brakes are aesthetically displeasing and some add length to the barrel without improving ballistic performance. I've used and like the Mag-Na-Port, which avoids most of these problems. Another good possibility is the KDF muzzle break that screws off. You use it on the range, where recoil is felt severely and where you wear hearing protection. When hunting, you hardly feel recoil so the KDF brake can be removed.

Every shooter has a different threshold of pain. I generally would not want a muzzle break on a .458 Winchester, but would want it on larger cartridges. Others will draw the line elsewhere.

However, a special problem arises when you mount a scope on the big gun. A recoiling scope can smack you in the eyebrow, causing a cut that needs four to seven stitches to close. Real men have no fear of "magnum eyebrows," but these injuries lead to several problems. First, since the wound is above the eye, blood flows into it, obstructing vision for any follow-up shots. Second, you typically loose three days of precious hunting time traveling to and from a hospital and searching for a doctor to sew you up. Third, if you have a really hard skull, it could damage the scope. A muzzle break does not eliminate the possibility of magnum eyebrow, but it reduces the probability. I know a chap who parted his eyebrow with a 7mm magnum.

Never shoot a scoped boomer with a stock that is too short. This almost guarantees a magnum eyebrow. I'm a bit taller than the average American, so I add an eighth of an inch to most of my stocks, but I like to add a quarter inch to my big-bore rifles.

Rifles built around the .375 present fewer problems. With luck, you might get by with less reinforcing of the stocks, and .375s tend to feed more smoothly than .458s. Those who are less sensitive to recoil can consider a lighter weight .375, especially if it is equipped with a muzzle brake.

Most guys put scopes on their .375s and use open sights on their .458s, but there is no firm rule on this. I prefer scopes on all my rifles. Most Americans use far too much scope. My favorite is a two-and-a-half- or three-power-wide field with four-plex crosshairs. Variable scopes do not hold up as well under heavy recoil and should not be used.

Every big-bore rifle should be equipped with open sights. Even the best, simplest scopes and mounts succumb to recoil or the constant bashing in safari cars and might have to be removed unexpectedly.

I dislike the shallow V rear sights, which are traditional on African rifles. In clutch situations, I tend to shoot high with all open sights, but the tendency is even worse with the shallow V sights. I prefer a coarse U at the rear, with vertical sides, and a flat-topped post up front.

Safari rifles traditionally have one standing rear sight set for a hundred yards, and two folding leaves set for 200 and 300 yards. These are useless and are potentially dangerous. About one time in five when you raise the rifle for a shot, you will find that the folding leaves have been accidently flipped up. You lose about three seconds reaching up to knock them down. Or, if you fail to notice them, your shot will go high. Folding leaves should be removed or epoxied in the down position. If you must borrow a rifle, tape the folding leaves down.

Traditional safari rifles also have deep magazines holding four or five rounds in addition to one in the chamber. These are unnecessary and undesirable. It is very unlikely that you will ever need to fire more than four rounds without having an opportunity to reload. Suppose you load one round in the chamber and five in the magazine, for a total of six rounds. The round in the bottom of the magazine will have been hammered five times by recoil before it is loaded into the chamber, even more if you reloaded during the shooting sequence. Under recoil, the front wall of the magazine hammers the point of the bullet, often driving the bullet back into the case until it contacts the powder. If the case was nearly full of powder, there will be little movement of the bullet and no problems will result.

However, I encountered serious problems with South African-made .375 ammunition. The mouths of the cases were heavily crimped into cannelures having square edges. The crimps held, forcing the necks of the cases to bulge out just below the mouths. The bulges prevented the cartridges from entering the chamber. After that, when hunting plains game, I loaded only one round in the magazine and one in the chamber. When hunting dangerous game, I loaded only three cartridges in the chamber and rotated the cartridges through the magazine. To reload, I emptied the magazine and put fresh rounds in the bottom, then put the hammered rounds on top and in the chamber. In this way, no round was hammered more than three or four times.

Big Rifles

Under heavy recoil, the front sling stud can rake the index finger of the left hand, tearing the skin open. During the 1990 hunting season in Botswana, the wound on my left index finger was reopened every weekend for about four months, leaving a small permanent scar. The best solution is to mount the sling stud on a barrel band forward of the fore-end. My solution is to always carry a couple of bandaids in my wallet.

Shooting the Big Guns

So you've finally come face to face with your masochistic tendencies. You've admitted to yourself that you want to shoot a big gun. Now you have to deal with two questions. First, how do you break the news of this psychological imbalance to your loved ones? Second, how do you shoot the boomers without developing a flinch and ruining your marksmanship? Since I'm not a psychologist, I will deal only with the latter question.

Not jerking the trigger on a .458 is like not gripping the armrest on the dentist's chair during a root canal procedure. Both are possible, but both require concentration.

People differ in their reactions to recoil. Three shotgunners can shoot a round of skeet, twenty-five shots. The next day, one will have a black-and-blue shoulder, one will have no discoloration but will have a sore shoulder, and the third will experience no reaction whatever. I fall into the middle category, suggesting that I am more sensitive to recoil than most. Yet, I routinely shoot one-to-two-inch groups at one hundred yards with the .458 Winchester and larger cartridges. If I can do it, the majority of shooters should be able to manage also.

The critical variable is not the reaction of the shoulder but the reaction of the mind. Shooting a shoulder cannon requires a lot of "want to."

Circumstances make a big difference. In chapter 15, I described how I rapid-fired four .458s into a buffalo and never felt a thing. Rapid-fire four .458s at the rifle range and you will need four codeine tablets and a half day of bed rest.

Take a seven-pound, 12-gauge shotgun to the range along with five rounds of three-inch ammunition with the full one-and-seven-eighths ounce of lead. Set up a stationary target and carefully aim the shotgun, squeezing the trigger as though you were shooting a rifle. If you can do that five times without flinching, you can shoot a .375 H&H Magnum. The fact that you can shoot fifteen rounds of three-inch ammunition from a goose pit is irrelevant. The circumstance is different.

When shooting the big guns, I first give myself the design advantages described in the previous chapter. Then, I find that I must prepare my shoulder. If I haven't shot for several months and then dump six or eight rounds through a .458, my shoulder suffers badly. I try to avoid the big bores until about ten weeks before I leave for Africa. At A minus ten (Africa minus ten weeks), I shoot one round of trap or skeet. This is simply a fun way to begin to toughen up my shoulder. At A minus nine, I shoot two rounds of skeet. At A minus eight, I sight in my .338 and allow maybe two rounds through a .458. At A minus seven, I allow four or five rounds with the .458 and try to maintain this level every week until departure. After conditioning my shoulder, I can shoot five or six rounds from a bench with no soreness.

I have no notion of what is happening here. Perhaps there are physiological changes in my shoulder. Perhaps it is all psychological. I know only that this procedure works for me. The conditioning process now takes half as long as it did ten years ago when I bought my first .458.

Every time I shoot a shoulder cannon, I also shoot a group or two with my .25-06. This rifle is super accurate and it never throws a flyer unless I jerk the trigger. It immediately discloses even a slight tendency toward flinching.

I often hear that shooters feel more recoil when shooting from a bench than when shooting from kneeling or offhand positions. It is true that recoil is felt more severely whenever you lean forward, as you do when shooting from a prone position or from a low bench. The secret, when shooting from a bench, is to stack enough sandbags under the rifle to bring the body to a vertical position. Then you can rock back with the recoil. Even when shooting from a bench, you should grip the fore-end with the left hand and rest the hand on the sandbags.

You will quickly learn to pad the elbows to keep them from being scraped across the bench. Always rest several minutes between shots. The pain from the first shot should subside completely before firing the next shot. When sighting in a new rifle or checking a new handload, it is necessary to shoot ten or more rounds at one sitting. For long shooting sessions, I insert a sandbag or a twenty-five-pound bag of lead shot between the rifle butt and my shoulder.

Big Rifles

All magnums produce a lot of noise, and muzzle brakes multiply the problem. On the range, I wear both custom-fitted earplugs and earmuffs. The earplugs take up almost no space in my luggage, so they go to Africa for use when checking the sights.

Have you ever shot skeet on a hot day? With every shot, your sweat-slippery glasses fall down on your nose, making it impossible to fire a quick second shot. This is an irritation on the range. In Africa, with a rifle producing double the recoil of a skeet gun, the loss of glasses could lead to disaster. Elastic bands attached to the bows are okay, but if you are a serious shooter, you need a more permanent solution.

I've tried every conceivable type of eyeglass frame, including some really ugly-looking athletic glasses. The best are conventional plastic frames with the old-fashioned bows that hook behind the ear. Thin wire bows are no good, only plastic is stiff enough. Unfortunately, plastic bows are not being manufactured at this time, so we have to choose between athletic frames and conventional glasses fitted with elastic bands.

If you use a scope, the recoil of a big gun will push the scope into the bill of your hat. If the bill is stiff, the scope knocks your hat off, which is almost as distracting as losing your glasses. Baseball caps, cowboy hats, and other hard-brimmed headgear are unacceptable. Your professional hunter wears a slouch hat with a soft brim. The scope still hits the brim, but doesn't knock the hat off.

We must realize that recoil is largely a psychological problem. If an athlete can convince himself that he can run a mile in four minutes, he probably will do it. If you really want to join the small group of shooters who can shoot a .458, you probably will succeed.

The problem with American shooters is that they grew up with .243s and .270s and they think a .30-06 is a heck of a big cartridge. Show up at the gun club with a .338 and you are treated with reverence. Boys growing up in Africa are not aware of these psychological barriers. When they get a little hair on their chins, they learn to drive a Land Cruiser and shoot a .458. There is no mystique about big guns in Africa.

Still, everyone has his threshold of pain. If you have trouble with a .458, have a muzzle brake installed, or drop back to a .375. If the .375 hurts you too badly, put a muzzle brake on it. If you cannot shoot a .375 with a muzzle brake, trade it for an easy chair. Quit punishing yourself and begin enjoying life.

Solo Safari

Bullet Placement

The best bullet and most powerful cartridge will not quickly kill a thirty-pound duiker unless the bullet hits a vital organ. With proper bullets, a shot through the lungs, just behind the shoulder, will kill any animal that walks on dry land. Head and neck shots are for inexperienced braggarts. With only a few exceptions, we experienced braggarts shoot for the biggest target, the lungs. Africans and Americans tend to disagree on how to reach the lungs.

In America, we eat most venison ourselves, so we do not want a lot of bloodshot meat. Therefore, most Americans aim to the place the bullet behind the shoulder, not through the shoulder. Africa has meat in abundance, so the white African shoots his animals through the shoulder, takes the tenderloins for himself, and gives the bloodshot meat to the blacks.

Even if we ignore the aesthetic qualities of bloodshot meat, the shoulder shot just doesn't make sense. The bullet wastes too much energy on muscle and bone, neither of which is immediately essential to life. Look at the rib cage of an animal. It is very wide behind the shoulders, but narrows considerably between the shoulders. Most of the lungs are located well aft of the shoulder bones. A bullet through the shoulder just clips the front edge of the lungs. It is far better to place the bullet behind the shoulder where the lungs are much wider.

A possible exception should be made when using solid bullets. A solid through the lungs will not cause much immediate hemorrhaging. Nevertheless, a solid that breaks the shoulder bone may carry bone splinters into the lungs and these will cause more rapid blood loss. Also, the solid may tumble off the bone. If it is traveling sideways, it will destroy more lung tissue.

Because Africans shoot through the shoulder, they use heavy bullets, such as 220-grain .30-06 bullets. Along comes an American with a box of 180s. He sees a 650-pound kudu. His professional hunter insists that he aim at the shoulder. The bullet fails. It is best to stick with bullet weights that work well for equivalent-sized American game and aim behind the shoulder, despite what your professional hunter says. Any discrepancies between his advice and the holes in the hide can be blamed on the wind, the light, or bad shooting. "Damn if my aim wasn't off ten inches. Lucky the bull fell dead in five yards."

Big Rifles

A problem arises when animals are quartering toward you. Then you have no choice except the shoulder. The solution is to use partition bullets. If you use enough gun, these bullets will get through.

Hippo nearly always must be taken through the brain with solid bullets. If they are in the water, the brain is the only available target. If they are on land, they typically are within ten yards of water, so they must be dropped immediately before they escape to water. On land, follow-up shots must be placed behind the shoulder, never through the shoulder. The hide and shoulder muscles on hippo are too thick and the bones are too heavy to allow passage of any bullet.

More than any other animal, buffalo require a careful match between bullet performance and bullet placement. The conventional wisdom is to place a solid through the shoulder or a softpoint behind the shoulder. The problem is that buffalo are very uncooperative. If you load with softpoints, the buffalo stand quarter to, presenting a shoulder. If you load solids, they stand broadside, exposing their ribs. As always, the solution is partition bullets which perform well from any reasonable angle. The Hornady or Remington 500-grain bullet fired from a .458 Winchester also will suffice.

Many hunters claim that the heart of a buffalo is lower in the chest than in other species. Therefore you should aim lower. In truth, the heart of a buffalo lies in the exact same place as in other animals, low in the chest, sitting atop the sternum. The secret to finding the heart in any animal is to measure up from the sternum, never down from the withers.

I've never understood why anyone would shoot for the heart when the lungs offer five or six times more target area. If you aim for the lungs and the shot goes low, you might hit the heart. If you aim for the heart and shot hits low, you get a leg and an angry professional hunter. For most animals, a softpoint bullet through the lungs kills as quickly as one through the heart. I've read that elephants die more quickly from heart shots than from lung shots. This probably is because everyone uses solids on elephants and solids are rather ineffective on lung shots.

Elephants have a unique shape that causes many errors in bullet placement. The front of the brain is protected by thick bone, so the frontal brain shot is notoriously unreliable. It should never be attempted on unwounded elephants. If the wind is in your favor, move around for a side brain shot. If the wind is unfavorable, either wait for the wind to change or for the elephant to move, or find another elephant. If an elephant charges, you have no alternative but the frontal brain shot. Aim for a line drawn between the eyes or just a bit above it. Good luck!

The best shot on elephants is the side brain shot. Many hunters advise that you aim one-third of the way along a line from the ear slit to the eye. This is incorrect. It might catch the front portion of the brain but it allows no room for error. A bullet hitting forward of the brain is a miss. A bullet hitting behind the brain might catch the spine, so it is better to aim too far back than too far forward. Next time, I will aim for the ear slit or no more than three inches along the line to the eye.

Africa is a hot place, so elephants spend much time in the shade where the ear and eye are not discernible. Elephant hunters should study photographs of elephants and learn where to aim when only the silhouette is visible. A low-power scope also is recommended.

Andy Kockott can judge the accuracy of a brain shot by the reaction of the elephant. If the brain is missed by a wide margin, the hind quarters sag, but the animal stays on its feet. The elephant will pause for a second, giving the experienced rifleman enough time to reload from the shoulder and fire again. If the bullet misses the brain by a narrow margin, the elephant will fall on its side but will attempt to regain its feet. If the brain is hit, the elephant will fall on its chest and will not roll over.

I missed the brains of both of my elephants rather badly, yet both went down. This confirms John Taylor's view that the concussion of a large-caliber rifle will effectively stun an elephant though the brain is missed. I used a .458 Winchester and a .460 Weatherby.

If you do not have a clear shot at the brain, and for follow-up shots, you can try for the heart and lungs. I've not tried this, but I believe two rules apply. First, avoid the leg and shoulder bones. No bullet fired from a hand-held weapon will reliably break an elephant's leg bone and continue on in a straight line. Unlike other animals, the shoulder bones of elephants are stacked vertically, straight above the legs, so they are easy to miss.

Second, if possible, hammer two or three or more bullets into the chest and ask your professional hunter and buddies to join in the shooting. Numerous written accounts indicate that a heart-shot bull can run a couple of hundred yards and a lung-shot elephant might cover many hundreds of yards before going down. Multiple hits might shorten these distances considerably.

CAMERAS AND BINOCULARS

O nce upon a time, I owned a pair of Leitz Trinovid 10X40 binoculars. These were the early model made in Germany, and they were among the best binoculars the world has ever known. They were worth a couple thousand bucks. One day they accidently fell off my Land Rover onto a dusty road in the Zambezi Valley. They were picked up by an army patrol and probably traded away for a six-pack of beer.

With binoculars, as with pocket knives, there is a direct relationship between price and the probability that they will be lost or stolen. Super-quality binoculars are great, but every doubling of price brings only ten percent more optical quality. I replaced the Trinovids with a pair of two-hundred-dollar Nikon compacts.

I've gotten more joy out of these 10X25 Nikons than out of the superior 10X40s. The larger glasses spent too much time in the glove compartment of my truck. The lightweight 10X25s are far more likely to be hanging around my neck, available for instant use. Superior twilight factors are meaningless when the glasses are in the glove compartment.

My only complaint against the 10X25s is the narrow field of view. The most common configurations for compact binoculars are 10X25 and 8X20. If you search diligently, you will find 8X25s, which may be the optimum compromise. They offer a much wider field of view than my 10X25s and fair amount of brightness, but the weight is still negligible.

Conventional binoculars have one massive hinge between the two barrels. Compact binoculars have two rather flimsy hinges. Therefore, perfect alignment between the two barrels is more difficult to achieve and maintain with compacts. You must check this very carefully before purchasing compact binoculars. Point the glasses at blue sky and adjust the width between the two barrels until you see just one circle. Then drop the glasses downward and immediately look at some small object and note whether you see one image or two. If you see two images, the two barrels are misaligned. By straining your eyes, you can bring the two images together, but you should not have to do this.

Every safari should include at least one 35mm camera. It often will be hung over a tracker's shoulder, so it should have a good case. The 35 to 70mm zoom lenses are perfect for safari use. When set at 35mm, they enhance the size of objects in the foreground. For photographing trophies, position the animal's horns in the foreground and place a person in the background. The 35mm lens tends to make the horns look large in relation to the person. Some guys use 28mm or wider lenses for this, but the results look exaggerated and grotesque. A 35mm lens enhances but still gives a natural, realistic look. At its top setting, a 35-70mm lens is great for portraits and candid shots of people.

For wildlife photography, the ideal combination would be a 200mm lens with a very large aperture (f2.8) for use in dim light and a compact 400mm (f5.6) lens for use in bright light. If you don't want to spend many thousands of dollars on lenses, compromise with a 300mm f4 lens. Virtually all the wildlife photos in this book were taken with a 300mm. This lens, coupled with a 1.4X teleconverter, would produce the equivalent of a 420mm lens. This combination provides good flexibility with only moderate weight.

Long telephoto lenses generally are used with tripods to reduce camera movement. Most African parks require tourists to remain in their vehicles at all times and all photography must be done through windows or from the roof hatches. You cannot step out to set up a tripod. A good alternative is to attach a photographic gun stock to the camera. If a camera could be likened to a pistol, the same camera with a gun stock could be likened to a rifle.

Casual photographers probably should carry only one type of film and it should have an ISO of 200. This fast film enables fast shutters, an advantage if an untrained African jabs the shutter while taking a photo of you with a trophy. Fast film also enables use of small apertures, which increase the depth of focus and cover the mistakes of untrained African photographers. Telephoto lenses amplify camera movement and therefore require fast shutter speeds. Again, fast film is the solution.

Cameras and Binoculars

More serious photographers will carry two camera bodies. One should be loaded with slower film (ISO 64 or 100) and the other with ISO 200 film.

Leopard hunters should include a small flash unit. Most leopards are taken within the last five minutes before sunset, and photos of the trophy are often taken in the dark.

Dr. Terrance Cacek

Dr. Terrance Cacek was raised on the banks of Indian Creek in southeastern Nebraska, near the small town of Odell. When not working on the family farm, he trapped muskrats, fished, hunted pheasants, and dreamed about faraway places. He earned degrees in agriculture and wildlife management and served a tour of duty in the United States Army, including a year in Vietnam. Dr. Cacek spent eighteen years working for natural resource management agencies in Oregon, Colorado, Washington, D.C., and Botswana, Africa. He now lives in the Virginia suburbs of Washington, D.C., where he spends most of his time dreaming about faraway places.

INDEX

Index

Index